THE FAMILY ROMANOV

MURDER, REBELLION & THE FALL OF IMPERIAL RUSSIA

CANDACE FLEMING

a·s·b
anne schwartz books

Text copyright © 2014 by Candace Fleming
Jacket photographs courtesy of the Library of Congress
Map of Russia and family tree by Holly Pribble

Visit us on the Web! rhcbooks.com

Educators and librarians, for a variety of teaching tools,
visit us at RHTeachersLibrarians.com

Library of Congress Cataloging-in-Publication Data
Fleming, Candace.
The family Romanov : murder, rebellion, and the fall of imperial Russia /
Candace Fleming.
pages ; cm
Includes bibliographical references and index.
ISBN 978-0-375-86782-8 (hc) — ISBN 978-0-375-89864-8 (ebook)
1. Russia—History—Nicholas II, 1894–1917. 2. Nicholas II, Emperor of Russia,
1868–1918—Family. 3. Romanov, House of. 4. Soviet Union—History—Revolution,
1917–1921. I. Title.
DK258.F5725 2014
947.08'30922—dc23
[B]
2013037904

The text of this book is set in 11-point Hoefler Text.
Book design by Rachael Cole

Printed in the United States of America
20 19 18 17 16 15

Also by Candace Fleming

Young Adult

The Lincolns: A Scrapbook Look at Abraham and Mary

On the Day I Died: Stories from the Grave

Middle Grade

Amelia Lost: The Life and Disappearance of Amelia Earhart

The Great and Only Barnum: The Tremendous, Stupendous Life of Showman P. T. Barnum

The Fabled Fourth Graders of Aesop Elementary School

The Fabled Fifth Graders of Aesop Elementary School

Younger Readers

Oh, No!

Clever Jack Takes the Cake

Imogene's Last Stand

CONTENTS

Part Four: Final Days

BEFORE YOU BEGIN . . .

The ruler of Russia is called the tsar or emperor (the titles are interchangeable), his wife is either the tsaritsa or empress, and his male heir is called the tsarevich. His other children are given the title of grand duke if male or grand duchess if female. These last titles are passed down just one more generation, so a tsar's grandchildren are also grand dukes and grand duchesses. But a tsar's great-grandchildren hold only the rank of prince or princess. Thus grand dukes and grand duchesses outrank princes and princesses.

Russians have three names: a first name; a father's name with *-ovich* or *-evich* (meaning "son of") added if male, or *-evna* or *-ovna* (meaning "daughter of") if female; and a last, or family, name. Therefore, Nicholas II's daughter's full name was Anastasia Nikolaevna Romanova; his son's full name was Alexei Nikolaevich Romanov.

Russian dates can be bewildering. That's because during Nicholas's reign, Russia used the old-style Julian calendar to record dates, when most of the world was using the new-style Gregorian calendar. This meant Russian dates lagged twelve days behind during the nineteenth century, and thirteen days behind during the twentieth. Thus Anastasia was born June 5, 1901, according to the Julian calendar, but June 18, 1901, by the Gregorian calendar. Since readers of this book are familiar with the Gregorian calendar, all dates in this book are given in the new style.

NICHOLAS & ALEXANDRA'S FAMILY TREE

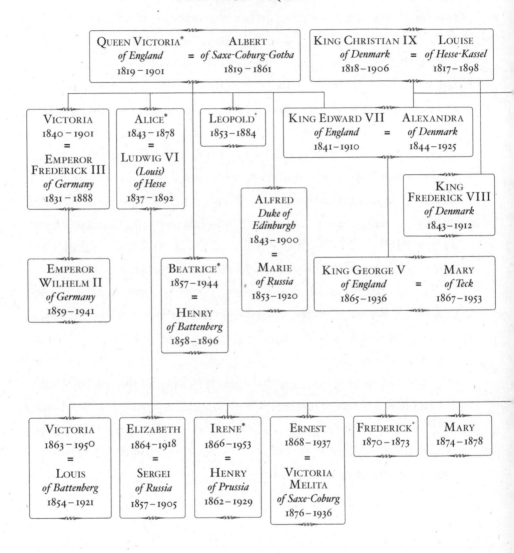

QUEEN VICTORIA* of England 1819 – 1901
= ALBERT of Saxe-Coburg-Gotha 1819 – 1861

KING CHRISTIAN IX of Denmark 1818–1906
= LOUISE of Hesse-Kassel 1817–1898

VICTORIA 1840 – 1901
=
EMPEROR FREDERICK III of Germany 1831 – 1888

ALICE* 1843 – 1878
=
LUDWIG VI (Louis) of Hesse 1837 – 1892

LEOPOLD+ 1853–1884

KING EDWARD VII of England 1841–1910
= ALEXANDRA of Denmark 1844 – 1925

KING FREDERICK VIII of Denmark 1843 – 1912

EMPEROR WILHELM II of Germany 1859 – 1941

BEATRICE* 1857 – 1944
=
HENRY of Battenberg 1858 – 1896

ALFRED Duke of Edinburgh 1843 – 1900
=
MARIE of Russia 1853 – 1920

KING GEORGE V of England 1865 – 1936
= MARY of Teck 1867 – 1953

VICTORIA 1863 – 1950
=
LOUIS of Battenberg 1854 – 1921

ELIZABETH 1864 – 1918
=
SERGEI of Russia 1857 – 1905

IRENE* 1866 – 1953
=
HENRY of Prussia 1862 – 1929

ERNEST 1868 – 1937
=
VICTORIA MELITA of Saxe-Coburg 1876 – 1936

FREDERICK* 1870 – 1873

MARY 1874 – 1878

*Hemophilia carrier
+Hemophiliac

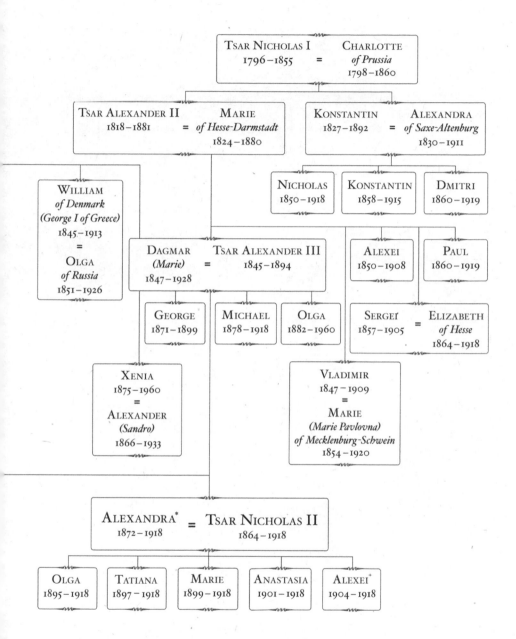

Note: Not all the royals are included on this family tree. Nicholas's and Alexandra's vast and tangled family relationships go back for centuries, making it difficult to include everyone who was or is related to them. For this reason, family members with less direct ties to the last tsar and his wife were reluctantly pruned from its branches.

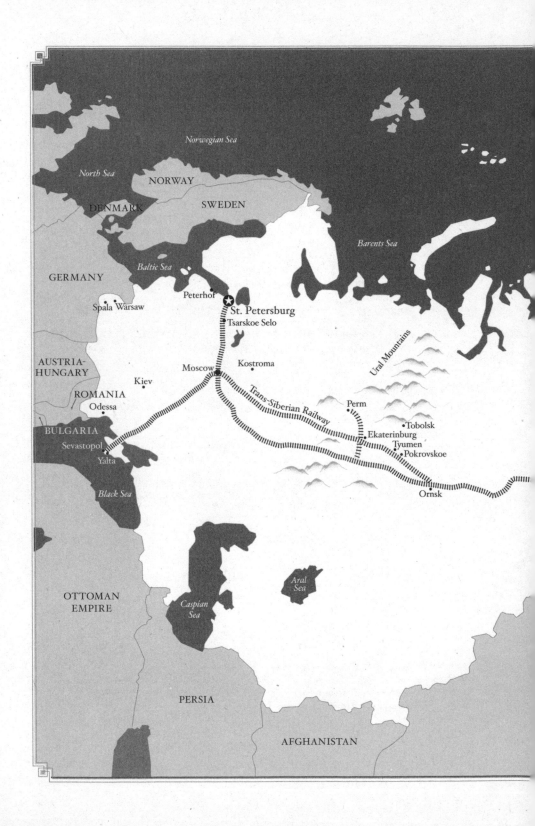

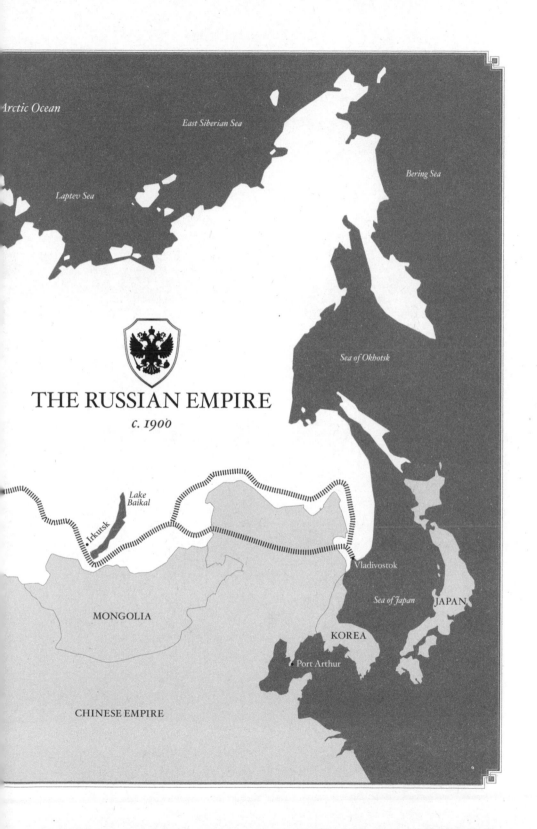

Arctic Ocean

East Siberian Sea

Laptev Sea

Bering Sea

Sea of Okhotsk

THE RUSSIAN EMPIRE
c. 1900

Lake
Baikal

Irkutsk

Vladivostok

Sea of Japan

JAPAN

MONGOLIA

KOREA

Port Arthur

CHINESE EMPIRE

"THE CHOSEN"

On the night of February 12, 1903, a long line of carriages made its way through the Imperial Gates of St. Petersburg's Winter Palace. The great mansion, which stretched for three miles along the now-frozen Neva River, blazed with light, its massive crystal and gold chandeliers reflected a hundred times in the mirrored walls of its cathedral-size reception rooms. The light cast a welcoming glow that contrasted sharply with the snow and ice outside. Bundled in sable, ermine, or mink wraps, the passengers alighted. Bracing themselves against the icy wind howling off the Gulf of Finland, they hurried through the arched doorway.

Inside, the strains of the court orchestra greeted them. Masses of fresh roses, lilacs, and mimosas imported just for the night from the South of France perfumed the air. Handing their furs to the wait-ing footmen, guests paused in front of the pier glass to straighten silk skirts and pat pomaded hair into place before ascending the wide marble staircase to the second floor.

A series of halls, each more grand than the last, met the guests. Gilded ceilings and doorways. Columns of malachite and jasper. White marble statues. Through these rooms the guests wandered, plucking flutes of champagne from silver trays, clapping each other on the back, laughing, joking, gossiping. They felt completely at ease in their opulent surroundings. That's because they were mem-bers of the nobility—the 870 families known in Russia as the *bélaya kost*—literally meaning "white bone," or what we would call blue blood.

Holding titles like prince and princess, duke, baron, count and countess, the *bélaya kost* represented only 1.5 percent of the population, but owned 90 percent of all Russia's wealth. Educated and sophisticated, many of them could trace their family roots all the way back to the ancient princes who had ruled the country centuries before. And most lived lives of incredible luxury that were, recalled one princess, "a natural part of existence." They built summer and winter palaces filled with fine antiques and priceless objets d'art, ordered designer gowns from Paris, vacationed in Italy or on the French Riviera, and spoke English or French (but seldom Russian because it showed a lack of breeding). Privileged from birth, the *bélaya kost* socialized only with each other. They belonged to the same clubs, attended the same parties, frequented the same shops, restaurants, and salons. Above all, they possessed an unshakable belief in their own superiority. As one member of the upper crust explained, nobles had "a certain quality of being among the chosen, of being privileged, of not being the same as all other people."

Tonight, they felt especially "chosen." Weeks earlier, the court runner had hand-delivered a stiff vellum card embossed with the imperial insignia—the gold double-headed eagle—to their palaces. It was an invitation from Tsar Nicholas II—an invitation to a ball!

St. Petersburg's upper crust buzzed. Even though the imperial couple was traditionally the center of society, Nicholas and Alexandra detested the social whirl. They rarely threw receptions or balls, preferring to remain in seclusion. This, however, was such a grand occasion—the two-hundredth anniversary of St. Petersburg's founding as the Russian capital—that even the party-shunning royal couple could not ignore it. And so Nicholas was throwing a costume ball. Guests were told to come dressed in seventeenth-century garb.

Giddy with excitement, the nobility flocked to dressmakers and tailors, where they spent fortunes on gold silk tunics, caftans edged in sable, and headdresses studded with rubies and diamonds.

Grand Duke Michael, Nicholas's younger brother, even borrowed an egg-size diamond from the crown jewels to adorn the cap of his costume. (During the festivities, the priceless bauble fell off his costume and was never found.)

At precisely eight o'clock came a fanfare from the state trumpeters. Then the great fourteen-foot-tall mahogany doors that led to the imperial family's private rooms swung open. The grand marshal of the court appeared. Banging his ebony staff three times, he announced, "Their Imperial Majesties!"

The room instantly fell silent. Men bowed. Women curtsied. And Tsar Nicholas II stepped into the hall.

Short, with a neatly trimmed beard and large, soft blue eyes, Nicholas hardly looked like the imposing ruler of Russia. And yet this unassuming man reigned over 130 million subjects and one-sixth of the planet's land surface—an area so vast that as night fell along the western edge of his territory, day was already breaking on the eastern border. His realm stretched from Poland to Japan and from the Arctic Ocean to the borders of the Ottoman Empire (modern-day Turkey) and China. He was the richest monarch in the world: his family wealth was once estimated at $45 billion (in today's U.S. currency). Every year he drew an income of 24 million gold rubles ($240 million today) from the state treasury, which derived most of *its* income from taxes and fees levied on the tsar's subjects. And if he needed more, he simply appropriated it. He owned thirty palaces; estates in Finland, Poland, and the Crimea (all part of Russia at the time); millions of acres of farmland; gold and silver mines, as well as oil and timber reserves; an endless collection of priceless paintings and sculptures; and five yachts, two private trains, and countless horses, carriages, and cars. His vaults overflowed with a fortune in jewels.

His wealth was on full display that evening. Dressed as Alexei the Mild (the gentle seventeenth-century tsar whom Nicholas nostalgically admired for having ruled, he believed, during a time of piety and morality), he wore a raspberry velvet caftan embroidered with gold thread, its collars and cuffs flashing with diamonds. He even carried the real Alexei's iron staff and wore his sable-trimmed cap and pearl bracelets. Too bad, sniffed one grand duke, Nicholas was "not sufficiently tall to do justice to his magnificent garb."

But it was the appearance of Empress Alexandra that caused many in the hall to gasp. Alexandra was wearing a gold brocade gown shimmering with the thousands of diamonds and pearls that had been sewn onto it—a costume that cost one million rubles ($10 million today). Her elaborate headdress glittered with diamonds and emeralds, and her pearl earrings were so heavy it was hard for her to hold up her head. Around her neck hung an enormous 400-carat blue sapphire. "[She] was just stunning," one guest admitted. But others disagreed. "She was dressed in the heavy brocade of which she was so fond," one catty countess recalled, "with diamonds scattered all over her in defiance of good taste and common sense."

With the imperial couple's arrival, the court orchestra broke into a polonaise, which was the traditional first dance, and Nicholas and Alexandra led the dancing with "appropriate pomp," recalled one grand duke, "though [they were] hardly full of enthusiasm." Even though he was "Emperor and Autocrat of All the Russias," as he was formally called, Nicholas often felt shy in society, while Alexandra acted nervous and awkward.

Now their guests followed suit, swirling and dipping. "The whirl of the waltz [puffed out] the skirts," recalled the French writer Théophile Gautier, who'd attended a ball at the palace two years earlier, "and the little gloved hands resting on the epaulettes of the waltzers looked like white camellias in vases of massive gold."

When the orchestra began playing a quadrille, a relieved Nicholas and Alexandra left the dance floor. He moved among the crowd, greeting guests, while she uncomfortably talked with a group of ladies. The empress's distaste for the event was obvious, leading some of the women to whisper behind their hands. "She danced badly," remarked one princess, "and she certainly was not a brilliant conversationalist. She . . . gave the impression that she was about to burst into tears."

At midnight, guests sat down to an exquisite French supper. There was soup with truffles, and delicate puffed cheese pastries served with fruit, followed by petite chicken soufflés in a rich sauce and roast duckling. As guests ate, servants bustled about serving wine and cognac from crystal decanters and coffee from engraved silver pots. The champagne bubbled and flowed. "It was," gushed one guest, "like a living dream!"

ALL DOES NOT GLIMMER

But beyond the golden glow of the Winter Palace, across its graceful courtyard and through its gilded gates, past mansion-lined avenues and the spires and domes of the city, lay the railroad tracks. Farther and farther across the frozen darkness they stretched, over silent steppes and across mountains to thousands of scattered villages where primitive log huts clustered around rutted dirt roads. Here lived the peasants.

In 1903—the same year as Nicholas's costume ball—four out of every five Russians were peasants. And yet the upper classes knew next to nothing about them. They didn't visit the peasants' villages or deal with the hired laborers who worked their estates. Instead, they remained comfortably ensconced in luxurious St. Petersburg. From there it was easy to romanticize the peasants' life. Most nobility (Nicholas and Alexandra included) envisioned peasants living in simple yet cozy huts, their "cheeks glowing with good health" and their teeth "whiter than the purest ivory," gushed one

Russian writer. It was common knowledge among the nobility that the country's fresh foods and clean air made the peasants healthier than the "vain city women who sickened themselves with rich food and tortured their bodies with laces, corsets, and shoes made only for fashion," declared one nobleman. And it was especially pleasing to picture the peasants enjoying life's simple pleasures "decked out in their holiday best, singing and dancing in fresh-cut meadows."

Nothing was further from the truth. Most peasants had never slept in a proper bed, owned a pair of leather shoes, eaten off a china plate, or been examined by a doctor. Most had never been beyond the borders of their villages.

These villages were dismal places. Along narrow, unpaved streets that were muddy in the spring and dusty in the summer stood a line of crudely built one- or two-room log huts called *izby*. Inside each, a wood-burning clay oven used for cooking and heating filled the room, taking up as much as a fourth of the space. Its large, flat top was a favorite sleeping place for the sick or elderly. Because most *izby* did not have chimneys (they cost too much), the smoke from the oven filled the room, leaving everything covered in a layer of black soot.

Most had no furniture, either. Instead, long wooden benches ran along the walls. Used for seating during the day, they were converted into beds at night. Without mattresses or pillows, peasants simply took off their coats and used them as blankets. Wrote one charity worker who visited a peasant hut in the 1890s:

> Stooping down, I creep through the low door, and enter the hut. A damp and suffocating air meets me, so that I am nearly fainting. A few rays of light struggle with difficulty through a small window. . . . A woman is at the oven, busy with a stone jar in her hand. Behind her, two children, covered with rags and pale and dirty, are sitting

on a bench, sucking on a hard crust. In another corner, something covered with a battered sheepskin cloak is lying on a bench. . . . It is a young girl, on the point of dying from starvation.

Often, there was little to eat but dark bread. It was a staple of their diet, and peasant housewives tried to stretch the loaves by mixing clay, ground straw, or birch bark into the flour. They also served a watery cabbage soup called *shchi* for supper, usually without meat. Recalled one elderly peasant, "It has been a year and a half since we've eaten any [meat]." Many peasants were so poor, even the cockroaches abandoned their huts. "A cockroach is a natural aristocrat," explained one observer, "and requires a greater degree of comfort than can be found in the dwellings of the rural poor."

Their poverty stemmed from a shortage of land. Most peasants did not own the land. Instead, each village had a group of elders called the commune that held title to *all* available acreage. It was the commune's job to decide the number of acres each family received to plant, based on the number of members per household. Unfortunately, the commune's holdings did not grow along with the population. Year after year, resentful families watched the size of their parcels shrink as communes tried to provide land to everyone. By 1903, the average peasant allotment had shrunk from eleven acres to six, and one out of every five families farmed less than three.

To make this shortage even worse, a family's parcels were usually not adjacent to one another. The acreage was scattered across a commune's entire territory. "Strips [of land] six feet wide are by no means rare," wrote one shocked journalist from the London *Times*. "Of these narrow strips, a family may possess as many as thirty in a single field!" Peasants wasted precious hours each day dragging plow and scythe from one scrap of land to another. Hitching their

sons and daughters to crude wooden plows (just one in three peasants owned a horse), they struggled to furrow the muddy soil before
planting their grain by hand.

But no matter how hard a peasant family worked, most could not
grow enough food to get through the year. A few managed to scrape
together the necessary coins to buy flour. Most, however, simply
tightened their belts even further. "There are many . . . households
that do not have the means to buy [even] cabbage," noted one visiting physician in 1907.

Most peasants were convinced that the best way to improve
their lot in life was to cultivate more acreage. And so they looked
with land-hungry eyes toward the nobility's estates. Remarked one
nobleman, "Every single peasant believed from the very bottom of
his soul that one day, sooner or later, the squire's land would belong
to him."

To the peasants' minds, the nobility—who possessed not only
half the land in Russia but also the most fertile acreage—did not
legitimately own their estates. Peasants believed the land should
belong to those who plowed it. Since the nobility did not work their
estates themselves, the peasants felt justified in taking whatever
they could. They picked fruit from the squire's orchards, fished in
his ponds, and gathered mushrooms and firewood in his forests.
They knew these activities were illegal, but most ignored the law.
After all, what was wrong with a hungry family stealing a few apples
from a man who had more than he could ever use himself? "God
grew the forests for everyone," they would say, quoting a Russian
proverb.

Some peasants did eke out a living. But during the first decade
of the twentieth century, hundreds of thousands more abandoned
their villages. Traveling by foot along the country's dirt roads, they
searched for work in the factories and mills that had cropped up
in Russia's cities. Most were young men looking to escape grinding

poverty. "All the healthy and able men ran away from our village to [the city] and took whatever jobs they could find," said one villager. Recalled another, "Everyone is trying as hard as he can to liberate himself from [farming] and find an easier means of existence."

Sadly, these men did not find an easier life. Instead, they crowded into city slums that reeked of human waste and unwashed bodies. Beggars stood on every corner; drunkards lolled in every doorway. Gangs of pickpockets, usually children, flitted through the crowds while prostitutes (many of them village girls who'd been unable to find work) plied their trade. In these miserable streets—beneath the constant fog of black smoke pouring from the factories' chimneys—people worked and ate, worked and slept, too tired to do much besides visit the tavern. "I did not live, but only worked, worked, worked," recalled metalworker Ivan Babuskin. "I worked morning, noon and night, and sometimes did not leave the factory for two days at a stretch." The factory owner expected him there six days a week, and if he didn't turn up, he would be fired. One's only thought, remembered Ivan, was that "it would be work again tomorrow—heavy, continuous, killing work—but there would be no real life and no real rest to look forward to."

For these efforts, a worker earned around eighty kopecks a day (forty cents), hardly enough to support himself when just a loaf of bread cost twenty-four kopecks and a two-room tenement without water, kitchen, or toilet cost more than an entire month's wages to rent. So to ward off starvation, a man's wife and children had little choice but to trudge to the factories as well. It was common for mothers to work eleven hours a day and earn one-third what men did. The children received even less. According to one historian, boys in Moscow's spinning mills "earned the equivalent of about a half cent for each frightening and dangerous hour spent darting in and out among the machines to tie threads, replace spindles, or oil moving gears." At the same time, children coughing through the haze of noxious fumes in Moscow's match factories earned a mere seventy cents a month!

Poisonous chemicals. Flying gears and belts. Razor-sharp graters. These posed dangers to anyone who worked in the factories. But owners did nothing to promote safety or protect their workers. Instead, they posted signs that read "In the event of an accident, the owner and director of the factory assume no responsibility." If workers thought their jobs were too dangerous, or their hours too long, they had no recourse. The tsar's government had left all decisions regarding the running of factories to their owners. And while some government inspectors did try to enforce child labor laws that had been enacted in 1897, they lacked any real power. Factory owners simply ignored them. Thus, explained one worker, "The factory owner is the absolute sovereign . . . constrained by no laws, and who often simply arranges things to suit himself. The workers owe him *unquestioning obedience* as the rules [of the factory] proclaim."

Afraid of being fired, most workers did not complain. For as bad as being a worker was, being unemployed was worse. "We slept in gutters and doorways," recalled one worker who'd lost his job, "and we survived by theft and begging. We had no other choice. The alternative was dying of starvation."

Outside the factory, workers suffered even worse conditions. With little affordable housing in the city, they squeezed into every available space—freezing attics, leaky basements. Sometimes as many as twenty men, women, and children lived in one small room. Overcrowding led to diseases such as cholera, typhoid, and tuberculosis that cut through the city's poor. Children were especially vulnerable. Said a woman weaver, "I had eleven [children], but only three grew up. You'd go to the factory, but your soul always was in torment. Your heart always grieved for your children."

Since their meager pay did not keep up with the rise in the price of goods, workers lived on a diet of cabbage soup, dried peas, and sour black bread. They wore rags. At the neighborhood taverns, they tried to drown their misery by squandering precious kopecks on cheap vodka and watered-down beer. Only then, in that misty, drunken haze, did many of them see "reflections of a better, less unjust world."

BEYOND THE PALACE GATES:
PEASANT TURNED WORKER

Sixteen-year-old Senka Kanatchikov arrived in Moscow in 1895. A far cry from his tiny village of Gusevo, the place both amazed and terrified him, as he recalled in his autobiography, originally titled From the Story of My Life:

What a stunning impression Moscow made on me. . . . Huge, multistoried houses—most of them with lighted windows—stores, shops, taverns, beer halls, horse-drawn carriages going by—all around us crowds of bustling people. . . . Compared with village hovels, what struck me about the houses of Moscow was their grandiose appearance, the luxury.

"Am I to live in a house like that?" I asked with delight.

"You'll find out in due course," Father responded.

And sure enough . . . we turned into a side street, and entered the gates of a huge stone house with a courtyard that looked like a large stone well. Wet linens dangled from taut clotheslines all along the upper stories. The courtyard had an acrid stench . . . [and] throughout . . . were dirty puddles of water and discarded vegetables. In the apartments and all around . . . people were crowding, making noise, yelling, cursing. My delight was beginning to turn into depression, into some kind of inexplicable terror. . . . I felt like a small insignificant grain of sand, lost in the unfamiliar and hostile sea of people that surrounded me. . . .

Here, in the hostile world of Moscow, I felt lonely, abandoned, needed by no one. While at work in the painting shop . . . which smelled of paint and turpentine, I would remember pictures of our village life and tears would come to my eyes, and it was only with great effort that I could keep from crying. . . . Awkward, sluggish, with long hair that had been cut under a round bowl, wearing heavy boots with horseshoes, I was a typical village youth. The skilled workers looked down on me, called me a "green country bumpkin" and other insulting names.

Our workday at the factory lasted eleven and a half hours, plus a one-and-a-half-hour lunch break. In the beginning I would grow terribly tired, so as soon as I got home from work . . . I would fall into my filthy, hard, straw-filled sack and sleep like a dead man, despite the . . . bedbugs and fleas.

I roomed and boarded not far from the factory, in a large, smelly house inhabited by all kinds of poor folk—peddlers, cabmen, casual laborers and the like. We rented the apartment communally [with] fifteen men. . . . I was put in a tiny, dark, windowless corner room; it was dirty and stuffy with . . . the strong smell of "humanity." There was a kerosene lamp hanging between the windows. Underneath the lamp was a cheap print of the Tsar's family. The room also contained two wooden cots. One belonged to [a man named] Korovin; the other I shared with Korovin's son, Vanka, who also ... worked in the factory's pattern shop.

Our food was purchased communally ... and on credit at [the factory] shop; our individual shares were assessed twice monthly and taken from our paychecks. Every day at noon, as soon as the factory's lunch bell rang, we would hurry ... to sit down at a table, where a huge basin full of cabbage soup was already steaming. All fifteen men ate from a common bowl with wooden spoons. The cabbage soup contained little pieces of meat. ... Everyone waited tensely for a signal. [Then] someone would bang his spoon against the ... soup basin and say the words ... "Dig in!" Then began the furious hunt with spoons for the floating morsels of meat. The most dexterous would come up with the most. ... Everyone was hungry as a wolf; they ate quickly, greedily. After lunch—if there was time—everyone threw himself down to rest without removing his boots or work shirt. Stomachs still grumbled and muscles ached. ...

PART ONE

BEFORE THE STORM

Were we all, the whole upper crust of Russian society, so
totally insensitive, so horribly obtuse, as not to feel that
the charmed life we were leading was in itself an injustice
and hence could not possibly last?
—Nicolas Nabokov
Bagázh: Memoirs of a Russian Cosmopolitan

Chapter One
❧ "I Dreamed That I Was Loved" ❧
1881–1895

The Boy Who Would Be Tsar

On a frosty March day in 1881, the boy who would become Russia's last ruler glimpsed his future. That morning, Nicholas's grandfather, Tsar Alexander II, was riding through the streets of St. Petersburg when a man stepped off the sidewalk. He hurled a bomb at the imperial carriage. Miraculously, the tsar went uninjured, but many in his retinue were not as lucky. Concerned about his people, Alexander stepped from his carriage. That's when a second bomb was thrown. This one landed between his feet. An explosion of fire and shrapnel tore away Alexander's left leg, ripped open his abdomen, and mangled his face. Barely conscious, he managed one last command: "To the palace, to die there."

Horrified members of the imperial family rushed to his side. Thirteen-year-old Nicholas, dressed in a blue sailor suit, followed a thick trail of dark blood up the white marble stairs to his grandfather's study. There he found Alexander lying on a couch, one eye closed, the other staring blankly at the ceiling. Nicholas's father, also named Alexander, was already in the room. "My father took me up to the bed," Nicholas later recalled. "'Papa,' [my father] said, raising his voice, 'your ray of sunshine is here.' I saw the eyelashes tremble. . . . [Grandfather] moved a finger. He could not raise his hands, nor say what he wanted to, but he undoubtedly recognized me." Deathly pale, Nicholas stood helplessly at the end of the bed as his beloved grandfather took his last breath.

"The emperor is dead," announced the court physician.

Nicholas's father—now the new tsar—clenched his fists. The

Russian people would pay for this. Alexander II had been a reformer, the most liberal tsar in centuries. He'd freed the serfs (peasant slaves) and modernized the courts. But his murder convinced his son, Alexander III, that the people had been treated too softly. If order was to be maintained, they needed to "feel the whip." And for the next thirteen years of his reign, Alexander III made sure they did.

Young Nicholas, standing beside his grandfather's deathbed, knew nothing of politics. Frightened, he covered his face with his hands and sobbed bitterly. He was left, he later confessed, with a "presentiment—a secret conviction . . . that I am destined for terrible trials."

ROMANOV RULE

Nicholas's family, the Romanovs, had sat on the Russian throne for almost three hundred years, ruling their subjects under a form of government called autocracy. In an autocracy, one person—in this instance, the tsar—holds all the power. The Romanovs claimed God had given them this power, had chosen them to rule the Russian people. As God's representative on earth, they maintained, the tsar should be left to run the country according to his own ideas of duty and right. This meant that *all* of Russia's political power was in the tsar's hands. Unlike most other nations, Russia had no constitution, no congress, no court of appeal for its citizens or supreme court to review or limit the tsar's power. There were only two restrictions: he had to abide by the teachings of the Russian Orthodox Church (of which he was official head), and he had to follow the laws of succession (those rules determining inheritance of the throne). On all other matters the tsar was supreme, and he made laws and policies according to his will . . . or whim.

The tsar's will was carried out by a multitude of officials and administrators. Below him sat thirteen ministers collectively called the Imperial Cabinet. Chosen by the tsar, each of these noblemen headed a large government department. There was a chief minister (or prime minister), as well as ministers of war, finance, justice, and the interior, to name a few. Their job was to implement the tsar's decrees and to offer advice. Whether the tsar chose to listen was his choice. The tsar could dismiss a minister at any time, and for any reason. Since they could be hired and fired on a whim, the tsar's ministers (with some exceptions) tended to be flatterers, telling him what he *wanted* rather than needed to hear.

Because of Russia's size, the tsar required a second tier of officials and administrators to carry out his will. Outside St. Petersburg, the country was divided into thirty-four provinces, each administered by a governor (also chosen by the tsar). Each had at his disposal an imperial army and police to help enforce the tsar's laws. Additionally, each province was divided into districts overseen by the *zemstvo,* or local council. The *zemstvo* managed the collection of taxes in their localities and dealt with issues like food supply and road maintenance. Not surprisingly, most members of the *zemstvo* were landowning nobility or wealthy townsmen.

Russia also required a huge imperial bureaucracy to enforce laws, impose fines and fees, and keep records. Because the majority of bureaucrats were neither well educated nor well paid, they were easily corrupted. It was common for low-ranking bureaucrats (those working closest to the citizens) to demand bribes for everything from issuing business licenses to approving land titles. Because of this, the lower classes despised bureaucrats. They viewed them as greedy, petty cheaters. Unfortunately, since the low-ranking bureaucrat was the most visible of all government workers, he became the public face of Romanov rule.

The tsar's government was propped up by both its military and its police force. Public safety was not the first priority of either organization. Instead, their most important function was protecting the autocracy from political dissent. If Russians so much as grumbled about the government, they could be arrested and exiled to far-off, frozen Siberia without recourse. To keep the peace and protect order, the tsar censored the press, banned books, limited public speech, and refused people the right to assemble for political reasons. Houses could be searched. Mail could be opened and read. Businesses and universities could be closed for no other reason than that the tsar commanded it. Even members of the nobility were subject to his will. The tsar could seize their property, refuse them permission to marry, and banish anyone from the country—all with just a snap of his autocratic fingers.

GROWING UP

Nicholas did not look forward to the day he would sit on the Russian throne. Shy and gentle, he enjoyed playing tennis, taking long walks, and reading in his bedroom. Every month the imperial librarian sent him twenty books from around the world. Nicholas, a fast reader, especially liked military history. He wasn't anything like his bullheaded, tough-as-nails father, Tsar Alexander III, who boomed when he spoke, and who had strong opinions and an even stronger will. How could he possibly live up to the expectations of his big Russian bear of a father?

And his father *was* bearlike. Standing six foot three, Tsar Alexander was so strong he could bend iron fire pokers and tie silver forks into knots. Once, while he was riding on the imperial train with his family, the locomotive jumped the rails, causing the roof to cave in. Using his tremendous strength, Alexander hoisted the roof onto his wide shoulders and held it until everyone escaped unhurt.

Alexander possessed incredible political strength, too. He demanded complete obedience from his subjects. "The tsar is swift and harsh. He shows no mercy," one of Alexander's courtiers noted. "He raises his iron fist, and the . . . people shudder, and obey." Once, when an adviser threatened to resign, the tsar picked up the man by his lapels and flung him to the marble floor. "Shut up! When I choose to kick you out, you will hear of it in no uncertain terms!"

That was how Alexander III held Russia together.

No wonder the thought of one day taking his father's place terrified mild-mannered Nicholas. He prayed for his father to live a long—*very, very long*—life.

Nor was Alexander eager for his son to become tsar. The boy's small size embarrassed him. (Nicholas would stand just five foot seven when fully grown, with narrow shoulders and short, stocky legs.) So did his high-pitched laugh and sloppy handwriting. "Nicholas is a *devchonka*—a bit of a girlie," Alexander once cruelly and publicly declared about his then thirteen-year-old son.

His opinion didn't change as the boy grew older. When Nicholas was in his mid-twenties, it was suggested he chair a government committee. Alexander snorted at the suggestion. "Tell me, have you ever spoken to His Imperial Highness, the Grand Duke Tsarevich? Then don't tell me you never noticed that the Grand Duke is a dunce!"

Alexander did almost nothing to prepare his son for his future role as "autocrat of all Russia." Nicholas never learned to deal with ministers or politicians. He never gave a speech, studied diplomacy, or grappled with national policy. In short, he never developed the qualities of a statesman. "It was my father's fault," Nicholas's sister Olga later wrote. "He would not even have Nicky sit in on Council of State. . . . I can't tell you why."

But living in his father's bear-size, ridiculing shadow *did* teach Nicholas one thing: to conceal his real feelings beneath a falsely patient smile. "I never show my feelings," he once admitted. During his lifetime, very few people would ever know how hurt, scared, or inadequate he truly felt.

THE EMPRESS

Most people agreed that Empress Alexandra was beautiful. She had flawless pale skin, golden hair, and clear blue eyes. But it was a sour kind of beauty. Alexandra's sharp nose gave her face a cold sternness, and her tight, thin lips rarely curved into a smile. "When she did [smile]," recalled her cousin Queen Marie of Romania, "it was grudging, as though making a concession."

She hadn't always been that way. As a child, the future empress— little Princess Alix Victoria Helena Louise Beatrice of Hesse-Darmstadt (now part of Germany)—was full of laughter, her broad smile deepening the dimples in her rosy cheeks. For this reason, her family nicknamed her Sunny. But when she was six years old, her mother died. Overnight, "Sunny" turned aloof, serious, and withdrawn. "Her attitude to the world [became] perpetually mistrustful," said Queen Marie, "strangely empty of tenderness and, in a way, hostile. . . . She held [people] at a distance, as though they intended to steal something which was hers."

She also became obsessed with God and the afterlife. "Life here [on earth] is nothing," she later wrote in her diary. "Eternity is everything, and what we are doing is preparing our souls for the Kingdom of Heaven."

With her mother's death, Alix's maternal grandmother—Queen Victoria of England—stepped in to raise the child. The most powerful monarch in all Europe, Queen Victoria was a no-nonsense woman used to getting her own way. Brushing aside any objections from Alix's father, Grand Duke Ludwig IV, the aging queen set out to mold her youngest and most favorite grandchild in her own image. Handpicked by Her Majesty, a string of English tutors and governesses traveled to Hesse with instructions to send detailed reports back to Windsor Castle. In return, they received a stream of orders from the queen: the princess must learn to speak proper English; high standards of taste and morality should be set; training in the avoidance of idle talk and gossip was imperative. And so, the German princess grew into a proper young Englishwoman. Duty to family and to country. Thrift and industriousness. Modesty and simplicity. And like Queen Victoria herself, Alix grew to be stubborn, iron-willed, and controlling.

Beyond the Palace Gates: A Peasant Boyhood

Before his experiences as a factory worker, Senka Kanatchikov lived in Gusevo, a village located just outside Moscow. Eleven years younger than Nicholas, Senka recalled his own, far different childhood in his autobiography:

My early childhood was not accompanied by any particularly outstanding events, unless one counts the fact that I survived; I wasn't devoured by a pig, I wasn't butted by a cow, I didn't drown in a pool, and I didn't die of some infectious disease the way thousands of peasant children perished in those days. . . . For a village child to survive in those times was a rare event. . . . My own mother . . . brought eighteen children into this world . . . yet only four of us survived. I . . . view[ed] my presence on earth as a great stroke of fortune. . . .

Our family consisted of nine or ten souls. There was no way we could live off the land alone, for our [acreage was] very paltry, and the earnings of my older brother [who went off to a factory in the winter] were inadequate. My father tried to sow more flax and get into commerce, but . . . nothing came of these efforts: the land was exhausted [from overuse], the price of flax was falling. . . . In this way we continued to struggle, year in and year out, barely able to make ends meet. . . . I tilled the soil. I harrowed, mowed, and threshed, and in the winter I went to the forest to gather wood. . . .

My father was strict . . . and despotic. . . . He kept the entire family in mortal fright. We all feared him and did everything we could to please him. There were times when he would "go on a binge" . . . as they'd say in our village. . . . [Then] he spent his time away from home, in the circle of his drinking companions. . . . [Often] he would drink to the point where he was seriously ill, and there were even occasions when he was close to death. When his binges were over . . . Father would become . . . morose and demanding. [At these times], he fell upon my unfortunate mother; my father was her deathblow. I loved my mother intensely and hated my father with an animal hate. . . . I passionately took my mother's side, and prevented him from beating her. This . . . usually ended up with Father beating me up as well, unless I managed to dodge his blows in time and run away. . . .

When I reached the age of fourteen . . . my mother took ill . . . and died. . . . For whole nights through, holding a waxen candle over [her] corpse . . . I read aloud from the [Bible]. . . . According to the popular belief . . . you had to read the entire Psalter forty times over to [send a soul to Heaven]. Great were my bitterness and suffering when, at the twenty-eighth reading . . . exhausted and worn out by sleepless nights, I [fell] asleep. . . . Without her, life in the village was unbearable. I wanted to rid myself of [it] as quickly as possible, to free myself from my father's despotism. . . . After long arguments and discussion, [Father] decided to let me go to Moscow.

A ROYAL COUPLE

Nicholas and Alexandra first met in 1884, when he was sixteen and she just twelve. Alix had traveled to Russia for the wedding of her oldest sister, Princess Elizabeth of Hesse, to Nicholas's uncle, Grand Duke Serge. Despite his small size, the future tsar of Russia was both handsome and charming. Smiling at the girl on the day she arrived at the Romanovs' Peterhof estate, he introduced himself. "I'm Nicky," he said.

"I'm Sunny," she replied stiffly.

"Yes, I know," he said. The two were second cousins, related through a royal tangle of relations. Plopping down beside the young princess, he spent the next few hours trying to break through her wall of reserve. He must have succeeded, because later that day he wrote in his diary, "I sat next to little . . . Alix whom I really liked a lot."

For the next four days, they enjoyed each other's company, walking in the Peterhof gardens. They picked flowers for each other, shared secrets, and even scratched "Alix, Nicky" with a diamond on a window of one of the houses.

The day before Alix and her family returned to Hesse, Nicholas gave her a small, jeweled brooch as a token of his affection. She accepted it, overwhelmed. But the next afternoon, worried about what her grandmother would think, she returned it. Offended, Nicholas gave the brooch to his little sister. Alix went home.

Five years passed before they saw each other again. In 1889, Alix arrived in St. Petersburg for a six-week stay with her sister. This time, she was seventeen and Nicholas twenty-one—the perfect age for romance. They saw each other constantly. He took her sledding and ice-skating, accompanied her to late-night suppers, ballets, and operas. He even hosted a dance in her honor. In the ballroom, which was perfumed with fresh roses and orchids, the couple danced in each other's arms until the orchestra's final note faded into the starry night. By the time Alix returned home, she was in love with Nicholas. And he was head-over-heels with her. Pasting her photograph in his diary, he later wrote, "My dream—one day to marry Alix H!"

DREAMS COME TRUE

Five more years passed. With no official responsibilities, Nicholas did little but attend the opera and ballet. He went to parties and dances and stayed out until the early-morning hours. "As always, I don't feel well after a ball," he confessed in his diary. "I have a weakness in the legs. . . . I am persuaded that I have some kind of sleeping sickness because there is no way to get me up."

He discovered a deep love for the army—its order and routine— after his father made him a junior officer, as Romanov tradition demanded. "[The army] appealed to his passive nature," recalled his best friend and cousin, Grand Duke Alexander Mikhailovich, known as Sandro. All Nicholas had to do was follow orders, while his superiors dealt with any problems. Freed from decision making,

Nicholas focused on what he enjoyed most—laughing and partying with his fellow officers. "We got stewed," he confided in his diary. "The officers carried me out." "Wallowed in the grass and drank."

He also embarked on a grand world tour that took him, among other places, to Egypt's pyramids and India's jungles. "Palaces and generals are the same the world over," Nicholas wrote. "I could just as well have stayed at home."

He and Alix did not see each other once during this time. Still, they wrote to each other—little notes filled with hopes and dreams and words of love. At last, on a balmy April morning in 1894, the two met again at a royal wedding in Coburg, Germany. Nicholas seized the chance to propose. But as much as Alix longed to say yes, she hesitated. Russian law demanded that the wife of the future tsar be a follower of the official state religion, Russian Orthodoxy, a branch of Christianity.

But Alix was a devout Lutheran. How could she abandon her faith? she sobbed. To toss it aside would, she believed, be an insult to God. Still, she adored Nicky. What should she do?

After hours of praying and sobbing, as well as discussion with her sister, Elizabeth, she found a solution. She wouldn't really be changing faiths, she reasoned. After all, Christianity was Christianity. She would merely be changing the way she expressed that faith.

Joyously, she told Nicholas her decision.

"Oh, God, what happened to me then," Nicholas wrote to his parents. "I cried like a child, and she did too. . . . The whole world was changed for me."

And Alix wrote poetically, "I dreamed that I was loved. I woke and found it true."

But her conversion was not casual. She embraced Orthodoxy, and an Orthodoxy of roughly the sixteenth century, at that. During a time when most modern, educated Russians looked upon their religion with indifference, Alix developed a deep belief in the miraculous and mystical. Within months of agreeing to convert, she began collecting icons, images of holy beings and objects. Believing, as the Church taught, that God and the saints helped and healed people through these icons, she surrounded herself with them, then spent hours each day on her knees in prayer. She also began putting faith in so-called holy men—hermits, soothsayers, wandering monks, and faith healers. They were, she believed, a direct link to God.

"WHAT WILL BECOME OF ME?"

Alix arrived in Russia at a gloomy time. Diagnosed with kidney disease, the once brawny Alexander III had wasted away almost overnight. Now he lay shrunken, sleepless, and spitting up blood in his palace in the Crimea. None of the doctors attending the tsar bothered to discuss his condition with Nicholas. Sweeping past the heir to the throne and his reserved fiancée, they reported only to Alexander's ministers and his wife, Empress Marie.

Their behavior offended Alix. How dare the doctors treat the future tsar like a nobody! It could not be tolerated. "Be firm and make the doctors come to you . . . first," she scolded Nicholas. "Don't let others be first and you left out. . . . Show your mind, and don't let others forget who you are." And then, in case he thought she was being too pushy, she added, "Forgive me, lovey."

Nicholas thought there was nothing to forgive. Eager and grateful for her guidance, he called himself "your poor little Nicky with a weak will," and thanked her for her "reprimanding words." He even promised "to do better . . . be firmer."

Alix was pleased. "Darling boysy," she gushingly replied, "me loves you, oh so very tenderly. . . . You must always tell me everything, you can fully trust me, look upon me as a bit of yourself. . . . How I love you, darling treasure, my very own One."

On the afternoon of November 1, 1894, Tsar Alexander died. The grief-stricken Nicholas suddenly found himself ruler of all Russia. Terrified, he pulled his cousin Sandro into his study. "What am I going to do?" he cried once he'd shut the door behind them. "What is going to happen to me . . . to all of Russia? I am not prepared to be tsar. I never wanted to become one. I know nothing of the business of ruling. I have no idea of how to even talk to the ministers."

Sandro worried, too. He knew Nicholas's father had held the empire together with his forceful personality and iron will. Now, with timid Nicholas on the throne, what would become of Russia?

THE FUNERAL BRIDE

Proper etiquette required Alix to return to Hesse to wait out the official mourning period before marrying the new tsar. But Nicholas would not hear of it. He needed his fiancée's forcefulness and strength of will. How else could he carry such a terrible burden? He insisted they marry as quickly as possible.

Alix agreed. "My poor Nicky's cross is heavy," she later wrote, "all the more so as he has nobody on whom he can thoroughly rely and who can be a real help to him." For now, Alix would become both wife *and* adviser. Reminding her future husband that beneath her long skirts she wore a pair of "invisible trousers," she vowed to "be all, know all and share all" with him. "Beloved," she would repeatedly say over the coming years, *"listen to me."*

But the couple could not marry until Alix was officially a member of the Russian Orthodox Church. And so, the day after Tsar Alexander's death, Nicholas and Alix, along with his mother, went to the palace chapel for the conversion ceremony. "Alix repeated her responses and the prayers wonderfully," said Nicholas. Afterward, he issued his very first imperial decree, proclaiming his beloved's new Russian name (as tradition demanded). Henceforth, the former Princess Alix of Hesse would be known as "the truly believing . . . Alexandra Feodorovna." (The name Feodorovna was in honor of Fyodor Romanov, father of the first Romanov tsar, and therefore founder of the Romanov dynasty.)

Four weeks later, on November 26, 1894, the couple married in the chapel of St. Petersburg's immense Winter Palace. Even though the court was still in mourning, black had been banished for the day, and Alexandra wore a silver brocade dress with a robe of gold cloth lined with ermine, and a sparkling diamond crown. "Our marriage seemed to me a mere extension of the [funeral rites]," the bride wrote to her sister, "with this difference, that now I wore a white dress instead of a black."

Meanwhile, the Russian people—Alexandra's future subjects— viewed the marriage with fear and superstition. Calling her "the funeral bride," they shook their heads and crossed themselves. "She has come to us behind a coffin," one subject muttered darkly. "She brings misfortune with her."

THE RESERVED EMPRESS

Before Alexandra's marriage, her grandmother had given her an important piece of advice: win the love and respect of the Russian people. It was, counseled Queen Victoria, her first duty as the new empress. But reserved Alexandra found this task overwhelming. In private with her husband, she was warm and affectionate and "lost her customary shyness," remarked one court official. "She joked and laughed . . . played a lively part in the games, and became very nimble-witted in general conversation." At public ceremonies,

however, she became a "different individual." Because she felt awkward and ill at ease, she stood ramrod straight, with her lips tightly
pursed. Said another courtier, "She kept herself aloof and seemed
unapproachable, unable to make small talk or to smile as a person
in her position should."

St. Petersburg society quickly judged her to be stuck-up, strait-
laced, and utterly boring. They made fun of her taste in clothes, her
dancing skills, her manners. She was, they claimed, "perpetually
unamused."

As for Alexandra, society's excessiveness shocked her. She dis-
approved of what she considered the aristocracy's idle and list-
less lives—sleeping until noon, then rushing off to hairdressers
or gambling clubs before returning home to dress for yet another
late-night party. Most of all, she was repulsed by the foolish and
vicious gossip that swirled through their drawing rooms, as well as
society's "unwholesomely precocious outlook on life." The higher
classes, she determined, were "corroded by a lack of [religious] faith
and marked by depravity." In disgust, she began striking names
from the list of people welcome at the palace. Members of the extended imperial family—aunts, uncles, cousins, even Nicholas's
brothers and sisters—suddenly found themselves scratched off.
"Oh, these young men of the family with . . . love of pleasure instead of duty," she grumbled to her husband. "They drag [in] so
much dirt."

"I trust you to always know best, Lovey-mine," Nicholas
would say.

Alexandra was relieved. Closing herself off, she grew gruff with
strangers, avoided coming down for meals if there were guests, and
often left social events early with the excuse that she felt ill. More
and more she stayed in her private rooms. When she did venture
out, she hid herself under a parasol so no one could see her face.
All she wanted, she confessed, was to escape the "spider's net" of

society and be alone with her "own Huzy." And so she begged him to abandon the Winter Palace (where most Romanovs had lived and reigned since the 1700s) and move to the country. Eager to please his "sweet Wifey," Nicholas agreed. Just six months after their wedding, the couple moved to the Imperial Park at Tsarskoe Selo, or "the Tsar's Village."

"A WORLD APART"

Located fifteen miles south of St. Petersburg on eight hundred acres of thick green lawn, the Imperial Park at Tsarskoe Selo was "a world apart, an enchanted fairyland," recalled one visitor. Ornate bridges crossed ponds and canals. Footpaths wound between rows of fruit trees and lush flower gardens. On warm spring days, bowers of lilacs perfumed the entire park.

Among the place's many wonders was a man-made lake that could be drained and refilled. On one shore stood a marble folly shaped like a Turkish bath, its gilt-tipped minaret stretching toward the sky. Nearby, an exact replica of a Chinese village glimmered exotically in the sunlight, while the tower of a medieval castle built intentionally to look like a ruin peeked above the treetops. Past the rose meadow crouched a granite pyramid, as well as the stone-turreted Elephant House. On warm days, the elephant—a gift from the king of Siam (modern-day Thailand)—bathed in a nearby pond while tame deer brought from faraway Mongolia wandered freely.

There were also two palaces within the Imperial Park. The first was the immense Catherine Palace, sprawling across the landscape in an extravagant profusion of blue, white, and gold. The second, located in a wooded corner of the park, was the simpler, yellow-and-white Alexander Palace.

Around all of it—palaces and park—ran a tall iron fence protected by Cossacks with sabers and pointed spears. Additionally, five thousand Imperial Guards patrolled both the gates and the footpaths inside the park, while hordes of plainclothes policemen kept an eye on the army of servants who worked on the grounds or in the palaces.

Just beyond the gates stood the town of Tsarskoe Selo with its stylish shops and mansions. A graceful, tree-lined road stretched from the train station to the Imperial Park's front gates. It was this road the imperial couple took the day they moved to the country.

Alexandra had already picked the smaller palace with its mere (by royal standards) one hundred rooms for their new home. Declaring it a "charming, dear, precious place," she began creating her own private world. In the palace's left wing, beyond the columned ballroom and the ornate reception halls adorned with carved pilasters and gilded moldings, Alexandra chose two dozen ordinary rooms to serve as her family's living quarters. She decorated them to her taste, replacing the crimson carpets and velvet curtains with chintz upholstery, wallpaper with flowered prints, porcelain knick-knacks, and potted palms. "It is incredible," said one visitor, "that these people can live surrounded by such bric-a-brac when they could have the most beautiful things in the world." Still, there was a cozy drawing room in maple and shades of green, a music room with two grand pianos, a library, two studies, and a large dressing room for Nicholas. There was also an indoor saltwater swimming pool.

But the room most gossiped about was Alexandra's lilac drawing room. Almost everything in it was a pale purple, her favorite color—the wallpaper, the curtains, even the furniture was purple and white. People who saw it were aghast. They accused the empress of having common tastes and called her a hausfrau. But Alexandra loved her room. It was, recalled one courtier, her "opal-hued" world, the one place where she felt completely safe. Here, she could recline on a low sofa beneath a large painting of the Mother of God, delighting in the scent of the fresh flowers brought in daily by the servants, while gazing happily at the jumble of family photographs that crowded her shelves, tables, and mantelpiece.

Double doors led to the imperial couple's bedroom. Here, too, lilac was the dominant color, but the walls, instead of displaying family photographs, were covered with more than seven hundred icons. Each had been hung on the silk wallpaper by the empress herself.

Once settled in, Alexandra did not want to leave. Nor did she want Nicholas to leave. They knew each other "through and through," she told him, and only needed to be together, "utterly cut off in every way."

Nicholas agreed. "It's inexpressibly wonderful to live here quietly, without seeing anyone—all day and night together!" he said. And so while the ministers, the treasury, and other government offices remained in St. Petersburg, the ruler of it all retreated to the country. He still read reports and spoke with advisers who came to him regularly from the city. He still signed orders and settled disputes. But secluded as he was in the country, tucked away from the happenings in the capital, Nicholas quickly lost touch with people and events. His and Alexandra's life together was "a sort of everlasting cozy tea-party," remarked one historian, fine for an ordinary private citizen, but not for the ruler of Russia.

CHAPTER TWO

❧ "WHAT A DISAPPOINTMENT!" ❧

1895–1901

ROYAL BABY

By the fall of 1895, Nicholas and Alexandra were expecting their first child. Once again, the Alexander Palace buzzed with workmen. When all was done, the rooms on the second floor of the private wing had been transformed into the imperial nursery, a cheerful complex of bedrooms, classrooms, and playroom. Big windows allowed the place to fill with light. Velvety carpets in shades of green and blue covered the hardwood floors. And at Alexandra's request, a private staircase (and later, a small elevator) was installed connecting these rooms to her own. She envisioned reclining on the sofa in her lilac drawing room while listening to the sounds of her children playing happily overhead.

Again and again, the couple visited the nursery. Just looking at it filled them with "utter delight," Nicholas admitted. "Sometimes we simply sit in silence . . . and admire the walls, the fireplaces, the furniture."

Both hoped for a son. For the past one hundred years, Russia's law of succession had specified that only males could inherit the throne. To ensure his family's future, as well as a stable succession of power, it was imperative that Nicholas have a son. Otherwise, when he died, his vast dynasty would pass to his younger brother and *his* son. Nicholas's own children would lose their direct link to the throne.

Still, the couple wasn't overly worried. Whenever Nicholas laid his hands on his wife's growing belly, he felt reassured. "[The baby] has become very big and kicks about and fights a great deal inside," he told his mother. Surely a rough-and-tumble son was on the way.

Early on the morning of November 16, 1895, Alexandra's pains began. As doctors tended to her in the bedroom, Nicholas hurried to his study. Excitedly, he ordered artillerymen in St. Petersburg to stand beside their cannons. Tradition prescribed that a thunderous three hundred rounds would be fired to announce the birth of a future tsar; one hundred and one shots would announce the birth of a daughter.

Hours passed. Nicholas paced and chain-smoked. At last, at nine o'clock that evening, a baby's cry was heard. "All the anxiety was over," Nicholas later remembered. He hurried to his wife's side.

Minutes later, the cannons in St. Petersburg began to boom. For miles around, Russians stopped what they were doing and started counting.

They listened for the hundred and *second* shot.

It never came. The empress had given birth to a girl—the grand duchess Olga Nikolaevna.

"God, what happiness!" Nicholas rejoiced in his diary. "I can hardly believe it's really our child!"

He knew some of his relatives were disappointed. But there was plenty of time to have a boy. After all, he and Alexandra were still young—she'd just celebrated her twenty-third birthday; he was twenty-seven. In the meantime, the couple was overjoyed with their "precious little one."

With her round face, blue-gray eyes, and button nose (which she later called her "humble snub"), Olga was a "sweet baby," said Nicholas. She was big and healthy, too, weighing a whopping ten pounds at birth. "She does not look at all new-born, because she is such a big baby with a full head of hair," her father bragged.

Unlike most members of the nobility, who handed off their infants to nurses and nannies, Alexandra cared for Olga herself. She nursed and bathed the baby, changed her diapers, and sang her lullabies. "You can imagine our immense happiness," she wrote to one of her sisters. "We have acquired a wonderful little one who is so nice to care for."

Olga remained in the lace-draped bassinet beside her parents' bed for several weeks before finally being sent upstairs to the nursery. "A pity and rather a bore," remarked Nicholas when the time came. Still, an empress could not devote *all* her hours to motherhood. It wasn't socially acceptable. So Olga was placed in the capable hands of a nurse.

Nicholas and Alexandra continued to fawn over their baby. Nicholas's sister Xenia recalled one afternoon at the palace. Before teatime, the proud parents took her up to the nursery. But rather than having the baby brought out for everyone's inspection as expected, the tsar and empress did something surprising. To Xenia's astonishment, they climbed into the playpen and played with their daughter!

ANOTHER DARK OMEN?

In May 1896, six months after Olga's birth, Nicholas and Alexandra traveled to Russia's old capital, Moscow. The twelve-month mourning period for Alexander III was finally over, and it was time to crown the new tsar.

Elaborate preparations had been made. No expense was spared, no detail overlooked. Beneath the five golden domes of an ornate cathedral, Nicholas swore his oath as tsar and judge of Russia. Afterward, he turned and crowned Alexandra "so carefully, so tenderly," recalled his sister Olga, that it brought tears to the eyes of the onlookers. Then Nicholas settled himself on the Diamond Throne, every inch of which was encrusted with jewels and pearls, while Alexandra sat on the Ivory Throne.

Meanwhile, on a nearby military field, hundreds of thousands of peasants gathered. They had traveled from all across the country to glimpse their new ruler. They had also come for the feasts and presents traditionally given to them by the tsar on such momentous occasions. But the next morning, panic broke out. Somehow rumor started that there was not enough beer or gifts to go around. The crowd pushed forward, eager to grab their share. Some wooden planks that had been placed over several deep ditches gave way. Men, women, and children tripped and fell. Unable to rise in the mass of pushing, shoving bodies, they were trampled, crushed, suffocated. When the frantic surge ended, an estimated fourteen hundred people were dead.

When Nicholas heard the news, he wanted to cancel that evening's festivities. Deeply distressed and in tears, he declared he could not possibly attend the ball being given in his honor by the French ambassador. But his uncle Serge (Alexander III's brother) convinced the still-inexperienced tsar otherwise. Failing to appear would insult their French allies, Serge told him. And that, he insisted, would only cause more scandal.

Nicholas bowed to the older man's judgment. And so, on the night of the tragedy, the imperial couple appeared at the glittering ball. They danced "on top of the corpses," noted one reporter.

The couple did try to comfort their subjects. They spent the next day visiting hospitals. They paid for all the funerals. And they gave a thousand rubles—an enormous sum equal to years of a peasant's income—to each of the victims' families. But it was too late. The people's first impression was the lasting one. And they took it as a bad omen. The reign of Nicholas II, many peasants predicted, would be beset with troubles from God.

A New Baby

By September, Alexandra was pregnant again—and feeling miserable. Her back ached. Her legs swelled. And she experienced such debilitating nausea that the doctor confined her to bed for seven weeks. When she was finally allowed up, she had to be pushed around in a wheelchair.

The entire family's expectations ran high. Surely this time Alexandra was carrying a son.

But on June 10, 1897, she gave birth to another daughter—the grand duchess Tatiana Nikolaevna. As the cannons boomed one hundred and one times, the dowager empress received a telegram announcing her granddaughter's birth. "Mama's emotion was intense," Xenia said with subtle meaning.

Nicholas's cousin Grand Duke Konstantin was just sitting down to lunch at the officers' club when he received word informing him of the baby's birth. "The news soon spread," he wrote in his diary. "Everyone was very disappointed."

Alexandra grew anxious. As empress, she knew her most important job was to produce an heir for Russia. And even though her new daughter was perfect, a little miracle from God, she'd failed.

The only person who did not seem discouraged was Nicholas. In his diary that night he wrote: "The second bright day in our life . . . the Lord blessed us with a daughter—Tatiana." Marveling at her fuzz of chestnut hair and large gray eyes, he was astonished by how much she looked like her mother.

BEYOND THE PALACE GATES:
LULLABIES FOR PEASANT BABIES

In 1898, a Russian author named Olga Petrovna Semyonova began closely observing several peasant villages near her family estate in Riazan province south of Moscow. She soon discovered that because more than half of all peasant children died, their mothers were emotionally distant. They were afraid to love their children. In fact, the death of an infant in these poor families was often regarded as a blessing, and a common saying when a child died was, "Thank goodness the Lord thought better of it!" The traditional lullabies sung to peasant babies—and recorded by Semyonova in her book, which was originally titled The Life of "Ivan": Sketches of Peasant Life from One of the Black Earth Provinces—*show how poverty affected the bonds between mother and child. Here is one example:*

> Hush, hush, hushaby my baby,
> A man lives at the end of the village.
> He's neither poor, nor rich,
> He has many children,
> They sit on a bench
> And eat straw.
> I'll make you suffer even more,
> I won't give you anything to eat.
> I won't make a bed for you.

"AND SO, THERE'S NO HEIR"

By fall 1898, Alexandra was again pregnant. And again hopes ran high. Surely *this* time there would be an heir. But when the cannons rumbled on June 26, 1899, they announced the birth of yet another girl—the grand duchess Marie Nikolaevna.

"And so, there's no heir," Cousin Konstantin grumbled. "The whole of Russia will be disappointed by this news."

This time, Nicholas and Alexandra were more than disappointed. They were alarmed. Every pregnancy was getting harder for Alexandra. While carrying Marie, the empress had not been able to walk without experiencing shooting back and leg pains. Forced to go everywhere by wheelchair, she'd even needed attendants to help her roll over in bed.

And then there was Nicholas's family—his mother, sisters, cousins, and nephews. Alexandra knew they scorned her for not fulfilling her duty. The country demanded an heir. The imperial line depended on her. More and more, she sank to her knees before her icons, begging God for the miracle of a son.

THE DARK SISTERS COME CALLING

Not long after Marie's birth, Nicholas's cousins came to tea—the grand duchesses Militsa and Anastasia. Known as the dark sisters because they dabbled in the occult, the two were notorious for the midnight séances they held in their St. Petersburg palaces. But that wasn't all. Both women believed in a host of psychic phenomena—ghosts, astrology, even magic.

Now, as each sister settled into one of Alexandra's purple-and-white upholstered chairs, they noticed how pale and strained the empress looked. Was she ill?

Not ill, Alexandra confessed, but afraid—afraid she'd never give birth to a son.

There *was* someone who could help, the sisters said. And they told the empress about a French mystic and "soul doctor" called "Dr." Philippe (though he was not a medical doctor), who could heal the sick by chanting, predict the future by praying, and make himself invisible just by donning a magic hat. Most incredible of all, he could tell the gender of an unborn child, even *change* it from a girl to a boy.

Alexandra accepted every word as truth. After all, the Russian Orthodox Church believed in seers, holy men, martyrs, and living saints as well as visions, miracles, and speaking in tongues. For centuries, it had taught that God often blessed ordinary men with the divine ability to heal bodies and souls, in addition to the ability to act as spiritual guides to the rich and powerful. "Holy Russia abounds in saints," declared one church official in 1901. "God sends consolation from time to time in the guise of simple men."

THE MYSTERIOUS "DR." PHILIPPE

Nicholas and Alexandra met with "Dr." Philippe in early 1901 when she was already pregnant with her fourth child. A portly man with wire-rimmed glasses and a black handlebar mustache, "Dr." Philippe gave the empress what he called a "moral examination" by peering deep into her eyes for several long moments. Confidently, he declared that her next child would be a boy . . . *if* she partook of his "astral medicine."

Alexandra eagerly followed his instructions. She prayed for hours on end, and forced down glass after glass of bitter herbal concoctions. She even bathed in the moonlight on what "Dr." Philippe called "astrologically auspicious nights." And as the months slipped by, Nicholas and Alexandra's confidence grew. This time—they *knew* it—they were having a boy.

IS IT A BOY?

Dawn was just breaking, the sky above St. Petersburg streaked with pink and violet, when the cannons once more began to boom. Already, working women wearing colored kerchiefs prowled in search of bargains at the fish market. Aproned vendors set up their stalls along the wide and sweeping boulevards. Laborers, their faces thin and careworn, trudged across the arching canal bridges toward their factory jobs. But with the first shot, many people stopped. The empress Alexandra had given birth to her fourth child! They began counting: *odin, dva, tri* . . .

But just as before, the boom of the one hundred and first shot was followed by . . . silence. It was another girl.

"My God, what a disappointment!" exclaimed Xenia.

Her words summed up the country's feelings.

Some people shook their heads in disbelief, or spat three times on the pavement, a traditional Russian gesture of disgust. A few even exclaimed, *"Doloi nemku"*—"Away with that German woman on the throne!"

Newspapers around the world gloomily reported the birth. "Czar Has Another Daughter," read the *New York Times* headline the next morning. "Russian People Again Disappointed."

Meanwhile, Nicholas struggled with his emotions. Whistling for one of his collies, he set off on a long walk through the gardens. They'd followed "Dr." Philippe's instructions exactly. So when Alexandra's pains began at three a.m. that June morning in 1901, they'd both felt utterly confident. And yet . . .

It was God's will, Nicholas now told himself. And God's will must always be accepted without complaint. After all, everything that happened in life was the result of God's will, so it was pointless to question the meaning of events. "God knows what is good for us," Nicholas often reminded himself. "We must bow down our heads [and] repeat the sacred words, 'Thy will be done.'"

Resigned, masking his true feelings behind a forced smile, he headed inside to kiss his wife and newborn. Then he set about sending telegrams to relatives and friends all around the world. Glad news, he told them: his fourth daughter—the grand duchess Anastasia Nikolaevna—was born.

"A SMALL FAMILY CIRCLE"
1903–1904

FOUR LITTLE ROMANOVS

By 1903, four little girls romped in the nursery. Seven-year-old Olga and six-year-old Tatiana shared one of the bedrooms, and were called "the Big Pair" by their parents. Four-year-old Marie and two-year-old Anastasia shared another of the bedrooms, and were called "the Little Pair."

By the look of their bedrooms, no one would have guessed their father was the richest ruler in the world. Fitted out with a hodge-podge of furniture that had been found around the palace, the rooms were a clutter of overstuffed chairs and mismatched tables. And unlike many of their royal cousins, who slumbered on silky-soft beds, all four of the girls slept on narrow, folding army cots. This was a Romanov family tradition meant to teach self-discipline and guard against self-indulgence. Each cot was covered with a blue satin comforter monogrammed with its owner's initials, and was so light that even little Anastasia could easily move it around. And she did. In the summer, along with her sisters, she dragged her cot closer to the open windows. In the winter, she moved it closer to the furnace grate. And at Christmastime, she hauled it into the playroom, where every year one of the family's six holiday trees was set up. There, under the sparkling ornaments, the sisters drifted contentedly off to sleep.

Just down the hall from the girls' bedroom was their bathroom, where two tubs waited: one made of ordinary porcelain, the other of solid silver and engraved with the names of all the imperial children who had ever splashed about in it. But as with the army cots, bath time was another chance for the girls to learn self-discipline. Every morning, they shivered in the porcelain tub as their nurse-maid poured buckets of cold water over their heads. Mercifully, warm baths were allowed at night. These were taken in the silver tub and, later in their teenaged years, would be scented with one of the few luxuries the girls were permitted: perfumes made just for them by Coty of Paris—rose for Olga, jasmine for Tatiana, lilac for Marie, and violet for Anastasia.

One item the empress did not stint on was the girls' clothing. She liked to outfit the grand duchesses by pairs in matching and expensive dresses. These were usually "fresh white frocks and colored sashes," recalled one family friend. Their long hair was tied back with blue satin bows.

A ROYAL DAY

And so the family's days passed comfortably and pleasantly. But most of all, they passed predictably. Every morning after their nanny, Margaretta Eagar, woke them, the grand duchesses—still sleepy and in their nightgowns—slipped down the narrow wooden stairs that connected their rooms to those of their parents.

Nicholas was long gone. Having risen at dawn, he'd already been at work in his study for hours, plowing through the mountain of documents that appeared on his desk each day. Alexandra, propped up on pillows in bed, put aside the letters she'd been writing to greet her daughters.

Good morning, "sweety darling Mama," the girls would chirp. Dutifully, they each kissed their mother's cheek, then perched on the side of the bed or curled up in a chair to listen as Alexandra went over the day's schedule, and reminded them yet again about proper manners: "Remember, elbows off the table, sit straight and eat your meat nicely."

Afterward, the girls scampered back upstairs to find the wardrobe maid waiting to help them bathe and dress, before the chambermaid served breakfast at the little table in the nursery playroom. Then it was time for their daily medical examination. Ticklish little Anastasia always giggled when Dr. Botkin, the court physician, pressed his stethoscope to her chest.

By midmorning, the grand duchesses headed for the park. Supervised by Nanny Eagar and protected by a dozen sentries, the girls pedaled their bicycles down the shaded lanes or played in the little house built on Children's Island. Located in the middle of a pond, the house had a sitting room and a study fitted out with child-size furniture. All they had to do was lower a drawbridge to cross over to the island. Sometimes Olga and Tatiana were allowed to paddle across the pond in a small rowboat, tying up to the island's tiny dock. In the winter, the girls built snowmen or whooshed down the sled run on their toboggans.

Soon it was lunchtime—the only formal meal of the day. That was when members of Nicholas's court gathered in the palace's semicircular hall. Though Alexandra rarely appeared, Nicholas always took his place at the head of the table. The grand duchesses—even little Anastasia—sat beside him. Before the army of white-gloved waiters served the cabbage soup, boiled fish, or suckling pig with horseradish, a priest stood to give the blessing. Sometimes their French chef stood in the doorway, waiting to accept compliments.

After lunch, Nicholas returned to his study, and the girls headed for the playroom. Marie liked to act out stories in the puppet theater, while Anastasia played with a one-eyed, one-armed doll she'd named Vera. Sometimes the girls went with their mother for a ride through the park or around the town outside the gates. That was when the stable boys pushed out the carriage and hitched up the horses. Two footmen took their places at the rear. The coachman took his place behind the reins. And squads of Cossack guards, sentries, and policemen took their places along the route. By the time the carriage rolled away from the palace, there was a protector hiding behind every tree and bush.

It wasn't until four o'clock, teatime, that the entire family finally came together. Just scrubbed and wearing fresh white dresses, the girls joined their parents in the lilac drawing room. Alexandra poured the tea, then handed around plates of hot bread, butter, and English biscuits. Nicholas smoked and read. Olga and Tatiana, who were just learning to sew, labored over their embroidery hoops. And Marie and Anastasia played on the thick green carpet. "It is very pleasant to spend [time] in a small family circle," declared Nicholas.

But the family circle was still incomplete. It needed a son.

Beyond the Palace Gates: Another Family Circle

Alexei Peshkov (later known as the writer Maxim Gorky) grew up in his grandfather's household in Nizhny Novgorod, an industrial city on the Volga River. In his book first published under the title My Childhood *(1913), he describes his life the year he turned nine:*

> Grandpa rented two dim cellar rooms in an old house at
> the bottom of a small hill. . . . Nearby rose factory stacks
> discharging a thick smoke, which the winter wind beat
> down over the whole city; there was always a burnt odor

in our rooms. In the morning hours we heard wolves howling.

Grandma was maid of all work from morning to night. She cooked, scrubbed, split firewood, kept the water pails filled; and when she came to bed she sighed with fatigue.

I, too, made my contribution. . . . I went through the streets and the backyards with a sack, collecting rags, paper, bones and metal scraps. Junkmen paid me two greven [ten cents] for a forty-pound bundle. . . . When grandma accepted the money from me, she hastily stuffed it into her skirt pocket, looked down and [said], "Ah, thanks, darling. This will get us our food." . . . A tear wobbled on the tip of her grainy nose. . . .

My stepfather had run up debts, lost his job and gone off, so [that summer] mama came back to grandpa's with my baby brother, Nicky, whom I had to tend. . . . Mama [was] so anemic and feeble she could hardly stand up . . . and the baby . . . was too weak to cry out; hunger only brought a whimper from him. In his naps, after meals, his breathing had a curious sound, like a kitten mewing.

After a good look at him, grandpa said, "What he needs is lots of rich food; but I haven't enough to feed all of you."

From the bed in the corner, mama . . . said hoarsely, "It's little enough that he wants."

"A little here and a little there makes a heap." Then, to me, with a wave of his hand, he said, "Nicky needs the sun—[take] him out[side]."

I . . . did as grandpa advised. . . . I felt an immediate attachment to my brother. I felt he understood everything

I was thinking. . . . The little one held out his hands to me, with a shake of his little white head. His scanty hair was almost gray, and there was a sage and elderly expression in his [tiny] face. . . .

The yard was small, foul and . . . gave off sharp scents of decay. Next door there was a place where cattle were butchered . . . [and] the bellow of calves was succeeded by the odor of blood which . . . [hung] in the air like a transparent, purple web.

When a beast bellowed . . . Nick would blink; his lips would puff out in attempted mimicry; but all he could do was blow out a "phoo."

At noon grandpa . . . would announce, "Dinner!"

He saw to the child's feeding. He took him on his knee, pushed bits of bread and potatoes into [his] mouth . . . and the dribble covered Nicky's thin lips and pointed chin. After the child had taken a little food, grandpa would raise the baby's shirt, prod the swollen abdomen, and consider aloud, "Has he had enough? Does he have to have any more?"

And from the dark corner would come mama's voice. "See how he's going after the bread?"

"Little fool. How could he know how much he needs?" But he gave Nick another morsel.

This feeding made me ashamed; I always felt a sickening lump in my throat.

"That's all," grandpa would conclude. "Give him to his mother."

I lifted Nicky, who whimpered and reached his hands toward the table. Mother, painfully raising herself, advanced toward me, holding out her dreadfully emaciated arms, dry and long and thin, like boughs off a Christmas tree. . . .

The end came on a Sunday in August about noon. My stepfather had just come back to town and gotten a job. Grandma had brought Nicky to him. . . . Mama was to be moved there in a few days. . . .

"Some water!" [mama called.]

I brought her a cup and, struggling to raise her head, she drank a little. . . . Slowly her long lashes closed over her eyes [and] a shadow invaded her face, occupying her every feature. . . . How long I stood at my mother's deathbed, I don't know; I stood there, holding the cup, watching her face turn gray and cold.

Just a day or two after mama's funeral grandpa told me, "Alex, I can't have you hanging around my neck. There's no room for you here. You'll have to go out into the world."

And out into the world I went.

MYSTIC MEDICINE

Despite the birth of a fourth daughter, Nicholas and Alexandra continued to meet with "Dr." Philippe, and the charlatan soon convinced the empress that she was pregnant with a son. Alexandra grew round. She began wearing loose clothing. Eventually, she retired to her drawing room too tired and heavy, she claimed, to appear in public.

News of her pregnancy swirled through the court. Everyone— the empress most of all—looked forward to the birth of an heir. But the miracle did not happen. Finally, court physicians were called in.

They told her the truth: there was no pregnancy, and there never had been. When she heard the news, recalled Nicholas's cousin Konstantin, "Alix cried a lot."

Scandalized, members of Nicholas's family insisted the fake doctor leave Russia immediately. To avoid further embarrassment, the imperial couple agreed. But Alexandra still had faith in the mystic. So "Dr." Philippe was called to the tsar's study for one last consultation. With the curtains closed tight and just a single candle flickering, the mystic took Alexandra's hand. Their wish for a son would be gratified, he told them, if and only if she prayed to Seraphim of Sarov.

Seraphim, a holy man who had lived years earlier, was remembered by common people as a miracle worker. But were the stories true? Orthodox Church officials, hoping to declare Seraphim a saint, had been searching for evidence of these miracles. But they had found nothing conclusive.

"Dr." Philippe now suggested the imperial couple step in on Seraphim's behalf. Make him a saint, he urged. Then he bent down and whispered the rest of his instructions into Alexandra's ear.

Eager to fulfill the mystic's instructions, Nicholas called in church officials. He commanded them to declare Seraphim a saint. But the churchmen refused. Saints are not made simply because the tsar orders it, they said.

"*Everything* is within the Emperor's province," Alexandra replied in a steely voice. He could even send *certain* Orthodox officials to jail.

The officials understood. They hastily declared Seraphim a saint.

And so, in July 1903, Nicholas and Alexandra traveled to Seraphim's hometown of Sarov in southeast Russia for the canonization ceremony. Publicly, they visited churches and marched in holy processions. But privately, in the dead of night, Alexandra followed a winding path through the deep forest to a spring said to be the source of St. Seraphim's healing powers. Following "Dr." Philippe's whispered instructions, she lowered herself into its moonlit waters and prayed for a son.

Just three months later, an overjoyed Alexandra learned she was pregnant. She was convinced it was because of "Dr." Philippe. He had interceded with the Almighty on her behalf, and God had blessed her.

This event cemented her belief in mysticism. From now on, she would blindly throw open the palace doors to many a strange or shady character who claimed to have holy powers. "Someday you will have another friend like me who will speak to you of God," "Dr." Philippe had also whispered to her that night in Nicholas's study.

Alexandra looked forward to that day.

THE HEIR

On August 12, 1904, as the imperial family was sitting down to lunch, Alexandra suddenly felt pains. She rushed to her bedroom. Just one hour later, she gave birth to an eight-pound baby boy. Wrote Nicholas in his diary, "A great never-to-be-forgotten day when the mercy of God visited us so clearly." The celebratory cannons began—three hundred salvos this time. Across Russia, bells rang and flags waved. In village churches and city cathedrals, special thanksgiving services were held where jubilant Russians packed the pews.

His Imperial Highness Alexei Nikolaevich, Sovereign Heir Tsarevich, Grand Duke of Russia looked like a healthy baby. Court official A. A. Mosolov recalled the first time he saw him: "The baby was being given a bath. He was lustily kicking out in the water."

Plucking the infant from the tub, the tsar dried him off and held him up. "There he was," said Mosolov, "naked, chubby, rosy—a wonderful boy!"

But just six weeks after his birth, Alexei started bleeding from the navel. In his diary, a worried Nicholas wrote: "A hemorrhage began this morning without the slightest cause. . . . It lasted until evening. The child was remarkably quiet and even merry but it was a dreadful thing to have to live through such anxiety."

The bleeding continued on and off for the next two days. Then it stopped. But his parents' fears continued to grow. What was wrong with their boy?

Hemophilia, the court physicians diagnosed.

Alexei's blood did not clot properly. Even a minor cut could take hours or even days to stop bleeding. But the greatest danger came from minor blows that might—or might not—start a slow oozing of blood beneath the skin that flowed for hours (or even days) into surrounding muscles and joints. This internal bleeding caused big purple swellings that pressed on Alexei's nerves. The pain from this pressure was so agonizing that he would scream out in pain for days on end, unable to sleep or eat. Relief came only when he fainted. This pressure, however, was his body's way of trying to slow the bleeding enough for a clot to form. Once this happened, the process of reabsorption would take place, the skin changing from purple to yellow to a normal color once again. The disease was, and still is, incurable. There was no effective treatment for hemophilia's symptoms as there is nowadays, and any episode meant weeks in bed. Far worse, every episode was life-threatening—if the bleeding did not stop, Alexei would die.

The only way to prevent internal bleeding was to keep Alexei from getting bumped or bruised. He would never be allowed to ride a bike or climb a tree, play tennis with his sisters, gallop on a horse, or wrestle on the ground with the tsar's collies. Instead, he would be watched carefully, kept from doing the things boys naturally did. His parents even appointed two sailors—Andrey Derevenko and Klementy Nagorny—to watch Alexei around the clock. Called the sailor nannies, the men stuck so close they could, claimed one historian, "reach out and catch [Alexei] before he fell."

FAMILY SECRET

Their son's illness devastated Nicholas and Alexandra. "Life lost all meaning for the imperial parents," recalled Nicholas's friend and cousin, Sandro. "My wife and I were afraid to smile in their presence. When visiting the palace, we acted as if we were in a house of mourning."

Typically, Nicholas believed Alexei's illness was God's will, and so he accepted it passively. "My own fate, and that of my family are in the hands of Almighty God," he said.

But Alexandra blamed herself for the boy's condition. Hemophilia—a genetic disease affecting predominantly males but transmitted by their mothers—was widespread in her family. Not only did several of her nephews suffer from the condition, but her own brother had died of it as a child. She knew she'd passed the disease to her son. But after she'd waited so long and prayed so hard, why had God allowed this terrible thing to happen?

Alexandra believed there could be only one explanation: God had found her unworthy. But if her unworthiness had caused Alexei's suffering, didn't it stand to reason that she could save him by becoming holier? And so she began to pray longer and harder, spending hours on her knees in the palace chapel. She covered the walls of the nursery, and even baby Alexei's crib, with hundreds of icons and religious images. She begged God to heal her son.

Until God granted that miracle, however, she and Nicholas chose to keep their boy's condition a secret. There would be no public announcement. Instead, doctors and servants were ordered to remain silent, and the word *hemophilia* was banned from palace use. Life at court became even narrower. The family, fearing the heir's condition would be discovered and talked about, rarely went out in public. And only a few family members and close friends were invited in. Convinced Alexei's illness was a threat to the tsar's regime, they withdrew completely into the protective bubble of Tsarskoe Selo.

Little did they know that the real danger to Nicholas's throne was not Alexei's hemophilia. It was the dark clouds of social unrest gathering across his empire.

PART TWO

DARK CLOUDS GATHERING

What a pity that Nicholas sleeps!
—Carl Joubert, 1904
Russia As It Really Is

CHAPTER FOUR

🌿 THE YEAR OF NIGHTMARES 🌿
1905

BLOODY SUNDAY

By 1905, the working class had begun envisioning a better life. And these visions began with books. "When I came in from work, I did not lie down to sleep immediately," recalled a weaver named Feodor Samilov. "Instead I picked up a book, lit a candle that I had bought with my own savings, and read until I could no longer keep my eyelids from closing."

He wasn't alone. The speed with which factory workers learned to read "was little short of astonishing," noted one historian. By 1905, six out of every ten laborers in Moscow were literate—an increase of twenty percent in less than ten years. And in St. Petersburg the number of working men and women who could read was three times greater than in the rest of Russia. Now the factory worker in St. Petersburg who could *not* read was the exception. The opposite was still true back in his peasant village.

These readers had almost no access to political writings. Censorship laws made such literature illegal, and newspapers faced stiff fines and forced closings if they included material considered offensive by the government. The result was that they steered clear of such writing. As for books, only those deemed appropriate by the tsar's censors were allowed on library shelves. "I read Jules Verne . . . and James [Fenimore] Cooper, and was captivated by their descriptions of journeys and discoveries," said weaver Samilov. "Over a period of five to six years, I read through the most diverse assortment of books imaginable . . . but I never encountered one that could have awakened my class consciousness." Even so, he added, "Books taught me how to think."

These literate workers were now able to picture a government more responsive to their needs; they had "caught sight of a new life," recalled factory worker Semën Balashov, "one very different from our life of servitude." In January 1905, he joined ten thousand other men, women, and children who had abandoned their jobs. Taking to the streets, they refused to return to work until their demands were met. What did they want? A living wage, an eight-hour workday, affordable housing, and public education.

An energetic young priest named Father George Gapon led them. Gapon had devised a new and dramatic way of drawing attention to the workers' demands. He would march them directly to the tsar and present him with a petition that began:

> We, the workers and inhabitants of St. Petersburg . . . our wives, our children, and our aged, helpless parents, come to THEE, O SIRE to seek justice and protection. We are impoverished; we are oppressed, overburdened with excessive toil, contemptuously treated. . . . We are suffocating in despotism and lawlessness. O SIRE we have no strength left, and our endurance is at an end. We have reached the frightful moment when death is better than the prolongation of our unbearable suffering. . . . We beseech thy help.

Gapon felt sure this would work. After all, most Russians still believed in the long-held Russian tradition of the *Batiushka Tsar,* the Father of the Russian People. While they cursed landowners, bureaucrats, police, and factory managers for their problems, they rarely blamed the tsar. It wasn't his fault, they said. He lived so close to heaven, he didn't know about his people's suffering on earth. But once they told him and handed over a petition, like a good and loving father the tsar would protect them from the greedy factory managers. He would help them win decent working and living conditions. Gapon saw himself at the head of a mass march to St. Petersburg's Winter Palace, where the tsar, stepping out onto the balcony, would receive their request with loving benevolence.

On Saturday, January 21, Gapon informed government officials about the march taking place the next day. He begged for the tsar to receive their petition at two o'clock in the afternoon. He didn't know that Nicholas was fifteen miles away at Tsarskoe Selo, or that the only people waiting for the marchers would be the soldiers Nicholas had ordered there after learning about the event. Now some twelve thousand bayonets and rifles stood ready.

The next morning, as snow swirled across the frozen rivers, workers organized themselves into processions. It was Gapon's plan for them to march along different streets, meeting at the Winter Palace Square. Wearing their best clothes for their meeting with the tsar, 120,000 men, women, and children walked peacefully along. Some carried crosses or icons. Others waved Russian flags or hoisted portraits of Nicholas and Alexandra high above their heads. As they went, they sang hymns, laughed, and talked excitedly. More than once, they burst into the national anthem, "God Save the Tsar."

But the marchers soon found their way blocked by soldiers. Unsure of what this meant, and not wanting to be late for their meeting, the workers pressed forward.

The soldiers fired.

Bullets shredded the flags, and icons, and portraits of Nicholas. Bodies fell to the snow-covered ground.

"The tsar will not help us!" cried one of the stunned workers.

"And so we have no tsar," added another darkly.

When the shooting stopped, between 150 and 200 men, women,

and children lay dead. Between 450 and 800 were wounded. And the traditional ideal of the tsar as the people's loving "father" was destroyed. No longer would Nicholas be held blameless for their troubles. Now he was a "blood-stained creature" and a "common murderer." The day itself became known as Bloody Sunday.

"Remember, son," said one father after the shooting had stopped. "Remember and swear to repay the tsar. You saw how much blood he spilled, did you see? Then swear, son, swear."

While his soldiers fired on St. Petersburg's citizens, Nicholas breakfasted with close friends and family in the semicircular hall of the Alexander Palace (as he did every Sunday morning), then attended services in the chapel. Afterward, he pulled the children around the park in their toboggan, before settling down beside the fireplace in Alexandra's drawing room with a glass of tea. It wasn't until early evening that his pleasant routine was interrupted by reports of the massacre. He was shocked. "Lord, how painful and sad this is!" he wrote later that night. But he did not blame himself. Nicholas insisted that his troops had been forced to shoot. What else could they do in the face of mob action? The workers, Nicholas asserted, should beg *his* forgiveness.

Alexandra, too, maintained it was all the workers' fault. "Yes, the troops, alas, were obliged to fire. . . . Had a *small* deputation brought, calmly, a *real* petition for the workman's good, all would have been otherwise."

A handful of Nicholas's advisers disagreed. They begged him to consider measures that would improve workers' lives. "I do not want to die without having told you . . . what great evil you will bring to yourself and to millions if you continue on your present course," Count Leo Tolstoy warned in a letter. Tolstoy, a great writer who had enjoyed wealth, success, and fame, wondered how Nicholas, "a free man not lacking for anything, and a reasonable and good man," could allow such misery to continue. He concluded that it was all the fault of their form of government. "Autocracy . . . no longer answers the needs of the Russian people," he asserted. "Give the masses the opportunity to express their desires and demands . . . improve men's lives," and prevent a revolution.

But Nicholas buried his head in the sand. "There are no labor problems in the city," he insisted. "No unrest in the countryside." Instead, he believed Russia was on the road to great progress that would, in the end, trickle down to everyone. Hadn't the imperial government, using money collected from Nicholas's subjects, built railroads that stretched across Russia? And hadn't mills, factories, and foundries sprung up all over the country? With such great changes, there were bound to be a few disruptions. But Nicholas firmly believed all would be well.

"FOOL'S PARADISE"

Over the next few months, violence spread across Russia as people reacted to Bloody Sunday. "It makes me sick to read the news," said Nicholas; "strikes in schools and factories, murdered policemen, riots." It was the beginning of what his mother called "the year of nightmares."

And yet he took almost no action to end the unrest. Instead, he remained isolated with his family at Tsarskoe Selo. In August, he took them for a two-week cruise on the Baltic Sea. Anchoring off the coasts of various Finnish islands, Nicholas and his daughters (Alexei was still too little to hike with them) explored the beaches and woods. Returning to the ship hours later, the children emptied their pockets of the treasures they'd brought back for their mother—shiny rocks, bits of shell, wildflowers. There was a reason to celebrate, too. "Baby Tsar has a new tooth!" Alexandra exuberantly reported.

Meanwhile, the country had suffered through sixteen hundred strikes since Bloody Sunday. Involving almost a million people, these labor walkouts surged and ebbed as workers joined them, then returned to their jobs, then struck again.

But then, on October 3, there was a walkout by Moscow's printers for better pay and working conditions. By mid-October, the printers in St. Petersburg and other cities went on strike, too. Then the railway workers joined the strike, bringing the country's entire train system to a grinding halt. Millions of other workers followed suit. Factory workers, schoolteachers, postal workers, telegraph operators—all walked off their jobs, as did doctors, lawyers, bankers, even the ballerinas of St. Petersburg's Imperial Mariinsky Theatre. Cities ground to a standstill. There were no newspapers or tramcars, and there was no electricity at night. Factories closed. Trains sat unmoving on the tracks. And fuel and food began to grow scarce. Day and night, mobs marched through the streets, waving red flags (a traditional revolutionary symbol) and threatening to destroy any business that did not shut its doors. No longer were people striking just for better wages and living conditions. The events of Bloody Sunday had shown them that they needed a voice in how their country was run. Only then could they hope to better themselves in society. And so they also demanded a legislature—a Duma—whose members they would elect.

This last demand was largely due to an organization called the St. Petersburg Soviet (*soviet* means "council" in Russian). Begun in early 1905 by a handful of workers from several of the city's factories, the soviet's purpose was to organize and coordinate all the strike actions happening across the city. Members urged workers to act with discipline and with common goals in mind (like the Duma the people wanted to establish). Because it took the form of a workers' government, it appealed to the city's voiceless classes. By October, the organization had over five hundred members from more than a hundred St. Petersburg factories and workshops. Perhaps more important, it inspired laborers in fifty other Russian cities to set up soviets, too.

But these soviets would be short-lived. Perceiving them as a political threat, Nicholas declared the workers' councils illegal. He had their leaders arrested, and their meetings suppressed. As quickly as the soviets had sprung up, they disappeared.

Despite the chaos in the city, Nicholas continued on as if nothing had happened. "The tragic aspect of the situation," one courtier wrote in his diary on October 14, "is that the tsar is living in an utter fool's paradise, thinking that He is as strong and all-powerful as before."

CHOICES

Ten days later, Prime Minister Count Sergei Witte took matters into his own hands. Having demanded an audience with the tsar, he bluntly told Nicholas that the country was on the verge of a revolution so potentially devastating that it would "sweep away a thousand years of history." The tsar had two choices: "Crush the rebellion by sheer force . . . and that would mean rivers of blood," Nicholas later explained to his mother, or "give to the people their civil rights, freedom of speech and press, also to have . . . a Duma."

Nicholas recoiled at the idea of these democratic reforms. "The heart of the tsar is in the hand of God," he told his ministers. Any change would weaken the sacred, moral power bestowed upon him by the Almighty. "I am not holding on to the autocracy for my own pleasure," Nicholas went on. "I act in this spirit only because I am certain that this is necessary for Russia."

Besides, it wasn't wretched living conditions that had caused the country's problems, claimed Nicholas. It was the fact that people had turned against the autocracy and their holy tsar. "We have sinned . . . and God is punishing us," he said. Therefore, strikes and protests were not a sign that the country needed democratic reform. Rather, they were God's way of telling the country it needed an even *stricter* autocracy.

His ministers tried convincing him otherwise. Better to make a few concessions than turn St. Petersburg into a battleground, they said. Count Witte even drew up a document for the tsar to sign. But Nicholas refused to give in.

Six days later, on October 30, Nicholas's cousin and commander of the St. Petersburg Military District, Grand Duke Nicholas Nikolaevich, stormed into the tsar's study. Waving a revolver, he shouted, "If the Emperor does not accept the Witte [document] . . . I shall kill myself in his presence. . . . It is necessary for the good of Russia."

Cornered, Nicholas backed down. That same day, he reluctantly signed Witte's document. Known as the October Manifesto, it granted "freedom of conscience, speech, assembly and association" to the Russian people. But most important, it promised a Duma that would allow even the lower classes of Russians to have a say in how the country was run. Among the powers given to this newly created legislature, the manifesto pledged that "no law may go into force without the consent of the Duma."

It was a stunning concession. By giving the Duma the final word on the creation of laws, Nicholas had essentially waived his autocratic rights. No longer would one man, the tsar, make all the laws affecting citizens' lives. Now a group of men, elected by the people, would decide what was best for them. "People have laid down their lives 'For the Faith, Tsar and Country'—and this is how Russia was created," fumed one nobleman. "But who is going to lay down his life 'For the State Duma'?"

Most of Nicholas's subjects, however, greeted the manifesto

joyfully. Calling off the strike, they cheered and sang. Speakers appeared on street corners, testing their new freedom of speech. People imagined a new Russia, a free Russia, a Russia that included them. Said one citizen, the country "buzzed like a huge garden full of bees on a hot summer's day."

CHAPTER FIVE

✤ LENIN, THE DUMA, AND A MYSTIC NAMED RASPUTIN ✤

1905–1907

REPRESSION AND POGROMS

On the very day the October Manifesto was proclaimed, a crowd of jubilant Moscow workers marched to the city jail. There, on this sunny autumn day filled with so much promise, they eagerly exercised their newly granted freedom of speech by peacefully demonstrating for the immediate release of all political prisoners. They sang hymns. They made speeches. And to their astonishment, the jail doors opened. One hundred and forty political prisoners—imprisoned for having spoken and written against the tsar—now stepped out onto the cobbled street. Roaring its approval, the crowd hoisted several of the released men high onto its shoulders. Triumphantly, they headed back toward the city's center. But they had not gone far before they met a large mob waving patriotic banners and carrying portraits of the tsar. As the still-celebrating workers grew closer, the mob pulled out knives and brass knuckles. Within minutes, the workers' triumph turned to terror as they were slashed and beaten. Some were forced to kneel before Nicholas's portrait, while others were made to kiss the national flag. When the attack was over, one of the prisoners lay dead, and dozens more were wounded.

Who had committed this crime? The Union of Russian People, later to be known as the Black Hundred. Staunch supporters of the tsar, members of the Black Hundred vowed to stamp out anyone they believed threatened the autocracy. This included "upstart" workers, students, and Jews—most especially Jews. Formed in early October, the Black Hundred's membership swelled with "uprooted peasants forced into towns as casual laborers; small shopkeepers . . . squeezed by . . . big business; [and] low ranking [government] officials" who felt their jobs were threatened by the new reforms. By 1906, the group claimed three hundred thousand members and one thousand branches across the country. Nicholas himself proudly wore the group's emblem and accepted one for his infant son, Alexei. Wishing the group "total success" in uniting "loyal Russians," Nicholas helped by financing the group's rabidly anti-Jewish, antiworker newspaper. He even secretly provided guns to its members. Meanwhile, policemen—acting under orders from Nicholas's minister of the interior—encouraged the Black Hundred to take to the streets, turning a blind eye as the mob attacked anyone who looked anti-tsar.

But the group's most vicious attacks were perpetrated against the Jews. In the two weeks after the signing of the October Manifesto, there were 694 separate pogroms across the country. Pogroms (derived from the Russian word meaning "to wreak havoc") were organized attacks against Jews. And while Nicholas did not instigate these attacks, he did little to discourage them. With staggering brutality, Russian subjects, provoked by the Black Hundred, rose up against their Jewish neighbors, burning homes, looting shops and synagogues, and murdering innocent men, women, and children. For the most part, police and government officials looked the other way. They took no action to stop the violence or arrest the attackers. Instead, they shared Nicholas's view that "the Yids," as he derisively called his Jewish subjects, "must be kept in their place."

Pogroms were hardly new to Russia. Attacks on Jews had been happening for centuries. One of the worst had occurred just two years earlier in the town of Kishinev. Incited by a leaflet (printed under the supervision of Nicholas's minister of the interior and paid for with the tsar's money) that read in part: "Brothers, in the name of our Savior, who gave his blood for us, in the name of our very pious Little Father, the Tsar . . . let us join on Easter Day in the cry, 'Down with the Jews!' Let us massacre these . . . monsters," Christians rioted for three days. When peace was finally restored, fifty-seven Jews (including two babies and a twelve-year-old boy) lay dead, and five hundred more were wounded. Homes and businesses—fourteen hundred in all—had been pillaged and destroyed, leaving almost two thousand Jewish families with little more than rubble. When Nicholas heard what had happened, he was pleased. "Good," he said. "The Jews needed to be taught a lesson."

Considered undesirable subjects, Jews had not only been the victims of dozens of pogroms, they'd been subjected to endless imperial decrees meant to discriminate against them. By the time Nicholas took the throne, his predecessors had already created more than fourteen hundred laws meant to limit the way Jews lived. Among them was a law forcing almost all Russian Jews (some 5.2 million, or nearly half of all Jews in the world) to live within fifteen western provinces known collectively as the Pale of Settlement. Additionally, Jews were forbidden from owning land, serving as army officers, holding a bureaucratic job, or practicing law. They were subject to special and steep taxes on their businesses, on kosher meat, and on synagogues. There were even strict quotas limiting Jewish admittance to high schools and universities. Nicholas himself decreed that those same quotas be applied to grammar schools. Because of his action, one-third of all Jewish children aged twelve and under were forbidden from going to school. Nicholas—who believed the world's Jews were conspiring against him—thoroughly approved of these restrictions.

By 1906, he also believed the uprising that had led to the October Manifesto had been entirely their fault. "They [have] been putting on airs and leading the revolutionary movement," he claimed. (While many Jews *did* join the ranks of revolutionaries, most were moderates who wanted to make changes through the Duma.)

Wrote Nicholas to his mother in November 1905: "In the first days after the Manifesto the subversive elements raised their head . . . and because nine-tenths of the trouble-makers are Jews, the people's anger turned against them. That's how the pogrom happened. It is amazing how they took place simultaneously in all the towns of Russia and Siberia. . . . [It] shows clearly what an infuriated mob can do; they surrounded the houses where revolutionaries had taken refuge, set fire to them and killed everybody trying to escape."

Alexandra agreed with her husband. "It's the Jews," she said. "[They have] filled the people's ears with bad ideas."

BEYOND THE PALACE GATES:
HOUSE NO. 13

It began on Easter Sunday—April 19, 1903—just after church let out in the Ukrainian town of Kishinev. Shouting, "Down with the Jews! Kill the Christ killers!" mobs of weapon-wielding, vodka-swilling Christians attacked the fourth district—the section of town where the Jews lived. Eight weeks later, journalist and author Vladimir Korolenko arrived in Kishinev. His goal, he explained, was to "pick one episode from the impersonal chaos known as massacre" so the world would know what happened there. He focused on one Jewish dwelling, which he called house No. 13. This is what he reported:

> About ten in the morning a policeman . . . a man well known in the neighborhood . . . strongly advised [Jewish residents] to hide themselves in their houses, and not to go out in the streets. The Jews naturally followed this advice, and they barred up the doors, gates and shutters. . . . The crowd arrived about eleven o'clock accompanied by

two patrols of soldiers, who unfortunately had "no orders" [to intervene during the pogrom] and remained in
the two by-streets above and below the doomed house.
The rioters consisted of about fifty or sixty persons,
among whom it was easy to recognize some of their good
neighbors. . . . The rioters set to work with the wholesale
destruction of everything that came to hand, and in a few
minutes the [town] square was littered with fragments of
glass and furniture and with down and feathers. It soon
became apparent, however, that the climax of horror was
to center round house No. 13.

To the left of the gate, stand some low-roofed out-
houses; in one of these the glazier Grienschpoun . . .
hid with his wife, two children, Ita Paskar, wife of the
shop assistant Gofsha Paskar, and her two children, and
a servant-girl. The door would not close on the inside,
and the structure itself was no stronger than a cardboard box. . . . The rioters rushed for the shed. . . . A
neighbor . . . was the first to stab the glazier in the neck.
The unhappy man rushed out, but they seized him and
dragged him on to the roof of the outhouse, where they
finished him off with sticks and clubs.

Some of the [other] Jews made a rush for the [attic].
Draper's assistant Berlatsky, who lived in the house with
his wife and four children, ran up first with his daughter.
He was followed by the landlord, Moses Macklin. . . . But
the murderers were not long in following the fugitives
into the loft. . . . The luckless fugitives realized that it
was impossible to hide themselves effectively in the close
and stifling attic. Hearing behind them the cries of their
pursuers, they began . . . to pull down the roof. Moses

Macklin was the first to get out. Berlatsky had first to help his daughter, Chaia, and as he was attempting to follow her, one of his pursuers reached the loft, and seized him by the legs. The daughter was attempting to drag her father up, and the pursuer was pulling him backward. But Chaia . . . suddenly ceased her efforts, and . . . implored the ruffian to let go of her father. He yielded to her entreaties. . . . The three crouched for some time on the roof of that house. Then the murderers emerged. The Jews began to run round the roof. The rioters followed at their heels. The same neighbor who [struck the glazier] was the first to wound Berlatsky. Finally all three were tripped over the edge of the roof. Chaia fell on a pile of feathers . . . and escaped with her life. The wounded Macklin and Berlatsky lay writhing with broken limbs on the pavement, where the cowardly crowd . . . finished them off with crowbars.

Nisensen . . . an accountant . . . was the last to be killed; he and his wife had hidden in the cellar, but he ran out into the street when he heard the cries of the murdered. . . . This drew the attention of the mob to himself. . . . He was caught and wounded . . . his legs and arms . . . broken in several places. . . . Then once more the same man who had first wounded Grienschpoun and Berlatsky stepped forward and struck Nisensen a blow on the head with a crowbar, which put an end to his sufferings. . . .

On the same day the news spread that the "order" . . . had at last come. It took [but] an hour and a half to restore [peace] in the town. No blood had to be shed, nor a rifle fired. A show of firmness was all that was necessary.

THE THREAT OF COMMUNISM

Meanwhile, the true revolutionaries—a handful of men and women who believed only a violent overthrow of the tsar could save Russia—still hoped to stage an armed insurrection. Most of them followed the teachings of the nineteenth-century German thinker Karl Marx. Marx saw all of history as a struggle between workers and property owners. That struggle, he believed, would end only when the people owned all natural resources (farms, forests, mineral deposits) as well as banks, railroads, utilities, and factories. Exactly how this commonly owned property would be organized was not addressed. Still, the goal was that everyone be equal. Because of this shared ownership, Marx called his new system communism. And it would come about, he theorized, only after total revolution by the working class.

Russian followers of Marx had been working toward this "total revolution" for almost thirty years. Calling themselves by the peaceful-sounding name Social Democrats (or SDs), they were, in fact, a radical group of communists who had done most of their work out of the country. Seen as a threat to the autocracy, SD party leaders had been forced by the tsar's police to flee Russia. In 1880, they had set up their party headquarters in Switzerland. From there they published anti-tsarist pamphlets and newspapers that were smuggled into St. Petersburg and other cities. Their goal was to spread communist ideas to workers as well as to the intelligentsia (academics and college students). One Russian who seized upon this dream was a short, stocky lawyer named Vladimir Ulyanov.

REVOLUTIONARY

Vladimir Ulyanov came from the very background he later claimed to scorn. His father was inspector of schools for Simbirsk province, a bureaucratic job of the first rank, entitling him to be addressed as "Your Excellency." His mother was a member of a landowning noble family. Born in 1870, little Vladimir was a difficult child. He told lies, cheated at games, and had a mean streak. But he was also smart, and an outstanding student. "Excellent in everything!" he would shout when he brought home his grades.

In 1887, Vladimir's older brother, Alexander, was arrested with seventy-two other university students for plotting to kill Tsar Alexander III (Nicholas's father). As one of the group's leaders, Alexander Ulyanov was hanged. No one knows how this affected seventeen-year-old Vladimir. Most historians believe it spurred him to join the revolutionary movement, although he never admitted as much publicly. That same year, he graduated from high school at the top of his class, without any outward signs of distress.

In the fall of 1887, he entered Kazan University. But within weeks, he was expelled for taking part in a small student demonstration. For the next five years, he lived on his mother's family estate, earning his law degree from home while also studying the works of Karl Marx and other socialist writings. He soon considered himself to be a professional revolutionary, vowing to devote all his energies to overthrowing the tsar and establishing a people's government. Since Marx's theory claimed revolution would begin in the cities, Vladimir moved to St. Petersburg in 1893. There he joined a like-minded group of revolutionaries involved in organizing workers' strikes and distributing antigovernment pamphlets. But in 1895, the police caught up with him. He spent one year in prison, followed by three years of exile in Siberia.

Because of his wealth and education, Vladimir's time in this frozen landscape was not one of hardship. Allowed to choose where he lived, he selected a village near the Mongolian border, taking along one thousand rubles and one hundred books. This made him both the wealthiest and most educated man in town. From his cozy rented rooms, he began a voluminous correspondence with other professional revolutionaries in Russia and across Europe. He wrote his own economic theories, and translated radical works from other countries into Russian. By the time his Siberian exile ended, Vladimir was no longer an obscure revolutionary—he was gaining a European-wide reputation as a leader of the communist movement.

He did not return to St. Petersburg. Instead, in 1901, Vladimir went abroad, where he wandered through Europe's cities—Munich, London, and finally Geneva—meeting other Russian revolutionaries. From these places, he also wrote and edited a newspaper called *Spark*. Although published in Europe, the paper was smuggled into Russia in hopes of inciting workers to revolution. Afraid to use his own name—it was not uncommon for the tsar's secret police to assassinate "enemies of the state" even when they lived outside Russia's borders—Vladimir began to write under the name Lenin. It stuck.

All iron will and ambition, Lenin cared for little but politics and power. He dressed and ate simply and stuck to a precise daily schedule, allotting no time for what he considered useless leisure. Neat and orderly, he kept detailed accounts of the money he spent; shelved his books (only social and political titles) alphabetically; and allotted himself exactly fifteen minutes each morning to tidy his desk. This way of life, he claimed, gave him the discipline needed for revolutionary work. He would not allow himself even to listen to music: "It makes me want to do kind, stupid things, and pat the heads of people," he claimed. "But now you have to beat them on the head, beat them without mercy."

Lenin agreed with most of Marx's ideas. But unlike Marx, Lenin did not believe the workers could bring about a revolution on their own. Instead, a few strong leaders, drawn from the most enlightened workers and activist intellectuals, were needed to guide events and encourage armed insurrection. This, Lenin insisted, was the only way Russia could move toward communism.

But many of his fellow Social Democrats disagreed. They wanted to take a more gradual approach to revolution. Immediate action to bring down the tsarist regime wasn't necessary, they argued. Instead, they should give the workers time to discover for themselves—through the experience of labor strikes and other social struggles—the necessity of revolution. Until that time, Social Democrats should continue publishing revolutionary propaganda in an effort to educate them. Revolution, they said, would happen only when workers were ready.

Lenin sneered at this idea. And in 1903, his insistence on an immediate revolt led to a split in the Social Democrat party. From then on, SDs who followed Lenin's lead were called Bolsheviks. Those who disagreed with him were called Mensheviks. But all were communists, intent on creating—in one way or another—a completely free, equal, and classless society.

LENIN IS TAKEN BY SURPRISE

Neither Bolshevik nor Menshevik leaders had much to do with the strikes of 1905. Their influence among the Russian workers was still too weak. In fact, news of the upheavals took Lenin completely by surprise. And yet he was in no hurry to leave Geneva for the fugitive life in Russia. As a known revolutionary leader, he would be arrested if the police found him. Instead, he tried to lead from afar, sending a stream of letters to the handful of Bolsheviks, urging them to armed insurrection.

Then Nicholas signed the October Manifesto. And Lenin grew worried. The newly granted rights, he feared, would let the pressure out of the revolutionary movement. He had to get home and rally Bolshevik Russians before their chance completely slipped away.

In mid-November—just two weeks after the October Manifesto was declared—Lenin crossed the border and made his way to St. Petersburg. Along with a small group of Bolshevik men and women, he began planning an uprising. But could it possibly succeed? Since the manifesto, most workers were not behind them. Lenin claimed it didn't matter. "Victory?" he cried. "The point is not about victory, but about giving the regime a shake and attracting the masses to the movement."

BATTLEGROUND

On the morning of December 20, the tsar's police attempted to arrest the leaders of the soviets, the organizations Nicholas had earlier declared illegal. This action incensed people in Moscow. Students, workers, and even well-dressed citizens surged into the streets to protest. Social Democrats, both Bolshevik and Menshevik, seized their chance and urged the people to fight against autocracy. And the people listened. Working together, they built barricades from whatever they could find—fences, overturned streetcars, telegraph poles, doors torn from nearby homes and shops. These barricades soon ringed the workers' section of the city. "The whole of Moscow has become a battleground," said one eyewitness. Homemade bombs exploded. From all directions came the sound of gunshots.

Revolutionaries from St. Petersburg and other cities rushed to join in the struggle. But not Lenin. The police had picked up his trail, and the Bolshevik leader could do little but shuttle from hiding place to hiding place. Still, the events in Moscow delighted him. "Go ahead and shoot!" he cried. "Summon the . . . regiments against the Russian peasants and workers. We are for a broadening of the struggle, we are an international revolution."

At Tsarskoe Selo, Nicholas chain-smoked furiously. Was this what he got from the people in return for his generous concessions? He decided to take matters firmly in hand. Deploying a special fighting unit to Moscow, he ordered them to clear the streets, using any means necessary.

The tsar's troops were ruthless. Bringing up artillery, they bombarded the workers' section until the whole district was nothing but smoldering rubble. Then soldiers entered the area. Their orders were to shoot anyone who had not already fled. Men, women, and children were systematically mowed down. By December 31, the rebellion was over. More than a thousand people had been killed, and thousands more were injured.

And a despairing Lenin slipped away into Finland. He felt sure he'd just lost the only chance for revolution in his lifetime.

BLOODY NICHOLAS

Back at Tsarskoe Selo, Nicholas decided to crack down on all his subjects. Now, he declared, they would "feel the whip." Perhaps then they would think twice before rebelling.

In cities all across Russia, police arrested anyone suspected of crimes against the tsar, imprisoning or exiling 38,000 so-called politicals, and executing another 5,000. Outspoken workers lost their jobs, their employers threatened with prison if they attempted to rehire them. Even children did not escape Nicholas's terror. Police routinely rounded up workers' children and beat them just to "teach them a lesson."

Things were worse in the countryside. Nicholas authorized what were known as Punitive Expeditions, detachments of tough, well-trained soldiers who restored order in the most brutal ways possible. Storming into a town or village, these soldiers killed citizens at random, burned entire communities without mercy, and left people wounded, homeless, and starving. "Don't skimp on the bullets" were the orders they received. And they didn't.

Their work delighted Nicholas. Once, after reading a particularly gruesome report of hangings and beatings, he turned to an aide. "This really tickles me," he said. "It really does."

It is estimated that between December 1905 and the start of the First Duma in April 1906, the Punitive Expeditions executed 15,000 people, wounded at least 20,000 more, and exiled another 45,000.

One more measure was taken. In January 1906, with Nicholas's agreement, his new prime minister—Peter Stolypin—established secret courts all across the country. The purpose of these courts was to allow for the quick arrest and conviction of anyone suspected of being a political revolutionary. Over the next two years, the tsar's "extraordinary security," as the police were called, rounded up more than 100,000 people. Stolypin's courts sentenced most of these "politicals" to hard labor, prison, or exile. But at least two thousand were executed. The hangman's noose soon became known as Stolypin's necktie.

Heads bowed, workers returned to their factories, peasants to their villages. By the saber and whip, order had been restored. The lower classes no longer acted out, recalled one noble, but their "courtesy, friendliness, bows [were replaced by] animosity [and] rudeness." Fear alone now kept the people in their place.

And the tsar had earned a new nickname—Bloody Nicholas.

PROMISES MADE AND PROMISES BROKEN

By the spring of 1906, Nicholas was also going back on the promises he'd made the previous October. "I am not convinced this [manifesto] requires me to renounce the right of supreme power," he said. So just one week before the First Duma met, he decreed some new laws. He now granted himself absolute veto power over any law the Duma might try to pass, thus making *his* the final word on all legislation. Additionally, he gave himself the right to dissolve the Duma whenever he wanted, as well as the power to issue laws by imperial decree when the Duma was not sitting. Last but not least, he kept complete control over foreign policy, the military, the police, and the day-to-day administration of the government. By doing so, Nicholas effectively stripped the Duma of its power before it had even convened.

And yet Nicholas still resented what he considered the Duma's interference in his government. Under no circumstances, he decided, could its members (called deputies) be trusted.

THE DUMA OPENS . . . AND CLOSES . . . OPENS . . . AND CLOSES

On May 10, 1906, men from all walks of life, including noblemen in gold-braided uniforms, tradesmen in tailcoats, peasants in rough tunics, and workers in plain cotton blouses and coarse boots, streamed up the carved marble staircase of the Winter Palace. These were the Duma's 524 duly elected deputies, representing all thirty-four provinces and three economic classes: landowners and wealthy businessmen; townspeople (including shop owners, tradesmen, doctors, lawyers, university professors, and factory workers); and peasants. Chosen through a complicated and indirect electoral process, the vast majority of deputies were noblemen and professionals. Still, one hundred peasants had found their way to the capital, as had twenty-five workers. And all had come to the Winter Palace for the opening ceremony of the nation's first legislature.

Entering the gold-and-white Imperial Throne Room, the deputies took their places on the left side of the hall. Some glared at the tsar's ermine-draped throne, and at the four little stools on which sat the symbols of his power—the crown, the scepter, the seal, and the orb. A regimental band began playing the national anthem.

On the other side of the hall stood the tsar's ministers, admirals, and generals as well as members of the Romanov family—Nicholas's sisters, brother, aunts, uncles, even cousins. The men had come in full dress uniform, their chests glittering with medals, while the women were adorned in silk and dripping with jewels.

"The two . . . sides stood confronting one another," recalled one eyewitness. "The court dignitaries . . . looked across in a haughty manner . . . at the 'people off the street' whom [events] had swept into the palace. One of the deputies, a tall man in a worker's blouse, scrutinized the throne and the courtiers around it with obvious disgust. As the tsar and his entourage entered the hall, he lurched forward and stared at them with an expression of hatred."

As Nicholas approached the throne, the nobility's side of the hall burst into cheers. But many of the deputies remained silent. "They neither crossed themselves nor bowed, but just stood with their hands . . . in their pockets," Nicholas's sister Xenia noted with shock. Instead, they watched, stone-faced, as the tsar mounted the dais.

Pale, nervously twisting a pair of white military gloves he clutched in his hand, Nicholas began reading from a prepared speech. He said nothing about the rebellion that had forced him to create the Duma. Instead, he clung to the notion that it was all God's will. "The care for the welfare of the country entrusted to me

by the Most High," he declared, "has caused me to summon representatives elected by the people to assist in the work of legislation."

While Nicholas spoke, Alexandra gripped her ostrich-feather
fan so tightly her knuckles were white. She looked "tragic," recalled
one onlooker, "and her face became alternately red and pale." When
he finished, tears rolled down her cheeks.

Nicholas, too, was overcome. As the imperial family filed from
the hall, he could not hold back his emotions. "Poor Nicky was
standing there in tears!" exclaimed Xenia.

Shaken by the sight of so many commoners in the palace, Nicholas's mother declared it a "terrible ceremony. . . . They . . . reflect[ed]
a strange hatred for us all."

Nicholas's sister Olga agreed. "The peasants looked sullen. But
the workmen [from the cities] were worse. They looked as though
they hated us."

Just two days later, the Duma demonstrated its anger over the
tsar's gutting of its power by demanding he release all political prisoners. The Duma knew that granting amnesty was Nicholas's right.
It also knew it could no longer enact laws without the tsar's agreement. In other words, the deputies knew their demand was nothing
more than a symbolic gesture. Their real goal was to give voice to
their frustrations, and perhaps force the crown to return some authority to the Duma.

Nicholas fumed. How dare the deputies make such a demand?
Agreeing with Xenia who declared, "The Duma is such filth . . . a
hearth of revolutionaries," Nicholas decided to exercise his right to
dissolve it. On July 21, 1906, the doors of the Tauride Palace were
locked and the tsar's imperial decree posted. Outraged deputies
could do nothing to stop this action. After just seventy-two days,
their legislative careers were over.

Nicholas did not intend to allow a second election. This denial was also his right. Prime Minister Peter Stolypin convinced him otherwise. Stolypin grasped what Nicholas could not. The government needed to appear to be working with the Duma. The Russian people saw the tsar's signature on the October Manifesto as a sacred promise. To violate it would anger the people. Did Nicholas really want to face another rebellion?

Reluctantly, Nicholas changed his mind. He allowed the election of a second Duma.

But when the Second Duma (whose makeup was similar to the first) met in February 1907, it proved just as troublesome. And just as radical. Deputies publicly raged against the tsar and demanded, among other things, that Nicholas end capital punishment, abolish government violence, and start distributing nobility-owned estates to land-hungry peasants.

And so, in June 1907—just three months after it was convened— Nicholas dissolved the Second Duma, too. "Slap! And they are gone," he told his mother.

But the legislative experiment was still not over. Another election for a third Duma, complete with new deputies, was set. Why did Nicholas bother? Because it gave the impression that Russia was becoming more democratic (especially important when making trade and military alliances with leaders of Western Europe who tended to see Russia as a backward country). Still, Nicholas could not stomach another hard-to-manage Duma. At Stolypin's suggestion, he decreed a change in the voting system. Under the tsar's new system, votes were heavily weighted by class. Now it took 230 landowners' votes to elect a single deputy, 1,000 votes for wealthy businessmen to elect a deputy, and 15,000 votes for members of the lower middle class to elect a deputy. Peasants needed 60,000 votes before they could send a representative from their class to the Duma. And workers? They needed a whopping 125,000 votes!

This electoral change placed power in the hands of the nobility, wealthy landowners, and businessmen—the very type of Russian that tended to support tsarism. Sarcastically called "the Duma of the Lords, Priests and Lackeys," this third group of deputies, who took their seats in November 1907, was highly acceptable to Nicholas. With no reason to dissolve it, he allowed the Third Duma to sit for the next five years.

RASPUTIN

"We made the acquaintance of a man of God," Nicholas noted in his diary in November 1905, just weeks after signing the October Manifesto. "Gregory from Tobolsk province."

Gregory Rasputin began his life as a peasant farmer. But one day, as he plowed the fields outside his Siberian village, he claimed to see a vision from God. Abandoning his wife and four children, he walked two thousand miles to a monastery in Greece. When he returned two years later, he declared himself to be what Russians called a *starets*—a holy man. Soon, he was wandering the countryside, blessing the poor and praying for the sick. By the time he arrived in St. Petersburg, he had gained a reputation as a healer and a prophet.

Meanwhile, Nicholas and Alexandra had been frantically searching for a way to help their sick son. Medical specialists from across Europe had been called in. Priests had been summoned. Even a Tibetan herbalist had appeared at court. But Alexei still suffered. So when the imperial couple heard about Rasputin from cousin Militsa, they eagerly invited him to the palace.

Did Nicholas and Alexandra cringe when Rasputin first appeared at Tsarskoe Selo that fall? According to some reports, the man was revolting, with his long, unwashed hair and scraggly, food-encrusted beard. Other eyewitnesses, however, contradicted this description. "Rasputin was exceptionally clean," remembered his friend Alexei Filippov. "He often changed his underwear, went to the baths, and never smelled bad."

If the *starets'* hands were soiled when he presented Alexandra with his gifts of holy icons and loaves of blessed bread, the royal couple surely looked past them. That's because it was the *starets'* astonishing eyes people noticed first. They possessed such a strange power, many people found it hard to resist his gaze. "[It] was at once piercing and caressing, naïve and cunning, far-off and intent," recalled the French ambassador, Maurice Paléologue. "His pupils seemed to radiate magnetism." No one knows what Rasputin and the imperial couple spoke about during their first meeting. But soon the *starets* began visiting the palace.

He usually came after dinner, joining Nicholas and Alexandra in her lilac drawing room. After kissing three times in the Russian fashion, they would talk—about God, miracles, and Alexei's health. Then the three would head upstairs to the nursery.

There Rasputin led everyone, parents and children alike, into Alexei's bedroom. "There was something like a hush," recalled Nicholas's sister Olga, "as though we had found ourselves in Church. . . . No lamps were lit; the only light came from the candles burning in front of some beautiful icons. [The children] stood very still by the side of the [*starets*], whose head was bowed. I knew he was praying. I also knew that my little nephew [and nieces] had joined him in prayer." Added Olga, "[All the children] were completely at ease with him."

But it wasn't just conversation and prayers that kept getting Rasputin invited to the palace. It was his apparent ability to ease Alexei's pain.

His aunt Olga remembered one such incident. Arriving at the palace, she learned her little nephew was sick. She immediately went up to the nursery to look in on him. "The poor child lay in pain, dark patches under his eyes, and his little body all distorted," she said. "The doctors were just useless . . . more frightened than any of us . . . whispering among themselves."

Alexandra sent an urgent message to Rasputin in St. Petersburg. He arrived at the palace around midnight, and closing himself up in Alexei's room, stood at the end of the bed, praying. Then he laid his hand on the boy's leg. "There's a good boy," he said, his voice low and soothing. "You'll be all right."

The next morning when Olga peeked in on her nephew, she could not believe her eyes. "[He] was not just alive—but well! He was sitting up in bed . . . [his] eyes clear and bright, not a sign of any swelling."

How had Rasputin done it? To this day, no one knows. Some historians have speculated that he used his strange, piercing eyes to cast a sort of hypnotic spell over the sick and frightened boy, calming him so the bleeding slowed. Others have suggested that the *starets* simply had good timing, that he waited until the symptoms had run their course before appearing at Alexei's bedside to take credit for his improvement.

But Alexandra believed Rasputin's healing powers were a gift from God, the answer to all her long hours of prayer. Here at last, she told herself, was the man whose coming "Dr." Philippe had foretold two years earlier: the man *"who will speak to you of God."*

CHAPTER SIX
❧ "PIG AND FILTH" AND FAMILY FUN ❧
1908–1911

SCHOOL DAYS

On a fall morning in 1908, Sydney Gibbes, a nervous man with painstakingly combed brown hair, arrived at the Alexander Palace. Strangely, he wore a long-tailed frock coat, black bow tie, and silk top hat. The unsuitableness of his outfit made him even more nervous. Still, "[court] etiquette was that gentlemen who had not a uniform wore evening dress," Gibbes later explained, "and so I set off to the Palace in evening dress at 6:00 in the morning. A ghastly experience!"

Gibbes's nerves could be chalked up to more than his clothing. Here he was, the new English teacher for the three oldest grand duchesses, and he had yet to meet a single member of the imperial family. Neither Nicholas nor Alexandra had even bothered to interview him. Seemingly summoned out of the blue, he found himself being led to a small schoolroom on the second floor. For several minutes, he was left there alone. Then the door opened. And Gibbes braced himself. The imperial children, he had heard, "generally behaved like young savages."

But Gibbes saw none of this—at least not right away. "I took my first lesson with the two elder girls . . . [thirteen-year-old] Olga and [eleven-year-old] Tatiana. . . . Then I had the third daughter [nine-year-old Marie] by herself."

Seven-year-old Anastasia and four-year-old Alexei were still too young for school. But while Gibbes was teaching, the tsarevich sneaked down the hall to visit the schoolroom. "A tiny little chap in wee white knickerbockers and a Russian shirt trimmed with . . .

embroidery of blue and silver," recalled Gibbes, Alexei "toddle[d] into my classroom ... look[ed] around and then gravely shook hands."

Gibbes was not the only tutor. The grand duchesses' lessons were taught by a string of teachers who arrived at the palace once or twice a week to focus on a particular subject. Among them was Peter Petrov, a friendly old man who taught Russian; Catherine Schneider, the German instructor; and Master Sobolev, the arithmetic teacher.

Sadly, these teachers were mostly a "mediocre bunch," recalled a family friend. "Not one of [them] enjoyed any prominence or had any outstanding achievement to his credit," agreed a member of court. Thus the grand duchesses' education was "to some extent neglected."

This was their parents' fault. Nicholas and Alexandra put little stock in education. "I was amazed that such a family, which possessed all the means, did not surround the children with the best possible teachers," remarked one observer. "Just how little attention was paid to the children's development could be judged by the interest with which they listened to the most ordinary things, as though they had never seen, read, or heard about anything. At first I thought this was simple bashfulness. But soon I came to realize that the situation concerning their education and intellectual development was very bad."

And for too long, remembered court official A. A. Mosolov, "the grand duchesses had *no* teacher. There were nurses to be seen in their apartments, but that was all. When the nurses had gone [because the children had grown too old for them] they had virtually no supervision, except, of course, that of their mother." But Alexandra did nothing to challenge their intellect. Instead, claimed Mosolov, she "remained always in an arm chair, motionless, and never spoke to her daughters in the presence of a third party."

Even with teachers, the grand duchesses' curriculum was an easy one. They studied some literature (although, curiously, none of Russia's great classics), religion, a little science, and only the most basic math. What they needed most, Alexandra felt, was languages—Russian, French, English, and German. "Four languages *is* a lot," she admitted, "but they need them absolutely." They were, after all, necessary for everyday living. English was the language spoken within the family circle because Alexandra's Russian was shaky. Russian, of course, was the children's native tongue, and they occasionally spoke it with their father and others but never when their mother was present. German was their mother's native tongue, and even though Nicholas spoke it fluently, he and Alexandra never used it to communicate with each other. And French was spoken at court.

The girls (including, later, Anastasia) detested languages. Calling them "piddle," they did just enough work to get by and nothing more. While they spoke English fluently, their great-uncle King Edward VII of England once declared their accents atrocious. And even with Gibbes's tutoring, they never mastered its spelling or grammar. As for Russian, some claimed they were hard to understand. "[The grand duchesses] had an accent that seemed English when they spoke in Russian, and Russian when they spoke English," said one acquaintance. "Never before or since have I heard anybody talk with that strange . . . accent." And French? "They never learned to speak it fluently," confessed their French teacher, Pierre Gilliard.

A courteous and observant man with a fastidiously trimmed mustache, Gilliard had arrived at the palace two years before Gibbes. In that time, he had grown to care for his young students. They, in turn, had come to trust him as a friend.

Olga, he wrote, "possessed a remarkably quick brain. She had good reasoning powers as well as initiative. . . . She picked up everything quickly, and always managed to give an original turn to what she learned." An avid reader, she was forever swiping novels and books of poetry from her mother's table before the empress read them. One day, when Alexandra complained, Olga replied, "You must wait, Mama, until I find out whether this book is a proper one for you to read." Still, for all her natural gifts, Olga did not fulfill Gilliard's hopes.

Less frank and spontaneous than her older sister, Tatiana liked painting, needlework, and playing the piano. Too bad, remarked Gibbes, "she showed no feeling when she played." Gilliard agreed. "She was not so gifted," he wrote, but she made up for it in "perseverance."

And then there was Marie. Unlike her two older sisters, who were at least diligent students, Marie paid little attention to her lessons. She preferred walking outside or painting pictures. In fact, according to Gibbes, she could paint with her left hand even though she was right-handed. More extraordinary, she could paint with her left hand *while* writing with her right. If that wasn't unusual enough, Marie was incredibly strong. She showed off her strength by occasionally grabbing her flustered tutors around the waist and lifting them off the ground.

Gilliard briefly pinned his academic hopes on little Anastasia. As a small child, she showed an interest in the classroom. But this fascination was short-lived. Just after her eighth birthday, she officially started school—and so did her teachers' troubles.

"A True Genius in Naughtiness"

Anastasia was a mischievous little girl, "wild and rough, a hair-puller and tripper-up of servants," wrote one historian. She possessed, recalled one family friend, "a true genius in naughtiness" that extended into the classroom. Said Gibbes, "The little grand duchess was not always an easy child to instruct. . . . We had, as a rule, charming lessons, but sometimes there were storms."

Once, she snatched up a bottle of black ink and threatened to throw it all over Gibbes's impeccable white shirt if he did not raise her English grade. The teacher refused, and the furious girl stormed out. Minutes later, she returned. This time, she was all smiles and sweetness, and she clutched a bouquet of flowers she'd grabbed from one of the palace's many blossom-filled vases.

Was this an apology for her earlier bad behavior?

No, it was a bribe—a fistful of flowers for a raised mark. Again, Gibbes refused.

Anastasia drew herself up. Chin high and with a loud huff, she marched into the classroom next door, where their Russian instructor sat. At the top of her voice, she said, "Peter Vasilievich, allow me to present *you* with these flowers."

Had Gibbes heard?

She shouted again just to be sure.

Anastasia was obviously a handful during Gilliard's lessons, too. While the French teacher did not share details, clues to her behavior can be found in a letter to her father. "What we [children] did to Monsieur Gilliard—just terrible!" she confessed. "We were pushing him with our fists and in any other way, he had it from us."

Another time, Alexei gleefully reported to his father, "Anastasia was trying to strangle Monsieur Gilliard!"

Anastasia's distaste for school was clear. "Now I have to do an arithmetical problem," she once grumbled in a letter to a friend, "and of course it doesn't want to solve, such pig and filth!" School, she added in a burdened tone, was nothing but "horrid lessons."

"ALEXEI THE TERRIBLE"

Still too young for school, the youngest Romanov was the center of his parents' world. They called him their "dear one," their "wee one," their "Sunbeam." And they fussed over him endlessly. "[He] was . . . the focus of all [their] hopes and affections," recalled Pierre Gilliard. "When he was well, the palace .... seemed bathed in sunshine."

A handsome child with chestnut-colored hair and big blue-gray eyes, Alexei was, despite his fragile health, romping and full of mischief. Once, when he was five, he crawled under the dinner table and snatched off one of the female guest's slippers. Carrying it above his head, he ceremoniously presented it to Nicholas.

The tsar was not amused. He commanded his son to return it.

Grudgingly, Alexei again crawled under the table.

Seconds later, the lady shrieked. That's because Alexei had stuffed a big, juicy strawberry into the shoe before putting it back on her foot.

He laughed uproariously at the joke—until he was banished to the nursery. He was not allowed in the dining room for several weeks.

Some guests wished Alexei's exile from the dinner table had been made permanent. "He wouldn't sit up, ate badly, licked his plate, and teased the others," Cousin Konstantin wrote in his diary after lunching with the imperial family one day. "The Emperor often turned away, perhaps to avoid having to say anything, while the Empress rebuked her elder daughter [fifteen-year-old] Olga, who sat next to her brother, for not restraining him. But Olga cannot deal with him."

His parents could deny him nothing. They loved him passionately and found it impossible to be firm with him. Because of this, most of his wishes were granted. If the tsarevich wanted a toy rifle, they bought it. If he wanted pancakes for dinner, they served them.

But nothing could substitute for what Alexei wanted most of all—to be like other boys. "Can't I have a bicycle?" he once begged his mother.

"Alexei, you know you can't," she replied.

"Mayn't I play tennis?" he persisted.

"Dear, you know you mustn't," Alexandra answered.

Alexei burst into tears. "Why can other boys have everything and I nothing?" he wailed pitifully.

Sometimes he seemed almost defiant in the face of his illness. Once, during a review of the palace guard, he hopped onto one of the gardeners' bicycles. Nicholas was in mid-salute when he spied his son zigzagging precariously across the parade ground. Frightened the boy might fall, Nicholas halted the review and ordered the soldiers to surround and capture the bicyclist. Squealing with excitement, Alexei led them on a merry chase. Another time, when he was seven, he sprang onto the tabletop during one of the few children's parties he was allowed to attend. Waving the other young guests up alongside him, he burst into a frenzied game of follow the leader. Wildly, the boy hopped from table to chair and back to the table. Horrified, his sailor nannies, Derevenko and Nagorny, tried to stop him before he hurt himself. But Alexei just hollered, "All grown-ups have to go!" and shoved them out the door.

The boy could be rude and domineering. As a six-year-old, he once walked into his father's office, where the foreign minister sat waiting for the tsar. Alexei expected the minister to leap to his feet. When he didn't, the boy stomped up to him and with fists clenched, shouted, "When the Heir to the Russian throne enters a room, people must get up." Another time, he was playing in the nursery with his sisters when he learned a group of soldiers wanted to meet him. "Now, girls," the six-year-old said dismissively, "run away. I am busy. Someone has just called to see me on business."

No wonder Nicholas once joked that he "trembled for Russia" under the rule of "Alexei the Terrible."

FAMILY FUN

The children found plenty of interesting things to do—playing tennis, hiking, dancing, bicycling, anything busy. All five of them adored animals, and at Tsarskoe Selo they had dozens of pets. Among them was Vaska the cat, and Ortipo, a French bulldog who snored so loudly he kept the girls awake at night. There was Vanka, a trained donkey from the Cinizelli Circus, who would snuffle through the children's pockets in search of treats and who loved to chew rubber balls. There was an elephant with his own elaborate stable; two llamas; a mouse who lived in the "Little Pair's" bedroom wall; and a parrot named Popov who resided—of all places—in the tsar's bathroom. And there was a King Charles spaniel who earned the family nickname *mersavetz* ("rascal") because, said Marie, he did his "governor-general" on the carpets. (Her parents gave the girls a little silver bucket and shovel with which to clean it up.)

One passion shared by the entire family was photography. Everyone, even little Alexei, had his or her own Kodak Brownie camera. The cameras were lightweight and easy to use, and the family took them everywhere, snapping away indiscriminately—dozens of photographs each day. Anastasia even attempted a self-portrait. "I took [one] picture while looking in the mirror," she told her father, "and it was hard, because my hands were shaking."

Most evenings after dinner, the family took time to carefully paste their photographs into special albums made of green Moroccan leather and engraved with the imperial eagle. Over the years, they filled album after album with snapshots, forming a detailed record of their everyday lives at Tsarskoe Selo . . . and wherever they went.

BEYOND THE PALACE GATES:
AN OCCUPATION FOR WORKERS' DAUGHTERS

Along St. Petersburg's fashionable Nevsky Prospect stood shop after expensive shop—furriers, perfumers, jewelers—all catering to the city's rich. Behind the shop's counters stood thousands of girls between the ages of fifteen and twenty. Older women were rarely hired because shop owners preferred what one called good-looking girls. Overworked, underpaid, and often exploited by their bosses, they were still expected to dress attractively and smile brightly. This is how one shop girl named Aizenshtein described her life, in a letter written to a newspaper in 1908:

The first thing the shop owner or manager says when you ask for a job is, "Are you ticklish?" If you bat your eyes or nod your head suggestively, the job is yours. But if you don't . . . you might as well forget it. . . . For this you get an unforgiving job. . . . Our workday in the winter is thirteen and a half hours, and in the summer, fifteen hours. Before the store opens and after it closes we have to clean, sort and put away all the merchandise that was taken out during the day. When the store is open, we have to stand out on the street [in any kind of weather] to attract customers. If we let anyone go by, the boss swears at us in the choicest language. The customers also swear at us for trying to drag them in by the coat tails.

We are very poorly paid; ten to fifteen rubles a month [about two dollars] is considered a good wage for a salesgirl. [But] they don't pay us each month, or even every two weeks, so we have to go to the boss each day and beg him for enough money for food. And when you ask the employer for [your pay] you are insulted: "You're always asking for money, but you never sell anything. How much money did you earn today, eh? I'm asking you! Answer my question!" screams the employer. "If you want money, you have to work." After a response like that, it's hard to approach the boss again. But when you've gone hungry for a few days, you try once more. You look around timidly, then go up to the boss again, and he either insults you, or, in the best circumstances, he gives you [a few] kopecks, saying, "Don't bother me again!"

We don't get time off for lunch. We eat behind the counter. A piece of bread and a cup of tea—that's our meal. We're not allowed to sit down, even when there aren't any customers in the store. . . . After that, you follow in the footsteps of many other salesgirls [who] get sick and wind up in the hospital.

THE ROYAL PROGRESS

Like clockwork, the family traveled throughout the year on what was called the royal progress. Every March, the Alexander Palace was abandoned, and the Romanovs headed south to the Crimea and warm weather. By May, they were ready to move again, this time to their summer mansion at Peterhof, where they could catch the cool breezes coming off the Baltic Sea. Four weeks later, in June, they boarded their imperial yacht, the *Standart,* for a cruise around the Finnish islands. When August rolled around, they made their way to Poland and their hunting lodges. Come September, they returned to the Crimea for a short time, before heading back to Tsarskoe Selo to sit out the long Russian winter. But they avoided St. Petersburg. Even though it was the country's capital and the seat of national government, the family never spent more than a few days a year in the cavernous Winter Palace, which Alexandra hated. In addition, with the hundreds of doors and passageways leading into the place, it was impossible to guarantee the family's safety.

Most of their traveling was done by imperial train—a chain of luxurious railroad cars "more like a home than a [locomotive]," recalled family friend Anna Vyrubova. It included a lilac-and-gray sitting room for the empress, a study of mahogany and green leather for the tsar, and a children's car filled with white painted furniture and chests of toys. There was also a kitchen with three stoves, a dining room that seated twenty, and a small room where the servants laid out *zakuski* ("appetizers") before every meal. Here Nicholas and the children helped themselves to small but savory delicacies—caviar, smoked herring, pickled mushrooms, and, a family favorite, reindeer tongue.

During these times, the empress "was frequently absent from . . . view," said Pierre Gilliard. This was because Alexandra, weakened by her five pregnancies and exhausted from the strain and worry over Alexei's illness, had grown sickly. Closing herself up in her sitting room with a backache, migraine, or some other ailment, she often spent days locked away from her children.

Her daughters especially missed her. Feeling isolated, and longing for any kind of contact, they ended up writing wistful little notes that they sent to Alexandra's sickroom. Some expressed love. Others apologized for being naughty. But all begged for Mama's attention.

"My sweety darling Mama," thirteen-year-old Olga wrote a bit ungrammatically in January 1909 after receiving a long note from

Alexandra exhorting her to be gentle, kind, polite, and patient. "It helps me very much when you write to me what to do, and then I try to do it better as I can."

Just days later, eleven-year-old Tatiana wrote, "My darling Mama! I hope you won't be very tired and you can get up to dinner. I am always so awfully sorry when you . . . can't get up. I will pray for you my darling Mama in church. . . . Please sleep well and don't get tired. . . . Perhaps I have lots of faults, but please forgive me. . . . Many, many kisses to my beloved Mama."

In May 1910, Marie, then eleven, longed for some motherly advice. "Mama, at what age did you have your own room . . . at what age did you start wearing long dresses?"

And Anastasia just wanted to share her day's events. "Madam dearest, I am afraid to go [to my bedroom] in the dark so I sat down on the W.C. picking my toe in the dark," her quirky, undated letter reads. "I hope you're well soon. Go to bed and be quiet. Good night. Sleep well."

Alexandra's response to her daughters' notes was always the same. Her suffering was a heavy cross they each must bear, she told them. "I know it's dull having an invalid mother," she wrote Marie in December 1910, "but it teaches you all to be loving and gentle. Only try to be obedient, then you make it easier for me."

The girls tried, always hoping that "darling Mama" would feel better tomorrow and rise from her sofa to join them.

CHAPTER SEVEN

GATHERING CLOUDS

THE LADIES LOVE RASPUTIN

Rasputin had become all the rage in St. Petersburg society. With Cousin Militsa's help, he'd gotten to know many members of the nobility. Now, when he wasn't expected at the Imperial Palace, the *starets* attended parties and soirées at some of the finest mansions in the city. Introduced as a man of God, he strode into opulent drawing rooms, wearing his peasant blouse and boots, his black hair hanging to his shoulders. Taking his hostess's soft hands in his rough ones, he gazed deep into her eyes. Was it hypnosis that swept so many noblewomen off their feet? It certainly wasn't his fine manners. Rasputin spoke with "coarse barnyard expressions," wrote one historian. If that wasn't enough, he bragged constantly about his relationship with the imperial couple. "See the gold cross?" he would say. "It's got 'N' stamped on it. The tsar gave it—did it to honor me." Or "Her Majesty sewed this shirt for me. I got other shirts she sewed."

Despite his crudeness, the ladies swooned over him. Dissatisfied with their pampered lives, many were searching for something new and exciting to fill their time. Rasputin fit the bill. Soon they formed a sort of fan club. Every day, dozens of noblewomen climbed the narrow, creaking stairs to his upper-floor apartment in St. Petersburg. Ignoring the stink of rancid butter and cabbage soup that filled the dark rooms, they gathered around him. Some even sat at his feet. Those unable to attend telephoned with tearful excuses, while one—an opera singer—called every afternoon just to sing him an aria. Telephone in his hands, the receiver pressed to his ear, he danced around the room.

Taking pleasure in insulting his wealthy guests, Rasputin sometimes dipped his finger into a plate of jam and, turning to one of them, said, "Humble yourself, lick it clean." He ridiculed the expensive gifts the women showered on him. "What's this, little mother . . . you could feed five villages of starving people with [this]." And he stepped far beyond the bounds of propriety by pulling the prettiest women into his lap to hug and kiss them. His rudeness, he believed, made him even more attractive to the bored nobility.

And it worked . . . for a while. But soon, rumors began swirling through society about the goings-on in Rasputin's apartment. And the upper crust was horrified. How dare the *starets* offend well-born ladies in that way? Rasputin, many nobles decided, wasn't a holy man. He was just a lecherous impostor. By 1911, doors began slamming in his face.

But not the palace doors. "They accuse Rasputin of kissing women," Alexandra grumbled to Nicholas. "Read the apostles; they kissed everybody as a form of greeting."

Because the *starets* was always on his best behavior in front of them, it was easy for the couple to ignore the truth: that Rasputin was a charlatan. Instead, they grew angry with anyone who criticized him. His enemies "are ours," Alexandra declared.

STOLYPIN VS. THE *STARETS*

All the rumors worried Prime Minister Peter Stolypin. He didn't trust the *starets'* hypnotic ways. What kind of advice was the crude charlatan giving the tsar? Deeply loyal to the throne, Stolypin decided to launch an in-depth investigation into Rasputin's activities.

He hoped solid evidence would force Nicholas to see the truth. For weeks, the police tailed Rasputin, questioning anyone he spoke with, and opening his mail. In February 1911, they turned over their findings to Stolypin. Although their report has been lost to history, rumors of its contents swirled. Some claimed it provided evidence that Rasputin had molested numerous women—maids, noblewomen, even nuns. And according to one member of Rasputin's family, the report contained obscene photographs. Whatever the truth, the report was obviously dark—so dark that Stolypin hurried to the tsar.

Nicholas read the report. But he refused to believe it. Why, he asked, was everyone so preoccupied with Rasputin? His relationship with the *starets* was his personal business, having nothing to do with political affairs. Naïvely, he did not see how Rasputin's bad behavior tarnished the reputation of the throne. Instead, he suggested that the prime minister meet with Rasputin. He was sure the two men would come to like each other.

Since a royal suggestion was the same as a command, Stolypin had no choice but to invite Rasputin to his office.

The *starets* arrived wearing an expensive fur coat (a gift from the empress) and a confident smile. He assured the prime minister that he was a peaceful man without a political agenda. "There is no need for the police to worry about me," he said.

"If this is true," Stolypin retorted, "then you do not need to fear the police."

When he heard these words, Rasputin's features changed. His eyes grew intense and piercing. Leaning forward, he locked gazes with the prime minister. "He mumbled mysterious and inarticulate words from the Scriptures," recalled Stolypin, "and made strange movements with his hands."

But Stolypin did not fall under this spell. Instead, he felt only "loathing" and "revulsion." "I could have you . . . prosecuted," he shouted, obviously referring to the mysterious findings of the police report. He gave the *starets* two choices: face the charges or leave St. Petersburg immediately. Which would it be?

Rasputin didn't answer. Snatching up his coat, he stormed from the office. He would complain to the empress about this rude treatment!

Knowing he needed to get to the tsar before Alexandra did, Stolypin hurried to Tsarskoe Selo. Pacing angrily, he told Nicholas about the meeting. The man was dangerous, he insisted.

Nicholas lit a cigarette. "Everything you say may be true," he conceded, "but I must ask that you never speak to me again of Rasputin. In any event, I can do nothing about it."

Stolypin thought Nicholas was talking about his inability to stand up to his wife. But he may have been referring to their need for Rasputin because of Alexei's hemophilia, which was still a secret.

Either way, Nicholas refused to take action.

So Stolypin took matters into his own hands. Without the tsar's permission, he wrote an order banishing Rasputin from St. Petersburg.

When Alexandra heard what the prime minister had done, she burst into hysterical tears and begged Nicholas to help "Our Friend" (the Romanovs' name for Rasputin).

For once, Nicholas stood firm. No matter how much his wife cried about the heartlessness of the separation, he refused to overrule his prime minister. (Some historians suspect this was the tsar's way of taking indirect action on the matter of the report.) He did, however, soften the blow. Summoning Rasputin to the palace, Nicholas said, "You have mentioned your desire to make a pilgrimage to the Holy Land. I think this would be a good time for it."

But how, wondered Rasputin aloud, could a poor man like him pay for such a trip?

"I will . . . give you the journey as a token of our esteem," replied

Nicholas. "The Lord knows you have earned it through your many services to the crown."

A pilgrimage to the Holy Land! It was the greatest gift possible for an Orthodox Russian. Pleased, Rasputin hurried home to pack.

He would be away from St. Petersburg until June. In that time, Nicholas hoped the controversy would blow over.

A PREMONITION OF DEATH

In September 1911, the entire imperial family, as well as a handful of ministers including Stolypin, traveled to Kiev. Because the city was celebrating the unveiling of a statue dedicated to his grandfather, Nicholas had agreed to make a public appearance. As his procession wound through the city, thousands of people lined the streets. But to their disappointment, most could not see the tsar through the circle of armed guards and policemen surrounding him. Since the events of 1905, Nicholas almost never ventured out. When he did, he went with heavy security.

Behind the tsar, riding in a separate carriage, came Stolypin. No guards on horseback protected him. No police held back the crowds. "You see, we are superfluous," he commented to a minister sitting beside him.

Neither man noticed the tall, bearded peasant who pushed his way to the front of the crowd. It was Rasputin, who had traveled to Kiev—on his own, and uninvited—to be near the imperial family. Now, as Stolypin's carriage passed, Rasputin reportedly began to shake. "Death is after him!" he shouted, raising a bony finger and pointing at the prime minister. "Death is driving behind him! Behind Peter [Stolypin]!" But only those in the crowd heard him.

The next evening, Nicholas attended a special performance being held in his honor at the Kiev opera house. Because Alexandra refused to appear in public, it was decided that fifteen-year-old Olga and fourteen-year-old Tatiana would go instead. The delighted girls followed Nicholas up the red-carpeted stairs and took their seats in the imperial theater box overlooking the stage. From there, they could see the dozens of soldiers posted throughout the theater.

Earlier, the tsar's security agents had searched the place for bombs and hidden assassins. Still, General Spiridovitch, chief of security, worried. "I was," he admitted, "obsessed by indescribable anxiety." From his aisle seat below the Romanovs' box, he had a clear view of the tsar, while beside him in the front row sat Stolypin, along with the other ministers.

The curtain rose. The music swelled. And Spiridovitch's anxiety grew. "Each instant I thought I heard steps in the aisle," he admitted, "and despite myself I would turn around."

The opera wore on. Then, during the second intermission, Nicholas and Olga stepped out in the hallway for a glass of tea, leaving Tatiana alone in the theater box. At that moment, a young man dressed in evening clothes rushed down the aisle. Pulling out a revolver, he aimed and fired twice.

Tatiana acted on instinct. Leaping from her chair, she slammed the door to the box shut, then flung her weight across it in an attempt to keep her father out. "Papa, don't come in," she shouted. "They are shooting!"

Her strength was no match for her father's. Shouldering open the door, he charged past her. Olga followed. As the three leaned over the railing, they saw Stolypin standing in the front row. "He slowly turned his face toward [us]," said Nicholas, "and with his left hand made the sign of the Cross in the air. Only then did I notice that he was very pale and that his . . . uniform [was] bloodstained. He slowly sank into his chair."

Around him, the theater erupted into chaos. As General Spiridovitch raced toward the tsar's box, and policemen tackled the shooter, audience members shrieked and pushed for the exits. Then calmer heads shouted for the national anthem to be played. The orchestra burst into music.

It was Nicholas's cue to appear—safe and sound—to the crowd below. From the box, he waved and saluted as the audience cheered.

Then General Spiridovitch and a phalanx of armed guards bustled the two very shaken teenagers and their father away. That night, said Nicholas, both girls "slept badly," and Tatiana "cried a lot."

Five days later, Stolypin died.

His assassin, a man by the name of Dmitri Bogrov, was hastily executed before an investigation could be made into his murderous act. Why had he killed the prime minister? The question went unanswered.

But Alexandra believed she knew. "Those who offend Our Friend may no longer count on divine protection," she said.

SWEET SIXTEEN

Weeks later, Olga glided across the state dining room of her family's palace in the Crimea, her pink tulle evening gown rustling, her white-gloved hand resting daintily on her father's arm. For the very first time, her long blond hair had been swept up into a fashionable coil. And around her neck glittered a birthday present from her parents: a necklace made of sixteen luminous pearls and sixteen flawless diamonds, one for every year of her life. They were Olga's first jewels, and they were being worn to her very first ball—her own!

Cheeks flushed, she greeted her guests—family, friends, courtiers, and young officers—before moving onto the dance floor with her father for the first waltz. The pair whirled across the marble floor to the strains of the regimental band. Because the night was so warm, the French doors had been thrown open, and the fragrance of the gardens' roses and orchids filled the room.

As the guests watched, did they whisper about the murder Olga had witnessed just weeks earlier? Did they look for signs of strain on her face? If they did, they would have noticed nothing. "She floated," recalled one guest, "like a butterfly" as she moved from her father's arms to those of the young officers who stepped forward to ask for a dance.

Unable to face even this social evening, Alexandra, along with Alexei and her other three daughters, watched it all from a balcony above the courtyard. But after the lavish midnight supper was served, the empress reluctantly made an appearance. "She looked," said one guest, "like a Greek icon, in a gown of cloth of gold. . . . The Tsarevich was next to her, his lovely little face flushed with the excitement of the evening."

Later, guests wandered along the winding paths of the luxuriant, rose-drenched gardens. Overhead, "the deep southern sky glitter[ed] with myriads of stars," recalled one lady, "and an autumn moon cast its silver light across the shining waters."

It was a moment of brightness in a world growing increasingly dark.

LETTERS TO RASPUTIN

Nicholas had hoped the rumors about Rasputin would run their course while the *starets* was away. Instead, things only grew worse. In late 1911, copies of letters began circulating around the city, letters from the imperial family to Rasputin. They revealed to all who read them just how much the Romanovs depended on the *starets*. In one letter, Olga spoke of her mother's invalidism. "God grant that dear Mama will not be sick any more this winter," she wrote, "[and that she will] not be so terribly melancholy and difficult."

Tatiana's letters begged Rasputin to "forgive all the sins I have committed against you," as if he were some sort of savior.

Marie's letters exposed the fact that she slept with a Bible Rasputin had given her. She wished her mother would "let me see you alone about God. It would be wonderful if I prayed to God with you."

And Anastasia wrote that she saw him in her dreams. No letters from Alexei appeared in print.

But it was Alexandra's letters that readers found most shocking: "I wish only one thing: to fall asleep on your shoulder. . . . I love you and believe in you. . . . I kiss you warmly." They took these words as proof that Alexandra and Rasputin were having an affair. They didn't know the empress wrote the same sort of gushing letters to everyone she knew—her sisters, friends, daughters.

Furious, Nicholas ordered the police to track down the originals. They did (although where they found them remains a mystery). When the minister of the interior turned the letters over to Nicholas, the tsar turned pale. He'd been hoping they were fakes. "These are not counterfeit," he said after sliding them from their envelopes. Then he tossed the pile into his desk drawer and lit a cigarette. His hands, recalled an eyewitness, trembled with barely restrained anger.

Alexandra was angry, too. She shot off a sternly worded telegram to Rasputin, scolding him for being so irresponsible with her letters.

Rasputin cabled right back. He tried to excuse himself by claiming the letters had been stolen. In truth, he had given them to an acquaintance while boasting—once again—about his close ties to the imperial family.

But the empress would not listen to his feeble excuses. Rasputin, she felt, had violated her trust.

Realizing he was in serious trouble, Rasputin rushed to Tsarskoe Selo. He begged Alexandra to see him.

She refused.

So Rasputin turned to the empress's good friend, Anna Vyrubova. He begged her to speak to the tsar on his behalf. Anna—a staunch believer in the *starets'* powers—agreed. She pleaded with Nicholas to include Rasputin in the imperial family's Easter trip to the Crimea. After all, wasn't the holiday a time for forgiveness?

Nicholas also refused.

Desperate now, Rasputin pleaded with Anna to help him stow away on the imperial train. Hiding out in the baggage car, the *starets* hoped the couple's anger would soften once they saw him disembark in the Crimea.

But somehow, Nicholas learned of Rasputin's secret travels. He ordered the guards to dump the *starets* and his luggage the next time the train stopped.

Frantic to get back into the family's good graces, Rasputin traveled on to the Crimea by himself. But his appearance merely caused gossip. "Now I can rest easy," said one courtier sarcastically. "Rasputin's here—everything will go well."

The imperial couple completely ignored him.

And so Rasputin returned to his Siberian village. And bided his time.

THE FAMILY NIGHTMARE

The spring and summer of 1912 passed pleasantly for the Romanovs. Sailing. Snapping photographs. Playing in the waves in front of their beachfront mansion at Peterhof. They even "walked barefoot," enthused Anastasia. "It was great!" Eight-year-old Alexei was so healthy and suntanned that Alexandra started to believe her fevered prayers had indeed worked a miracle.

In August 1912, as they always did, the imperial family traveled to two of their three Polish hunting lodges. They went first to Bialowieza in eastern Poland. "The weather is warm and my daughters and I go for [horseback] rides on these perfect woodland paths," Nicholas wrote his mother.

Alexei cried to go with them. His pleading broke his mother's heart. She knew he felt smothered and overprotected. And so she let him go rowing on a nearby lake.

But instead of stepping carefully into the rowboat, the high-spirited boy leaped . . . stumbled . . . smashed his upper thigh into an oarlock. The accident caused a small bruise and enough swelling to land Alexei in bed for a few days. But it soon disappeared, and he felt fine. "All in all," Nicholas wrote, "it did not seem like [much] to bother about."

Two weeks later, the family moved to their forest lodge in Spala. Days passed. Nicholas hunted. The grand duchesses played tennis. And Alexandra and Alexei rested in the sunshine.

One afternoon, Alexandra took the boy for a carriage ride. At first, all seemed fine. Mother and son, as well as Anna Vyrubova (who often traveled with the family), happily bounced along the rutted road. Suddenly, Alexei cried out in pain. His stomach hurt. So did his back. Alarmed, Alexandra ordered the driver to return home. But there were miles to go, and every carriage bump caused the boy to cry out. It was "an experience in horror," recalled Anna. By the time they got back to the lodge, Alexei was "almost unconscious with pain."

Dr. Botkin quickly diagnosed the problem. The torn blood vessels from the rowboat accident had been seeping blood—first into Alexei's leg, then into his groin, then into his lower abdomen. To make more room for the blood filling his tissues, Alexei's leg had involuntarily drawn itself up, until it pressed awkwardly against his chest. Still the blood kept flowing. Soon, there would be no place else for it to go. Dr. Botkin and several specialists who had been called in could do nothing.

Curled on his side and semiconscious, Alexei shrieked with pain. His face, recalled Anna, "was absolutely bloodless, drawn and seamed with suffering while his almost expressionless eyes rolled back in his head."

"Mama, help me," Alexei wailed over and over again. "Won't you help me? Won't you?"

Like the doctors, Alexandra could do nothing. For the next eleven days, she held her son's hand, sponged his feverish forehead, and prayed. She felt sure her son was dying.

Alexei believed he was, too. "When I am dead it will not hurt anymore, will it, Mama?" he asked one day. His words brought her to tears.

Still, she coped with her son's illness far better than Nicholas. Recalled Anna, "Seeing his boy in agony and hearing his faint screams of pain . . . [the tsar's] courage completely gave way and he rushed, weeping bitterly, to his study."

Servants stuffed cotton in their ears and went on with their work. Since they did not know the cause of Alexei's illness, they could only guess at the reason for his suffering. Meanwhile, Nicholas went on with his hunting. The grand duchesses went on with their walks and tennis games. Even Alexandra went on giving the obligatory teas expected by the Polish nobles who arrived at the lodge. It was, noted one historian, "an extraordinary situation; the heir to the throne lay dying, but everyone carried on as normal." All of this just to keep Alexei's hemophilia a secret.

On the eleventh night of his ordeal, Alexei weakly grasped his mother's hand. "When I am dead, build me a little monument of stones in the woods," he whispered.

There was, it seemed, nothing more they could do.

Members of the grief-stricken family—Nicholas, Olga, Tatiana, Marie, and Anastasia—waited for the inevitable.

But Alexandra refused to give up. There was still Rasputin. Since the incident with the letters, her faith in the *starets* had dulled. Should she contact him? The situation, she decided, left her no choice. She sent a telegram to Siberia.

Rasputin immediately cabled back: "The Little One will not die. Do not allow the doctors to bother him too much."

Early the next morning, Alexandra entered the drawing room where her family sat waiting for Alexei's death. Looking around at their sad, tired faces, she smiled. "The doctors notice no improvement," she said, her tone suddenly confident, "but I am not a bit anxious myself now. . . . Father Gregory . . . has reassured me completely."

Twenty-four hours later, Alexei's bleeding stopped. Astonished doctors could find no explanation for it. The boy had been at death's door. In fact, the episode had been so severe that it would be a whole year before he could walk again. His sudden improvement seemed to defy science. "It is wholly inexplicable from a medical point of view," said one of the doctors.

The event wasn't inexplicable to Alexandra. Rasputin, she believed, had interceded with God on her behalf, wrought a miracle through his power of prayer, vanquished death. Any lingering doubts she may have had about the *starets* were now completely swept away. Convinced that he spoke with God's voice, she vowed to always listen . . . no matter what.

Rasputin understood perfectly his strengthened hold over the royal family. Time and again, he warned the empress, "[The boy] will live only as long as I am alive."

CHAPTER EIGHT

❧ THREE CENTURIES OF ROMANOVS ❧

GROWING UP

One day in early 1913, Dr. Botkin arrived at the Alexander Palace to check on Alexei, who was still recovering from his illness in Spala. As the doctor headed along the second-floor corridor, he heard a thump-thumping sound coming from one of the rooms. Curious, the doctor peeked in.

There was Anastasia, red-faced and sweating, and hopping on one leg.

Struggling to keep a straight face, Dr. Botkin asked what she was doing.

Without missing a hop, Anastasia breathlessly replied, "An officer . . . told me that to [jump] around . . . on one leg helps one grow." And she desperately wanted to grow, "or something," she admitted.

At eighteen, her oldest sister, Olga, had a round face and high cheekbones.

Sixteen-year-old Tatiana was willowy and tiny-waisted.

Fourteen-year-old Marie had a peaches-and-cream complexion.

And Anastasia?

At twelve, she was short and chubby. True, people often commented on her good, strong Russian features. But they were lost in a face that one courtier called "lumpy and lacking elegance." And in the past few months she had gotten so round her family had given her a nickname—*kubyshka*. It meant "dumpling."

But it wasn't the girls' appearance that worried some members of the court. It was their emotional immaturity. They blamed this on Alexandra's obsessive desire to protect her daughters from the outside world. "Even when grown, the empress continued to regard them as little children," recalled Anna Vyrubova. Isolated from society with no company but one another, the girls existed in a kind of time warp, one in which they never really grew up. Recalled one courtier, "When the two eldest had grown into real young women, one would hear them talking like little girls of ten and twelve." They would giggle, poke each other, and run into corners.

The teenaged girls thought it especially fun when Olga led them all in a mock battle involving using toy guns and racing their bicycles through the palace rooms. And they still erupted into embarrassed giggles whenever the palace censor—whose job it was to clip out any unsuitable scenes from the films the family watched in the semicircular hall every Saturday night—missed an on-screen kiss or hug.

Isolated. Immature. Naïve.

These were the grand duchesses on the eve of the biggest celebration Russia had ever seen.

THREE-HUNDREDTH ANNIVERSARY

Feeling betrayed by their subjects, Nicholas and Alexandra had rarely appeared in public since the events of 1905, eight long years ago. Once, when the English ambassador urged them to "break down the barrier that exists between you and your people, and regain their confidence," the tsar had drawn himself up and replied haughtily, "Do you mean that *I* am to regain the confidence of my people, or that they are to regain *my* confidence?" The rift between ruler and subjects had continued to widen.

But now a momentous event was approaching—the three-hundredth anniversary of Romanov rule over Russia. Nicholas and his advisers saw it as the perfect opportunity to reestablish the tsar's relationship with his subjects. They planned an extravagant, weeklong jubilee in St. Petersburg, complete with balls, operas, parades, firework displays, fairs, and concerts in the park. Pictures of every Romanov tsar would be hung on the fronts of stores. And thousands of colored lights would be strung. Each night, the words *God save the Tsar,* as well as a double-headed Romanov eagle, would be illuminated; the Winter Palace would blaze with a huge portrait of Nicholas.

In the workers' district, factories would be closed for the first day of the celebrations, and free meals served to the poor. Additionally, Nicholas would show his benevolence by granting amnesty to two thousand political prisoners—all from the lower classes. "Thousands of invisible threads center in the tsar's heart, and these threads stretch to both the huts of the poor and the palaces of the rich," read one piece of jubilee propaganda.

Nicholas and Alexandra felt sure this display of power and opulence would inspire loyalty from their subjects. "No hope seems too confident or too bright," reported one British journalist.

March 6, 1913—the first day of the long-planned celebrations—dawned with heavy clouds, a cold mist, and the occasional roll of thunder. As the imperial family's carriages traveled from the Winter Palace, where they had moved weeks earlier in preparation for the anniversary festivities, to a special thanksgiving service at the Cathedral of Our Lady of Kazan, nothing seemed especially celebratory. The imperial banners of white, blue, and red that decorated the family's route hung dripping and dispirited. And the crowds, far smaller than anyone had expected, were subdued when the tsar passed. Where was the cheering? The shouting? The singing? Instead, there was "little real enthusiasms, little real loyalty," recalled one spectator. "I saw a cloud over the whole celebration."

The triple row of guards and policemen standing between the tsar's procession and the people added to the gloomy mood. Fears over bombs and assassination attempts had turned the capital into an armed camp.

Meanwhile, inside the cathedral, five thousand invited guests—nobles, diplomats, visiting dignitaries, generals, admirals, and government officials, as well as hundreds of policemen—waited. Everywhere in the flickering light of the candles, gold glinted, from the altar and icons to the priests' vestments and the great dome overhead. Candlelight reflected off the women's jewels, too, in "a fantastic shower of diamonds, rubies, sapphires, emeralds . . . a blaze of fire and flame," recalled French Ambassador Maurice Paléologue.

But just minutes before the imperial family arrived, a scuffle took place at the front of the cathedral. All eyes turned to see Duma President Michael Rodzianko glowering at Rasputin.

The *starets* had taken a seat in a block of prominently placed chairs reserved for Duma members. Rodzianko could not believe the man's audacity. By doing so, Rasputin was publicly proclaiming his close ties to the throne.

Infuriated, the Duma president (who believed all the rumors about the *starets*) shouted, "Clear out at once, you vile heretic."

Rasputin waved his invitation. "I was invited here by persons more highly placed than you," he replied.

"Clear out," repeated Rodzianko, "or I'll order the sergeant-at-arms to carry you out."

Refusing to budge, Rasputin looked at him coolly. Then his gaze grew intense. He looked deep into Rodzianko's eyes.

Rodzianko felt a "tremendous force" surge through his body. Believing the *starets* was using hypnosis, "I suddenly became possessed of an almost animal fury," he later recalled.

"You are a notorious swindler!" the Duma president shouted.

At that, Rasputin dropped to his knees and began praying.

Unable to control his rage, Rodzianko began kicking the *starets* in the ribs.

But Rasputin remained on his knees.

Finally, Rodzianko grabbed him by the scruff of the neck and heaved him into the aisle.

Rasputin recognized defeat. Pulling himself up off the marble floor, he cried dramatically, "Oh, Lord, forgive him such sin!" Then as all eyes watched, he strode from the cathedral and into his waiting automobile (yet another gift from the empress).

Shocked whispers rippled through the congregation.

The empress's expression as she entered the cathedral minutes later only added to the gossip. "Her face was cold and expressionless, almost austere," said Meriel Buchanan, the British ambassador's daughter.

The sight of eight-year-old Alexei didn't help, either. Still unable to walk, he was carried to his seat by a Cossack guard. Behind him, people put their heads together and whispered yet again. What was wrong with the future tsar?

At last, the four grand duchesses entered. In their white silk gowns with trains of red velvet, they looked like fairy princesses. All eyes watched as they took their places behind their parents and brother. "Is that Olga Nikolaevna?" some people might have whispered. "Who is the little one?" Hardly anyone could tell the grand duchesses apart. Almost always photographed in matching white dresses, they tended to be considered as a whole, rather than as individuals. The grand duchesses obviously accepted this. Recently, they'd begun signing the letters and gifts they gave jointly as OTMA—a combination of the first letter of each of their names.

As the music began, the congregation turned back toward the altar and the imperial couple. Alexandra stood stone-faced and straight as a stick, the diamonds covering her gown's bodice trembling with each nervous breath she took.

Nicholas, too, appeared uneasy. Despite the tight security in and around the cathedral, he kept "anxiously and furtively scanning the

faces of the assembly as if afraid of meeting some secret danger," recalled one observer. It was obvious the tsar no longer felt safe even
among his most loyal subjects.

That's when some people noticed the imperial couple looking
up into the shadowy heights of the cathedral dome. Two doves circled over their heads. Believing in religious omens as they did, they
took this as a good sign. "A symbol," Nicholas later said, "that the
blessings of God, after three centuries, continue to rest on the . . .
Romanov[s]."

Two months later, as part of the anniversary celebration, the
family took a weeklong trip to Moscow. Along the route, people
flocked to see them. In Kostroma on the Volga River, people ventured waist-deep into the water for a closer look at the family. And
in villages, old peasant men and women fell to their knees as the
royals' cars whizzed past. From their open-topped Renaults, the
family hardly noticed the little tables that stood before many of
the huts. On them, peasants had laid flowers, salt, and bread—the
traditional Russian offering to guests. But while the people acted
curious or reverent, on only one occasion was the family greeted
with spontaneous good feelings.

It happened during a visit to an ancient monastery. An old peasant woman stepped from the gathered crowd and approached Alexandra. Falling on her knees, she begged the empress for a blessing.
Alexandra made the sign of the cross above the woman's bent head.
Then impulsively, she unwound the silk shawl she was wearing and
gave it to the peasant.

The crowd burst into cheers. "God save the Tsar!" they cried.
"Let your Sovereign Family live forever."

This single experience convinced both Nicholas and Alexandra
that the jubilee's mission had succeeded. Said the empress to a friend
shortly after the celebrations, "You can see it for yourself—we need

merely to show ourselves and at once their hearts are ours." Added Nicholas, "My people love me."

"Nobody . . . could have imagined that in less than four years Nicky's very name would be splattered with mud and hatred," his sister Olga later said.

TEACHING ALEXEI

Not long after the tercentenary celebrations, Pierre Gilliard, who had discovered the truth about Alexei's illness at Spala, and Sydney Gibbes, who still knew nothing about it, began tutoring the tsarevich. It was long past time for the almost nine-year-old to enter the classroom, but his frequent illnesses had delayed his education. Now, with the boy on the mend, the teachers began their lessons. Sadly, recalled Gilliard, Alexei had not been taught the "habits of discipline." The boy hated to be corrected, and tended to be lazy. He also blamed his teachers for his being in the classroom. "I had a definite impression of his mute hostility," Gilliard wrote, "and at times it reached a stage of open defiance." What sort of defiance? The always-reserved Gilliard did not elaborate.

But Sydney Gibbes did. One day, he taught Alexei to make a "telephone" by holding one end of a wire to his ear and the other between his teeth. But the project quickly turned into a scuffle, Gibbes fending off his student as Alexei struggled with all his might to wrap the wire around the teacher's teeth.

Another time, the two skirmished over scissors. "I had rather a bad [time]," Gibbes wrote in dismay. "[Alexei] wanted to cut my hair, and then his own, and when I tried to prevent him, he went behind the curtain and held it round him. When I opened it he had actually cut some hair off and he was rather disconcerted when

I told him he had a bald place.... He would insist on cutting or pretending to cut everything. The more I tried to prevent him, the more he shrieked with delight." Concluded Gibbes, "Lessons with the tsarevich were more exciting than pleasant."

Still, Alexei was "sensitive to the suffering in others because he suffered so much himself," claimed Gilliard.

He could also be introspective. One bright summer day in 1913— six months after Alexei's ordeal at Spala—Olga found Alexei lying on his back in the grass, gazing wistfully up into the sky.

What was he doing? she asked.

"I like to think and wonder," he replied.

"About what?"

"Oh, so many things," he said. "I enjoy the sun and the beauty of summer as long as I can. Who knows if one of these days I shall be prevented from doing it."

BEYOND THE PALACE GATES:
A DIFFERENT KIND OF EDUCATION
FOR A DIFFERENT KIND OF BOY

Around 1913, poverty forced the peasant father of eight-year-old Nicholas Griaznov into an apprenticeship agreement with St. Petersburg shop owner A. Kasatkin. The father agreed that little Nicholas would work in the shop for four years, receiving a mere three rubles a month (not even enough to buy a cup of milk) plus room and board for his labor. In return, the shop owner promised to teach Nicholas a useful trade. But like most shop owners, Kasatkin looked upon his apprentices as nothing more than cheap labor. Expected to rise earlier than anyone else (around four thirty), the boy was on the go all day, delivering purchases, unpacking merchandise, or standing on the sidewalk in every kind of weather, coaxing customers into the store. Not until midnight did he finally drop onto his straw mattress in the kitchen. More than five other child apprentices were also squeezed into this space. All were poorly fed, badly clothed, and regularly beaten. Desperate to call attention to his son's plight, Nicholas's father sent a letter to the newspaper New Russia. *Because censorship allowed for public discussion of social problems as long as they weren't blamed on the tsar or his government, the newspaper ran the letter. It read:*

> I tried to take my son away and put him in another shop, but his boss wouldn't let him go. He said there was some kind of law which let him keep my son until the apprenticeship was over, that is, for three and a half more years, and until then he wouldn't give him up. Kasatkin told me, "The law gives me the right to teach the boy to be a human being and to hit him and even beat him with a rod if he is disrespectful to my family. If you want your son back . . . then you will have to pay me . . . 300 rubles for my expense in training the boy. Then I'll give him to you." Now where is a poor peasant like me supposed to get that kind of money? I don't even have a crust of bread, not to speak of [300] rubles to give Mr. Kasatkin for my child.

Days later, the newspaper printed Kasatkin's response:

> I would like to direct your attention to the following fact. I paid a middleman a good bit of money for [Nicholas], just like all the other merchants who buy apprentices for their stores. These middlemen travel around to impoverished villages . . . during the winter months when food is scarce. They collect eight- to ten-year-old boys and

send them to stores as apprentices without obtaining the consent of either the parents or the children. An honest press should not attack particular individuals but should attack this system of buying and selling children, which exists in [St.] Petersburg and in other cities. I alone do not have the power to fight against such established custom. Competition forces me to use as much cheap and unpaid labor as I can.

PART THREE

THE STORM BREAKS

Arise, lift yourselves up, Russian people,
Arise for battle, hungry brother,
Let the cry of the people's vengeance ring out—
Onward, onward, onward!

We've suffered insult long enough,
And submitted too long to the nobles!
Let us straighten our powerful backs
And show the enemy our strength!

So arise, brothers, arise and be bold,
And then shall the land be ours once more,
And from bitter aspens shall we hang
Every last lackey of that Vampire-Tsar.
—"The Peasant Song," 1917

CHAPTER NINE

"MY GOD! MY GOD! WHAT MADNESS!"

1914

SUMMER ON THE *STANDART*

Many Russians would remember June 1914 as being glorious, with clear skies, a golden sun, and soft, cooling breezes. Feeling almost carefree, the Romanovs set off on holiday aboard the *Standart*. They cruised the coast of Finland. Here and there along their meandering route, the ship dropped anchor. Then Nicholas and the children rowed ashore to forage through pine forests for berries and mushrooms. Because of her back problems, Alexandra rarely left the ship. Instead, she reclined on deck, sewing and reading until her family returned for dinner. Afterward, there was dancing beneath the ship's canvas awnings. In their white dresses, the teenaged grand duchesses bantered and flirted with the young officers as they whirled to the strains of the *Standart's* brass band. Bored by all the mush, Alexei scrambled across the deck, climbing up ladders and swinging from ropes as his sailor nannies chased after him. At day's end, the family gathered for evening prayers sung by the sailors' choir. Alexandra especially loved this time of day, when the rays of the setting sun danced on the water, and the deep voices of the sailors, singing the Lord's Prayer, echoed across the vast, watery silence. Retiring to their staterooms, they fell blissfully asleep to the waves' gentle rocking.

But just four days out, terrible news shattered their idyllic days. Archduke Franz Ferdinand, prince and heir to Austria-Hungary, had been murdered.

WAR CLOUDS LOOM

Austria-Hungary was an empire made up of a group of provinces located in Central Europe. While its two largest ethnic groups were German and Hungarian, in 1914 there were also forty million Slavs—Poles, Croats, Bosnians, Serbians, Czechs, and Slovaks— living within the empire because their territories had been occupied by the Austrians. Most of these Slavic people hated being ruled by the Austrians. Burning for the day they would be free, some plotted to break up the empire and return the Slavic provinces to their rightful people.

The small Slav kingdom of Serbia supported these desires. Its government looked the other way as extremist groups, bent on using violence and destruction against Austria, organized within its borders. It was one of these terrorists, a nineteen-year-old named Gavrilo Princip, who calmly stepped out in front of Archduke Ferdinand's car during the prince's ceremonial visit to the city of Sarajevo (in modern-day Bosnia). Aiming carefully, Princip fired twice. The archduke's wife, Sophie, instantly crumpled, and blood gushed from the archduke's neck. Fifteen minutes later, both the future ruler of Austria-Hungary and his wife were dead.

Over the next two weeks, political tensions in Europe grew. Blaming the Serbian government for the assassination, Austria-Hungary moved to punish the tiny country. It began threatening war.

Fearing attack, Serbia turned to Russia for help. Years earlier, the two Slavic countries had signed a mutual defense agreement. This meant they were treaty-bound to defend each other.

Meanwhile, Germany—which had a defense treaty with Austria-Hungry—quickly let it be known that it sided *against* Russia and Serbia.

That was when France, because of *its* mutual defense treaty with the tsar, weighed in on the side of the Slavs.

And England? It, too, allied itself with Russia because of a treaty it had signed with France.

"My God! My God! What madness!" exclaimed French Ambassador Paléologue. All of Europe tottered precariously on the brink of catastrophe. An Austrian attack on Serbia could mean the start of a war the likes of which the world had never seen.

"I HAVE KILLED THE ANTI-CHRIST!"

On June 30, Alexandra cabled Rasputin from aboard the *Standart*. "It is a serious moment," she wrote. She begged him to pray for peace.

Her telegram arrived in the Siberian village of Pokrovskoe just hours later, and a messenger delivered it to Rasputin's house (the *starets* was visiting his family for the summer). Rasputin ripped open the envelope and read the telegram while standing in the doorway. Realizing it required an immediate response, he went after the messenger. But as he stepped through his gate and into the street, an unknown woman appeared. "Her mouth and face were veiled so I could only see her eyes," he later recalled. "At that moment a dagger flashed in her hand and she stuck it once into my stomach. . . . I could feel the blood pouring out of me."

"I have killed the anti-Christ! I have killed the anti-Christ!" the woman screamed hysterically.

Clutching his wound with both hands, Rasputin stumbled toward the church. Dagger raised, the woman came after him. But a crowd, attracted by the commotion, stopped her. Pushing her to the ground, they held her until the police arrived.

Meanwhile, Rasputin was carried to his house, where he lay moaning and bleeding until a doctor from the town of Tyumen, forty-seven miles away, arrived eight hours later. Recognizing the seriousness of Rasputin's condition, the doctor chose not to move the patient. Instead, he performed surgery by candlelight in the *starets'* bedroom. Rasputin, who refused anesthesia, instantly fainted.

When he came to hours later, he did two things: he called a priest to pray for him, and he cabled Alexandra. "That hunk of carrion stuck me with a knife," he wrote her, "but with God's help, I'll live."

He was barely conscious when her reply arrived. "We are deeply shaken—praying with all our hearts."

But Alexandra did more than pray. She sent a specialist to Siberia. He immediately transferred Rasputin to the hospital in Tyumen, where another, more delicate surgery was performed to repair the *starets'* internal organs.

For the next forty-six days, Rasputin recuperated in the hospital. Feverish and weak from loss of blood, he read the newspapers and worried. What if war broke out? Germany, he believed, would defeat Russia. The kaiser would take Nicholas's place on the throne, and when that happened, the pleasant life he'd built for himself would be swept away. His privileges. His influence. All would be gone. Rasputin couldn't let that happen. In hopes of averting war, he began sending almost daily cables to Nicholas.

Surely, the diplomats "should be able to keep the peace," he wrote in one. In another, he said, "We don't have a war yet, and we don't need one." He even went so far as to advise Nicholas not to "give [our enemies] a reason to start yelling again."

On July 28, Austrian-Hungarian troops began bombing the Serbian capital of Belgrade. The next day, Nicholas—who had cut short his vacation and returned to his summer mansion at Peterhof—ordered his army to mobilize along the border his country shared with Austria.

According to some reports, when Rasputin heard this news, he thrashed about in bed so wildly that he ripped out his bandages. "[Do] not plan for war," he urgently telegrammed the tsar, "for war will mean the end of Russia and yourselves, and you will lose to the last man."

When Nicholas received this telegram, he ripped it up in frustration. He felt so conflicted. His instincts told him that war could be "a good thing, especially from the standpoint of morale." An event like that would unite the Russian people, heal class divides. But Alexandra, who believed all Rasputin's warnings, pleaded with Nicholas to maintain the peace and listen to Our Friend. He spoke, she insisted, for God. At the same time, Nicholas's generals pressured him to prepare for a war they claimed was just one shot away.

Nicholas wavered, unable to decide on a course of action. But events soon made the decision for him.

WAR COMES TO THE ROMANOVS

On August 1, 1914, everyone except Alexei (who was bedridden because of a twisted ankle) attended vespers in the little Alexandria church at Peterhof. Standing before the altar in the candlelight, Nicholas wore, observed Pierre Gilliard, "an air of weary exhaustion, [and] the pouches that always appeared under his eyes when he was tired [were] markedly larger." Hands clasped, he prayed with all his might for God's help.

Beside him, Alexandra's face bore the same "care-worn . . . look of suffering so often seen at [Alexei's] bedside." She, too, prayed "fervently . . . as if she could banish an evil dream."

The girls added their prayers to their parents'. Bowing their heads, the family chanted the familiar and comforting words:

O Lord, save the people,
And bless thine inheritance.
And give peace in our time, O Lord;
For it is thou, Lord, only that makes us dwell in safety.

When the family returned from church, Nicholas—promising he'd be only a moment—stepped into his study to read the latest reports. The others went into the dining room to wait for him.

As the minutes passed and the always-punctual Nicholas did not come, the family grew more and more uneasy. Finally, Alexandra sent Tatiana to fetch him. But before the girl could push back from the table, he appeared in the doorway.

Pale, his voice shaking, he told them the news. Germany, allied with Austria-Hungary, had declared war on Russia.

At the table, all four girls began to cry.

As for Alexandra, she may have thought of the telegram she'd received from Rasputin earlier that day. "I say a terrible storm cloud hangs over Russia," he'd written ominously. "Disaster, grief, murky darkness and no light. A whole ocean of tears, there is no counting them, and so much blood . . . Russia is drowning in blood. The disaster is great. The misery is infinite." She, too, began to weep.

"GOD SAVE THE TSAR"

The next morning, everyone but Alexei, still in bed with his bad ankle, traveled by yacht to the Winter Palace in St. Petersburg. There Nicholas would formally declare war on both Germany and Austria-Hungary—a war that would one day be known as World War I.

How different it was from the last time the family had appeared in the city. This day the streets teemed with people. In a patriotic frenzy, they packed roads, bridges, and the Palace Square, waving banners, singing, and cheering. When the tsar's boat came into view, they shouted "*Batiushka, Batiushka* [Father Tsar, Father Tsar], lead us to victory!" In a sudden rush of loyalty to Russia and their tsar, the people had forgotten their bitterness and resentment. War had done what Nicholas could not. "For Faith, Tsar and Country!" shouted nobility and worker alike. "For Defense of Holy Russia!"

The family arrived at the Winter Palace. Inside its packed corridors, people stretched out to touch them as they passed. They pressed kisses to their hands and to the hems of their dresses. Some dropped to their knees before them, bowed, or made the sign of the cross as they passed.

In the vast white marble Nicholas Hall, a special altar had been set up. On it stood the icon known as the Vladimir Mother of God. At least six hundred years old, the icon was said to have the miraculous ability of turning back invaders. Now, at the beginning of this new war, Nicholas knelt before it and asked its blessing. Then raising his hand, he took the traditional Russian oath: "I solemnly swear that I will never make peace as long as a single enemy remains on Russian soil."

At last the family moved toward a balcony high above the crowded Palace Square. The grand duchesses hung back, pressing against the velvet curtains as their parents stepped out.

At the sight of their tsar, the huge crowd fell silent. Then, as one, they dropped to their knees on the cobblestones.

Overwhelmed by emotion, unable to make his voice carry that far, Nicholas could only make the sign of the cross. Then he lowered his head as tears ran down his cheeks.

From below, five thousand voices burst spontaneously into song:

> God save the Tsar,
> Mighty and powerful,
> Let him reign for our glory,
> For the confusion of our enemies,
> The Orthodox Tsar,
> God save the Tsar.

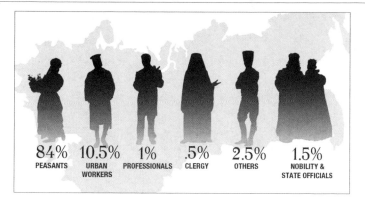

84%	10.5%	1%	.5%	2.5%	1.5%
PEASANTS	URBAN WORKERS	PROFESSIONALS	CLERGY	OTHERS	NOBILITY & STATE OFFICIALS

An approximate breakdown of Russia's social classes at the turn of the twentieth century.

HOLLY PRIBBLE

In this official portrait taken in 1888, twenty-year-old Nicholas stands behind his father, Tsar Alexander III. Surrounding them are the other members of his family. His mother, Maria, stands behind brother Michael. Sister Olga leans against her father; beside her sits brother George. Sister Xenia is to the right of Nicholas.

THE STATE ARCHIVE OF THE RUSSIAN FEDERATION, MOSCOW

This photograph of Alix and her sisters posing with their grandmother was taken shortly after their mother's death in 1878. From left to right: Princess Irene, seated; Princess Victoria, standing; Queen Victoria seated and holding six-year-old Alix's hand; and Princess Elizabeth (who later married Nicholas's uncle the Grand Duke Serge) standing behind Alix.

The Winter Palace in 2011, looking very much as it did when Nicholas and Alexandra lived there.

A view of the Great Palace at Peterhof, a large seaside park that became the Romanovs' summer residence.

The Alexander Palace, where Nicholas and Alexandra made their home. The family's private rooms were located in the left wing.

ERIC ROHMANN

Nicholas and Alexandra's bedroom in the Alexander Palace. Note the numerous icons on the walls.

COURTESY OF BRANSON DECOU COLLECTION DIGITAL ARCHIVE,
SPECIAL COLLECTIONS, UNIVERSITY OF CALIFORNIA, SANTA CRUZ, CA

Bejeweled Nicholas and Alexandra pose in the seventeenth-century costumes they wore to their fancy dress ball in 1903.

CORBIS

The little grand duchesses posed for this portrait in 1900. From left to right are three-year-old Tatiana, one-year-old Marie, and five-year-old Olga.

Alexandra and baby Anastasia in 1901. The empress signed this portrait *Alix*.

Baby Alexei in 1904, looking bright-eyed and healthy despite his diagnosis of hemophilia.

In 1896, peasants from all across Russia converged on Moscow for Nicholas's coronation to receive small gifts and food from the tsar, as was the custom. This photograph shows what was called the People's Feast on the day after the tragic events. Note the long tables and the communal bowls.

Barefoot peasants living in a traditional village, outside their *izba,* c. 1910.

Peasant women washing laundry in the Volga River, c. 1900.

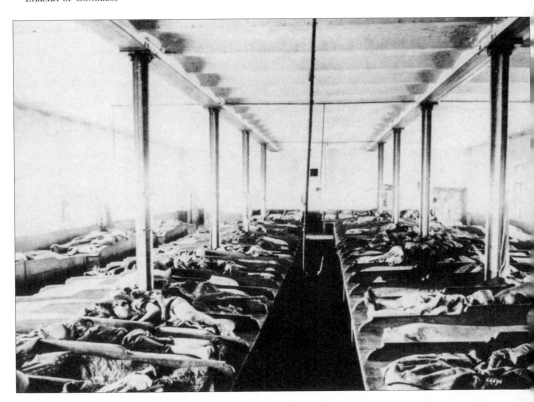

Plank beds in the workers' dormitory of a factory in St. Petersburg, c. 1900. As many as seventy-five workers slept in one room on long wooden platforms divided into individual spaces by foot-high partitions. Factories charged workers to live here, docking the cost from their pay.

Some of Moscow's poorest citizens pose outside a shared three-story house, c. 1900. As many as a thousand people squeezed between the walls of these ramshackle buildings, paying five kopecks a night (the equivalent of twelve hours' work) for a space no bigger than a closet.

IMAGNO/AUSTRIAN ARCHIVES, VIENNA

Two Moscow workers share a space and a drink, c. 1904.

ZENO, BERLIN

St. Petersburg factory workers—both men and boys—pose for this 1910 photograph.

LIBRARY OF CONGRESS

This painting depicts the injuries inflicted on protesting workers by tsarist soldiers shown stationed (at right) before the Winter Palace on Bloody Sunday, 1905.

LIBRARY OF CONGRESS

The opening of the Duma in the Winter Palace, 1906. On the left stand the autocratic nobles of Russia, and on the right, the newly elected deputies. Before them, Nicholas reads his speech in front of an ermine-draped throne—a sign of royal supremacy. To the far left, a ramrod-straight Alexandra, along with Nicholas's mother and other members of the royal entourage, watches.

CORBIS

The Duma in session at the Tauride Palace, 1907. Note the portrait of Nicholas looming over the proceedings, a constant reminder to deputies that they were ever under the watchful eye of the tsar.

A photograph of Vladimir Lenin taken around 1918.

The tsar's police round up villagers as part of Nicholas's crackdown, 1906. The officer on the far right is checking identification papers.

A group of Jewish children gather for a photograph in 1905 in Warsaw, Poland (then part of the Russian empire).

An apprentice boy, c. 1900.

A rare snapshot of a relaxed and smiling Alexandra picnicking on the coast of Finland, c. 1908.

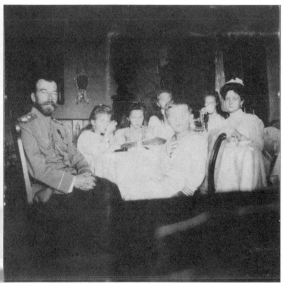

Afternoon tea at the family palace in the Crimea in 1909. Alexei sits front and center, while from left to right are Nicholas, Anastasia, Olga, Marie, Tatiana, and Alexandra.

Even though he was supposed to be careful, Alexei took all sorts of physical risks, as this photograph taken around 1909 shows. As Anastasia looks on worriedly, Alexei swings exuberantly from a pole.

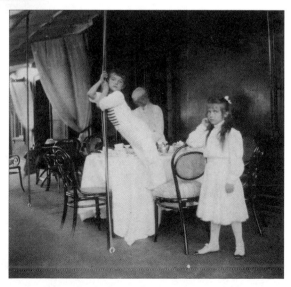

Olga (front) and Tatiana (left) play in the surf in the
Crimea, c. 1909. On the right, holding a Kodak Brownie
box camera, is Alexandra's good friend Anna Vyrubova.

The imperial couple in the Crimean scenery, c. 1910.

A retouched lantern slide showing Rasputin with the Romanovs, c. 1910. In the front row from left to right are the children's nurse, Tatiana, and Marie. In the second row from left to right are Alexandra, Rasputin, Alexei, and Anastasia. Standing behind the *starets* is Olga.

LIBRARY OF CONGRESS

Prime Minister Peter Stolypin, one of Rasputin's greatest foes.

LIBRARY OF CONGRESS

Anastasia and Alexei cuddle in a chair on the terrace of the family palace in the Crimea, 1910.

ROMANOV COLLECTION, BEINECKE RARE BOOK AND MANUSCRIPT LIBRARY, YALE UNIVERSITY

Olga (center) and Tatiana study with Pierre Gilliard at the palace in the Crimea, c. 1911.

ROMANOV COLLECTION, BEINECKE RARE BOOK AND MANUSCRIPT LIBRARY, YALE UNIVERSITY

Anastasia looks over Olga's shoulder as the older girl reads, c. 1912.

ROMANOV COLLECTION, BEINECKE RARE BOOK AND MANUSCRIPT LIBRARY, YALE UNIVERSITY

Alexandra reveals both her weariness and sadness in this candid
photograph taken in the doorway of Alexei's sickroom at Spala in 1912.

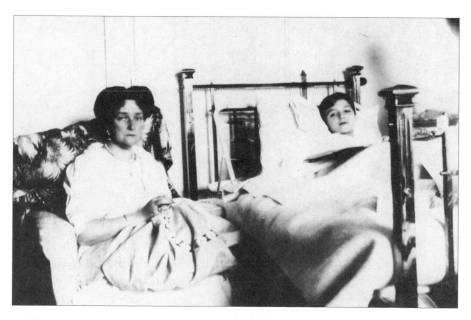

Alexandra sits at her recovering son's bedside just days after the hemophilic
episode that almost killed him.

Nicholas and Alexei on the balcony of the Alexander Palace, c. 1913.
By tradition, the family maintained close ties with the armed forces, and both
father and son liked to wear uniforms. The boy's leg is still bent at the knee,
owing to the events at Spala.

This portrait of the Romanov family is one of
a series taken to mark the tercentenary in 1913.
Eight-year-old Alexei sits before his parents,
while eleven-year-old Anastasia sits next to
Nicholas. In the back from left to right are
thirteen-year-old Marie, seventeen-year-old
Olga, and fifteen-year-old Tatiana.

CHAPTER TEN

❧ IN DEFENSE OF MOTHER RUSSIA ❧

MARCHING TO WAR

In the days after Nicholas's declaration of war, hundreds of thousands of peasants were mobilized all across Russia. In Siberia and along the Black Sea, in the already chilly far north, and in the fertile Ukrainian steppe, where the crops stood ripe in the fields. Over and over, young peasant men kissed their sobbing wives, mothers, and sweethearts good-bye, before climbing aboard trains that carried them far from their villages. As in all Russian wars, it was the peasants who did most of the fighting and dying. They marched away, obediently answering the tsar's call to defend Russia. But the expression on most of their faces, wrote one foreign correspondent, "was somber and resigned."

Many Russians believed they could beat the Germans within six months. "[They] don't know how to fight," scoffed one of Nicholas's commanders. "All [we] have to do to annihilate their whole army is simply throw our caps at them."

To this end, the Russian High Command launched an invasion into the German territory of East Prussia (modern-day northeastern Poland). On August 26, just weeks after the war began, 250,000 Russian soldiers marched into Tannenberg Forest. And the Germans, lying in ambush, mowed them down. In just four days, the Russians lost every single man—an entire army either killed or captured—and vast amounts of badly needed military equipment.

The Russians did better against the Austrians, taking the province of Galicia (between the borders of modern-day Poland and Ukraine) in mid-August, as well as several Carpathian Mountain passes before Christmas. They even toppled the Austrian fortress of Przemysl. But there they stalled. All they could do was hold their position.

The German and Austrian armies held their positions, too. Stalemate ensued. With neither side strong enough to push the opposing army back, the combatants resorted to defensive warfare. Digging trenches, they hunkered down inside them. Machine guns trained on each other, they waited, hoping to wear out the enemy's resolve.

But Russia was ill-prepared for a long, drawn-out war. The Ministry of War—run by the incompetent Vladimir Sukhomlinov—had counted on a short campaign, lasting no longer than six months. And so it had made no plans for the wartime production of guns and ammunition. Instead, Minister Sukhomlinov assumed the country's existing weapons stockpiles would be more than enough.

He was wrong. Just six weeks into the conflict, the chief of the Artillery Department warned Sukhomlinov that Russia would soon be forced to surrender if something wasn't done about the situation immediately.

"Go to the devil and quiet yourself," the war minister snapped. He did nothing.

By the following spring, the shortage had grown so severe that many soldiers charged into battle *without* guns. Instead, commanders told them to pick up their weapons from the men killed in front lines. At the same time, soldiers were limited to firing just ten shots a day. Sometimes they were even forbidden to return enemy fire. "Our position is bad," one soldier wrote to his father, "and all because we have no ammunition. That's what we've got to, thanks to our minister of war, making unarmed people face up to the enemy's guns because we don't have any of our own. That's what they have done."

Those Russian troops stalled on top of the Carpathian Mountains now found themselves without enough ammunition to push forward. All they could do was hold the ground they'd taken. Their commander, Alexei Brusilov, repeatedly telegrammed the war ministry for ammunition. He also demanded warm clothes and boots for his men.

But Sukhomlinov had not made plans for clothing the soldiers, either. When he finally looked into the possibility of manufacturing soldiers' boots, he learned that all the country's tannin extract (used for processing leather) was imported from Germany! And so Russia ordered boots from the United States. It took months for the order to be filled. In the meantime, recruits went barefoot. "They haven't given out overcoats," one soldier wrote home. "We run around in thin topcoats. . . . There is not much to eat and what we get is foul. Perhaps we'd be better off dead."

Back at Tsarskoe Selo, Nicholas knew very little about his soldiers' plight. Daily reports from Sukhomlinov reassured him that both "morale and equipment are in splendid order." When he inspected troops in January 1915, "[the commanders] prepared one company and collected all the best uniforms from the other regiments for it to wear," recalled one soldier, "leaving the rest of the men in the trenches without boots, knapsacks . . . trousers, uniforms, hats, or anything else."

It was obvious that Russia's war effort was on the verge of collapse, and everyone in the tsar's government knew it . . . everyone, that is, except Nicholas himself.

BEYOND THE PALACE GATES: VASILY'S DIARY

Trainload after trainload of untrained military recruits found themselves swept from the countryside and onto the battlefield. One, Vasily Mishnin, was a twenty-seven-year-old furniture salesman from the sleepy town of Penza in Central Russia. He began his diary on the day he left behind his pregnant wife, Nyura, at the train station.

25 DECEMBER 1914

The third [train] whistle. Everybody breaks down. Loud crying, hysterics, whole families weeping. I kiss my Nyura for the last time and all of my family kiss me. I can hardly hold back the tears. . . . Beside myself I climb into the [train car] with the rest [of the men] and look out at the crowd. I can hear wailing, and a tumult of voices, but I've suddenly grown numb. My nerves are in shreds . . . my eyes fix on Nyura again and I want to jump out of the [car] and kiss her again, for the last time. Too late, the long whistle of our steam train screams out, it's ready to separate us from our loved ones and take us—God knows where.

5 JANUARY 1915

We go to the depot to get our rifles. Good Lord, what's all this? They're covered in blood, black clotted lumps of it are hanging off them. All this horror is piled up in the yard, and we all have to rummage about looking for a decent one—a soldier with a bad rifle is like a teacher without a pencil.

26 JANUARY 1915

At 7 a.m. the division commander walks down the trench and orders us to oil and clean our rifles. "As soon as you see a German, shoot him!" (He is shaking, as if he has a fever.) "But don't let him see you, and don't leave the trenches." [At] midnight I have to go and relieve the guard under the cover of fire that's pouring on [our] trenches. My heart pounds, it is a terrifying thing to walk to your death. The seven of us climb out of our trench and go up to the barbed wire boundary. We find a hole and crawl through it like cats. Bullets and shells keep flying out of the German trenches. . . . We get to the guard post. . . . It is frightening even to sit or lie down here—the rifle is shaking in my hands. My hand comes down on something black: it turns out there are corpses here that haven't been cleared away. My hair stands on end. I have to sit down. . . . All I can feel is fear. . . . I want the ground to open up and swallow me. . . . What next?

27 JANUARY 1915

Suddenly a screeching noise pierces the air, I feel a pang in my heart, something whistles past and explodes nearby. My dear Lord, I am so frightened. . . . One explosion follows another, and another. Two lads are running out shouting out for nurses. They are covered in blood. It's running down their cheeks and hands, and something else is dripping from underneath their bandages. They are soon dead, shot to pieces. There is screaming, yelling, the earth is shaking. . . . And at that moment a shell flies right into our dugout. . . . [Then] we're running, but God knows where. Our [Commanding Officer] has run off into the forest. I suppose he thought it was safer in there. As if. None of us can understand what's going on. . . . We scramble into a peasant hut . . . press ourselves against a wall, sit down and wipe our eyes. Our eyes are full of tears, we wipe them away, but they just keep coming back because the shells are full of gas. . . . [We] lie facedown and we just want to dig ourselves into the earth. Under our breath we pray to our Lord God to save us from this, just for this one day. Dear [Nyura] . . . we will probably never see each other again—all it takes is an instant and I will be no more—and perhaps no one will be able to gather the scattered pieces of my body for burial.

NURSES ROMANOVA

With the war, Alexandra "became overnight a changed being," recalled her friend Anna Vyrubova. Under her patronage, the Catherine Palace at Tsarskoe Selo was converted into a hospital, as were eighty-five other mansions and palaces in the St. Petersburg area. Still, Alexandra wanted to do more. So she enrolled in nursing courses, and she took nineteen-year-old Olga and seventeen-year-old Tatiana with her. "To some it may seem unnecessary my doing this," she told Nicholas, "but much is needed and every hand is useful."

Now Alexandra no longer stayed in bed until noon, complaining of headaches and back pains. Every morning, she and the "Big Pair" walked across the park to their nursing classes at the newly created hospital. Working in the wards, the students "washed, cleaned and bandaged maimed bodies, mangled faces, blinded eyes," remembered Anna, who joined the Romanovs in their nurses' training. It was gruesome work. "I have seen the empress of Russia assisting in the most difficult operations," continued Anna, "taking from the hands of the busy surgeons amputated legs and arms, removing bloody and vermin-ridden field dressings, enduring all the sights and smells and agonies of the most dreadful of all places, a military hospital in the midst of a war."

After two months of intense training, Alexandra and her daughters earned their nursing certificates as well as the right to wear the Red Cross uniform. With its apron and nurse's wimple, the gray uniform was extremely plain. Yet it made its wearers look "dignified and courageous," said Anna.

Fifteen-year-old Marie and thirteen-year-old Anastasia wanted to be nurses, too. But Alexandra said they were too young. Instead, she allowed them to be "patronesses," establishing their own little hospital just across the pond from the Alexander Palace, in a cluster of buildings Nicholas had built years earlier. Called the Hospital of Grand Duchesses Marie and Anastasia, it had enough white iron beds for two dozen wounded officers. Because they were not noble-born, infantrymen were sent to separate hospitals. There were dominoes, chessboards, and even a pool table.

The "Little Pair" took their patroness duties seriously. Every few days, they hurried along the path that led from the palace to their hospital. Sitting at the wounded soldiers' bedsides, they read to them and wrote letters for them. Sometimes they knitted little gifts—scarves and lap rugs. And if their patients felt well enough, they challenged them to a game of checkers or a few hands of bezique, their favorite card game. Upon their discharge, they gave the men little mementos of their stay—watches and medals inscribed with the girls' initials.

Hospital work was fun at first, especially for girls who had lived so long in isolation. "There was a concert [at our hospital]," Anastasia told her father. "There were singers and then dancers. . . . Everyone applauded at the end." But the reality of war soon pushed its way into their little hospital. Every day, Red Cross trains brought hundreds of wounded and dying men from the front. Moaning and bloody, their flesh burned and torn, they called out, "Stand near me. Hold my hand that I may have courage." The girls did. "Two more poor things died," Anastasia now mournfully told her father. "[I] sat with them only yesterday."

THE WAR GRINDS ON

In May 1915, after a long winter of being mired in the trenches, a combined Austrian-Germany force attacked the Russian troops still hunkered down in the Carpathian Mountains. A thousand shells a minute pounded the Russians' trenches. Terrified troops "jumped up and ran back weaponless," recalled one German soldier. "In their gray fur caps and fluttering unbuttoned coats, they looked like a flock of sheep in wild confusion." The Russians tried to make a stand, but without supplies or ammunition, they finally retreated, giving up the hard-won territory they'd spent the winter defending.

But the enemy kept coming, pushing the Russians farther and farther back. When it was all over, Russia had not only lost the territory it had earlier won from Austria, but all of Russian Poland as well. "They've screwed it all up," General Brusilov heard one of his soldiers grumble, "and we've been landed with cleaning up the mess." Said another, "A fish begins to stink from its head. What kind of tsar surrounds himself with incompetents? It's as clear as day that we're going to lose this war."

The Great Retreat, as it came to be known, ended in September 1915, only after German forces got bogged down in Russian rain and mud. By that time, one out of every three men on the front line had been killed or captured. Thousands more deserted, returning to their farms, only to discover that in many cases the government had requisitioned all their crops and livestock. For many, it was the last straw, wrote one historian, "the vital psychological moment . . .

when [soldiers'] loyalty to the monarchy finally snapped. A government which had dragged them into a war which they could not hope to win, had failed to provide them adequate weapons and supplies . . . was not worthy of further sacrifices."

DARKNESS DESCENDS

With the continued defeat of its army, gloom and misery fell across the country. Gone were the cheering crowds, the merrily waving banners, the Russian people's bravado. Now groups of bleak, shivering citizens gathered on snow-packed sidewalks to read the ever-lengthening casualty lists posted in shop windows. Wounded and dying soldiers filled hospitals. And the spirit of patriotism flickered out. It was replaced by anger, suspicion, and a hatred of anything German. Across the country, German books were burned, German businesses were looted, and music written by such German composers as Bach and Beethoven was banned from public performances. Even the name of the capital was changed from the German-sounding St. Petersburg to the Slavic Petrograd.

Ugly stories began to circulate about the country's unpopular German-born empress. The people accused Alexandra of being a spy, and of supporting the kaiser's army. The mood grew so dark that in Moscow a mob gathered in Red Square to demand her imprisonment in the Peter and Paul Fortress as a traitor to her country.

Nicholas now realized something extraordinary needed to be done to quell the nation's anger.

COMMANDER TSAR

When the war began, the tsar had put his cousin Grand Duke Nich-olas, known in society as Nikolasha, in charge of battlefield oper-ations. But by the summer of 1915, with the mood of the country darkening and the army in retreat, Nicholas considered firing Niko-lasha and taking command himself. Many of his ministers advised against it, fearing that any military failures would be tied to him. In addition, he lacked war experience and knew almost nothing about military strategy. Still, Nicholas believed he was the people's *Batiushka Tsar,* and just his presence—symbolic and emotional—would spur the soldiers to even fiercer fighting.

But could he walk away from the day-to-day governing of the country?

Alexandra insisted he could. So did Rasputin—but not for patri-otic reasons. The *starets* held a grudge against Nikolasha that dated back to the fall of 1914. That's when Rasputin, recovered from his knife wound, had finally returned to Petrograd. Recognizing Niko-lasha's powerful new position, Rasputin had immediately offered to visit Stavka (military headquarters) and bless an icon. In this man-ner, he hoped to weasel his way into the commander's good graces.

But Nikolasha would have none of it. He hated Rasputin for his influence over the imperial couple. "Yes, do come," the commander had insultingly replied. "I'll hang you."

Rasputin seethed. Such a dangerous enemy had to be eliminated. Now, whenever he was with Alexandra, he began sowing seeds of doubt and suspicion.

"The Grand Duke is deliberately currying favor in the army and overshadowing the tsar so that one day he can claim the throne," the *starets* would say; or "The Grand Duke cannot possibly succeed on the battlefield because God will not bless him. How can God bless a man who has turned his back on me, a Man of God"; or "If the Grand Duke is allowed to keep his power, he will kill me, and then what will happen to the Tsarevich, the tsar and Russia?"

Alexandra, in turn, repeated Rasputin's words to her husband. Again and again, she reminded Nicholas that Nikolasha was "Our Friend's enemy, and that brings bad luck. His work cannot be blessed, nor his advice be good." He had to be replaced.

Nicholas was easily persuaded. But he still needed someone to take care of state affairs while he was five hundred miles away at Stavka. He turned to Alexandra. "Think, my wifey . . . will you not come to the assistance of your hubby?" Later he added, "Yes, truly, you ought to be my eyes and ears there . . . while I [am at Stavka]. It rests with you to keep peace and harmony among the Ministers."

Alexandra, who had never before shown any interest in running the country, agreed. After all, she would not be alone. At her side, his "prayers arising day and night," would be their "Friend," Rasputin. What could possibly go wrong?

On August 22, 1915, Nicholas boarded the imperial train and headed for military headquarters. In his pocket he carried a letter from Alexandra, cheering on his decision, and a farewell gift—a pocket comb Rasputin had given her. "Remember to comb your hair [with it] before all difficult tasks and decisions," she told him. "The little comb will bring its help."

LIFE AT STAVKA

Nicholas soon took up residence at Stavka, moving into a comfortable mansion located hundreds of miles from any actual fighting. Leaving important military decisions to his chief of staff, the tsar set up a leisurely schedule for himself. He began his official duties at ten a.m., listening to reports from various ministers and officers.

After that, he had lunch, followed by two hours for walks, naps, or car tours of nearby troops. From three to six p.m. he did a bit more work, followed by dinner served on bone china and a nice glass of port wine. During the evenings, he sometimes watched movies in a makeshift theater set up especially for him. Other times, he listened to music on his phonograph. There were some discomforts. "My field bedstead is so hard and stiff," Nicholas wrote to Alexandra, "but I must not complain—how many sleep on damp grass and mud."

Lonely for his family, the tsar soon begged his wife to allow eleven-year-old Alexei to live with him at headquarters. She had a hard time letting the boy go. Since his birth, he'd rarely been out of her sight for more than a few hours. But she finally agreed. After he left, she sent dozens of fretting letters to Stavka. "See that Tiny doesn't tire himself on the stairs," she wrote. "He cannot take walks. . . . He forgets he must be careful. . . . Take care of Baby's arm, don't let him run about on the train so as to knock his arms." And every night at nine o'clock—the time when she and Alexei had said their prayers together—she went into his bedroom by herself. Kneeling before his icons, she prayed for his safety.

Meanwhile, Alexei adored life at Stavka. Sleeping on a cot in his father's bedroom, he took lessons each morning with Pierre Gilliard, who had accompanied him. Afterward, he played with his toy rifle in the garden. "He . . . walks backwards and forwards on the path, marching and singing loudly," wrote Nicholas. At mealtimes, he often pulled pranks on the staff gathered around the table, bombarding them with little pellets of bread and soaking them with the garden fountain. And in the afternoon, father and son took car rides or swam in a nearby river. Sometimes, wearing identical khaki uniforms, they reviewed troops or visited factories.

Not surprisingly, Nicholas's presence made no difference in the war's course. Shortages of military equipment and supplies, raw materials for factories, and food for the cities and the troops grew worse. Prices soared. Soldiers went without boots, coats, guns, and bullets.

The result was "more of the same," said French Ambassador Paléologue. More military disasters. More retreats. More dead and wounded men.

Still the tsar clung stubbornly to his belief that God would set things right. "It is His plan," he said. "You will see . . . everything [is] for the best." And so Nicholas remained at Stavka.

CHAPTER ELEVEN

"THE REIGN OF RASPUTIN"

LEAPFROGGING MINISTERS

In Petrograd, Rasputin had a new apartment. Located on the third floor of an ordinary brick building in a working-class neighborhood, it was not an elegant place. But it was very close to the train that ran between the city and Tsarskoe Selo, making trips to the palace easy. Living in a modest apartment also helped Rasputin preserve his image as a holy man whose interests were heavenly rather than earthly.

This, of course, was far from the truth. Every day, a long line of people from every walk of life snaked down his apartment stairs—shopkeepers, countesses, college professors, peasants. Knowing Rasputin's influence with the empress, they came seeking favors: one to have her husband transferred from the front, another to obtain a job promotion, still another to be given a lucrative government contract. One musically untrained woman even wanted Rasputin to have her made the lead singer at the Imperial Opera!

If he chose to help, Rasputin would scrawl a note in his almost illegible handwriting to high-ranking officials within the government. "My dear and valued friend," it would read, "do this for me. Gregory." Many of these notes appeared at the palace. "All were drawn up in the same way," recalled one court official, "and they opened all doors in Petrograd." In return for granting these requests, the *starets* accepted money, wine, food—whatever the favor seeker had to offer.

Another group of people also hung around Rasputin's apartment—a unit of policemen. Placed there by Nicholas to protect the *starets,* they took detailed notes of all his comings and goings. And their notes did not paint a holy picture. "Rasputin took part in a drinking party with some [college] students," read one. "A musician struck up and there was singing and Rasputin danced with a maidservant."

Read another: "Rasputin came home dead drunk at 1 a.m. and insulted the concierge's wife."

And another: "Rasputin came home at 7 a.m. He was dead drunk. . . . He smashed a pane of glass in the house door; apparently he had had one fall already, for his nose was swollen."

These reports—thousands of pages taken over the course of a year—were given to Alexandra. But she refused to see the truth. The reason people hated him, she claimed, was because they hated her. Furiously, she threw the pages into the trash.

The contents of these reports, however, leaked to the public. Soon, the "Staircase Notes" were being whispered about by court officials, countesses, factory workers, even soldiers. And almost everyone was outraged. Not only was the citizenry convinced that Rasputin was a fake, but they saw the empress as a narrow-minded, reactionary, hysterical woman because she remained under the fraud's spell. Such gossip could only further degrade the monarchy, making them appear less near to God than ever before. For the good of the country, many now believed the *starets'* power had to end.

But no matter how much gossip swirled, the telephone in Rasputin's apartment kept ringing as, time and again, Alexandra summoned him to Tsarskoe Selo, where they met at Anna Vyrubova's house on the estate to avoid the gossipers.

Rasputin would rush to her side, somehow managing to sober up before arriving. Once there, he ingeniously acted the role of a holy man. So convincing was his performance that Alexandra firmly believed Rasputin was God's messenger, sent to guide them through the war. "I fully trust in Our Friend's wisdom endowed by God to counsel what is right for you and our country," she wrote Nicholas soon after he departed for Stavka. "He sees far ahead and therefore his judgment can be relied upon." It would be fatal, she insisted, not to listen to his advice.

And Rasputin had lots of advice—especially about Nicholas's ministers. The *starets* felt threatened by these powerful men, most of whom hated him. He wanted them out of his way. But not so he could rule Russia; Rasputin never wanted that. He merely wanted to be left alone to continue his depraved lifestyle. And so, as he'd done with Nikolasha, he began talking against the ministers.

Alexandra was an avid listener. Since her earliest days as empress, she had divided her world into a large group of "enemies" and a much smaller group of "friends." And over the years, she'd grown increasingly paranoid. In her mind, the war was really a struggle between the few "good" and "moral" people who supported Nicholas against the ever-growing circle of people who opposed him. Rasputin easily convinced her that the ministers were scheming against her husband, herself, and the *starets*.

Within weeks of Nicholas's departure, Alexandra began bombarding him with letters, sometimes several a day, filled with her paranoid suspicions about so-called rotten ministers. "Forgive me, but I don't like the choice of Minister of War. Is he not an enemy of Our Friend?" she would write. Or "Long-nosed Saznov [the foreign minister] is such a pancake." Or "Why do we have a [useless] rag as Minister of Court?"

Once the seeds of doubt had been sown, she suggested replacements:

"Our Friend finds Ivanov would be good as Minister of War."

"Really, my Treasure, I think he is the man Our Friend hinted [about]; I am always careful in my choice."

"Our Friend begs very much that you should not name Makarov

as Minister of the Interior—you remember how he . . . never stood up for me—it would indeed be a mistake to name him."

Rasputin chose all the replacements. Unfortunately, he did not care about these men's ability or knowledge. Instead, he picked them, wrote one historian, "because they liked him, or said they liked him, or at least didn't bother him." One time, the *starets* discovered a candidate in a Petrograd nightclub. Drunk yet again, Rasputin loudly declared the band's bass singer too weak. Glancing around the club, he spied a plump aristocrat named A. N. Khvostov. Slapping his back, Rasputin said, "Brother, go and help them sing. You are fat and can make a lot of noise." The equally drunk Khvostov agreed. Staggering onstage, he burst into song. Rasputin clapped with delight.

Not long afterward, Khvostov was unexpectedly appointed to the post of minister of the interior.

And so it went—a crazy game of "ministerial leapfrog"—as ministers were appointed and fired by Nicholas at the behest of the empress and her *starets*. Between September 1915 and March 1917, four different men held the position of prime minister. In that same time, Russia had five ministers of the interior, four ministers of agriculture, and three ministers of war, transport, and foreign affairs. At one point, unable to find a man fawning enough to suit Rasputin, the Ministry of Foreign Affairs went without a leader for four months. Alexandra solved the problem by having Nicholas turn over the foreign ministry's responsibilities to the prime minister. But the prime minister was already doing the job of the minister of the interior, also a vacant position. Overworked, the prime minister handed over the interior's work to the minister of justice, who in turn handed the justice work over to the minister of agriculture. This complicated leapfrogging deprived Russia of its most able statesmen at a time when they were most needed. Instead, a group of incompetent, mediocre men now held the most important positions in government.

It did not take long for the people—upper and lower classes alike—to lose all confidence in the ministers and, by extension, the tsar's government. "It is a terrible thing," one Duma member remarked glumly. "The tsar offends the nation by what he allows to go on in the palace . . . while the country offends the tsar by its terrible suspicions. The result is the destruction of those centuries-old ties which have sustained Russia. And the cause of all this? The weakness of one man and one woman. . . . Oh, how terrible an autocracy without an autocrat!"

THE POINT OF NO RETURN

By late 1916, Russia was reaching the point of no return. Hundreds of thousands of men continued to die in a war that now seemed pointless to many. Away from the fighting, the country was falling into economic chaos, and the tsar's government was crumbling.

The Russian people blamed much of it on the empress and her *starets*. Obscene pamphlets about them began circulating around Petrograd. Cartoons showed Rasputin as a puppet master who had the imperial couple on a string. By fall 1916, anger against Rasputin reached the boiling point. People everywhere believed he was the actual ruler of Russia. Despite censorship laws forbidding criticism of either the tsar or his government, the newspaper the *Siberian Trade Gazette* boldly called Rasputin a "thief" and a "half-educated peasant." Across Russia, citizens began calling the government "the Reign of Rasputin."

In the Duma, too, members publicly raged about the *starets*. "Dark forces are destroying the Romanov dynasty," shouted deputy Vladimir Purishkevich during a legislative session in December

1916. Purishkevich, who had never before breathed a word of criticism against the tsar, now pounded furiously on his desk. "If you are truly loyal to Russia, then on your feet. Have the courage to tell the tsar . . . an obscure [*starets*] shall govern Russia no longer!"

The hall erupted into wild cheering. Only one man did not leap to his feet—Prince Felix Yusupov, the dashing and rich husband of Nicholas's favorite niece, Irina. Instead, he paled and trembled as he realized what needed to be done. There was only one sure way to break the empress's dependence on the *starets*. Kill him.

But Yusupov couldn't do it alone. So he begged Purishkevich, as well as the tsar's cousin Grand Duke Dmitri Pavlovich, to help. He also asked an army physician, Dr. Stanislaw Lazovert, and an army officer named Sergei Sukhotin to join them. "We will be heroes," he told the men. "The Empress will land in an asylum within two weeks of Rasputin's death. . . . And if the Emperor is freed of the influence of Rasputin and his wife, everything [will] change; he [will] be a good . . . monarch. And . . . we will have saved the empire." Inspired by Yusupov's words, the men threw themselves into murder plans. For the next four weeks they plotted. By December 29, all was ready.

DEATH TO THE *STARETS*

It was just before midnight and snowing heavily when Rasputin arrived at Prince Yusupov's palace. The *starets* had been lured there by the promise of finally meeting the prince's wife, Irina, reportedly the most beautiful woman in Petrograd. He came dressed in his best—a silk blouse embroidered with cornflowers and tied with a red cord, black velvet pants, and brand-new boots. At first, everything went according to plan. Yusupov showed Rasputin into a basement room where he plied the *starets* with wine and cakes that

Dr. Lazovert claimed to have laced with cyanide. He waited for his guest to fall to the floor, writhing in pain. But to his amazement, the poison had no effect at all.

At this point, according to Yusupov, Rasputin pointed to a guitar in the corner. "Play something cheerful," he said. "I like your singing."

As Yusupov strummed, Rasputin helped himself to another glass of poisoned wine.

Two hours later, the still-guitar-playing prince finally lost patience. Excusing himself, he hurried to the top of the stairs, where his fellow murderers sat listening. What should he do? Yusupov later claimed that Grand Duke Dmitri wanted to give up. But Purishkevich objected. He didn't think it wise to send Rasputin home half poisoned. Said Yusupov, "Then you wouldn't have any objections if I just shot him, would you?"

Grabbing Dmitri's pistol, he returned to the basement. The *starets* was gulping still more poisoned cakes, when Yusupov shot him in the back.

With a wild scream, Rasputin fell to the floor. He looked, Yusupov later recalled, "like a broken marionette."

The others rushed into the room. They found the prince standing over the body wearing, recalled Purishkevich, "an expression of loathing."

Feeling for Rasputin's pulse, Dr. Lazovert declared the man dead.

Yusupov handed the gun back to Dmitri. Then, while the others went in search of something to wrap the body in, he collapsed with relief into a chair beside the corpse. "That's when I saw both eyes—the green eyes of a viper—staring at me with an expression of diabolical hatred," claimed the prince.

Rasputin wasn't dead after all! Staggering to his feet, his mouth foaming, the *starets* lunged at his would-be murderer. His long, bony fingers dug like steel claws into the prince's shoulders. Terror-stricken, Yusupov struggled and broke free from the death grip. He pounded up the stairs. Behind him wheezed Rasputin. "Felix!" he called, using the prince's first name. "Felix!"

"He's alive!" Yusupov screamed to the others as he reached the top of the stairs. "He's getting away."

Incredibly, the *starets*—who just minutes earlier had been dying on the cellar floor—was now *running* across the palace courtyard toward the gate. "I will tell everything to the empress!" he shouted over his shoulder.

Purishkevich could not let that happen. Pulling out his own pistol, he chased after the *starets*. "I fired," recalled Purishkevich. "The night echoed with the shot. I missed. I fired again. Again I missed. I raged at myself. Rasputin neared the gate. . . . I fired a third time. The bullet hit him in the shoulder. He stopped. I fired a fourth time and hit him in the head."

And yet, Rasputin kept breathing. Yusupov came running from the palace, a rubber club in his hand. "In my frenzy, I hit anywhere," he later said. Rasputin soon stopped moving. Then the murderers rolled the body in a blue curtain, tied it with ropes, and shoved it into the backseat of Purishkevich's car. Driving a few blocks to the frozen Neva River, they shoved the body through a hole in the ice.

Three days later, police divers pulled the body from the icy river. They were surprised to see that Rasputin's right arm was freed from the ropes and slightly raised. This left people with the notion that the *starets* had still been alive when his murderers dumped him in the water, that he struggled with incredible strength until he finally drowned.

An autopsy performed that very day, however, refuted this notion. According to the senior autopsy surgeon, Dmitri Kosorotov, the body was riddled with bruises. This was consistent with Yusupov's story about the rubber club. Curiously, though, while the autopsy *did* reveal cakes and wine in Rasputin's stomach, no traces of the cyanide Dr. Lazovert had supposedly put in them was found. Had Lazovert changed his mind without telling the others and not poisoned the food? Was this why Rasputin continued to eat and drink that night with no ill effects?

Dr. Kosorotov also noted three gunshot wounds. The first bullet had entered Rasputin's chest, slicing through the *starets'* stomach and liver. The second had gone through his back, piercing his kidney. And the third had struck the back of the head. Either of the first two wounds would have killed Rasputin in minutes, the doctor determined. But the third injury would have killed him instantly. There was no way, he concluded, that Rasputin was alive when his killers dumped him in the river. This was corroborated by the fact that no water was found in the lungs. Rasputin had not died from drowning. The cause of his death was a gunshot wound.

The discovery of Rasputin's body touched off public celebrations across Russia. Bells rang. Flags waved. "People kissed each other in the street," recalled Ambassador Paléologue, "and many went to burn candles [of thanksgiving] in Our Lady of Kazan." Some shops even posted photographs of Yusupov and the others in their front windows. Banners beneath them boldly proclaimed the men heroes.

THE NEWS

The morning after the murder, the telephone in the Alexander Palace rang. It was the minister of the interior calling with grave news. "A patrolman standing near the entrance of the Yusupov palace was startled by the [sounds] of a pistol," he reported. "Ringing the doorbell, he was met by . . . Purishkevich who appeared to be in an advanced state of intoxication. [He said] . . . they had just killed Rasputin."

Struggling to stay calm, Alexandra ordered an investigation. Then she closed herself up in her lilac drawing room. "I cannot, and *won't* believe He has been killed," she wrote to Nicholas. "God have mercy. Such utter anguish."

The children could not stop crying. Why would anyone want to hurt their friend? "[They] sat on the sofa, huddled up close together," recalled one courtier. "They were cold and visibly terribly upset. . . . They evidently sensed that, with his murder, something terrible and undeserved had started for . . . themselves, and that it was moving relentlessly toward them."

CHAPTER TWELVE
❧ It all Comes Tumbling Down ❧
JANUARY–MARCH 1917

The Nobility's Petrograd

In the weeks following Rasputin's death, the weather turned bitter cold. At times, the mercury dropped to fifty below zero in Petrograd, and great drifts of snow buried railroad cars and supply depots, making delivery of desperately needed goods impossible. With millions of peasants fighting instead of working in the fields, food shortages loomed and prices soared. A loaf of black bread cost three times as much as it had at the start of the war, a pound of potatoes eight times as much. Rents tripled even as thousands of workers found themselves unemployed, their factories shut for lack of coal. Fewer and fewer people could afford even the most basic necessities, even *if* those items could be found in the city.

Still, the nobility's palaces blazed with light. Music still floated from their ballrooms. And lavish midnight suppers of cold sturgeon, stuffed eggs, and rose cream cakes were still laid out temptingly in elegant dining rooms. Jewels glittered. Gold braid dazzled. And both champagne and laughter bubbled up as partygoers discussed the latest craze in card games and the shocking price of caviar. Above all, they gossiped about Rasputin's murder.

Had they heard about the *starets'* private funeral in a secluded corner of the Imperial Park at Tsarskoe Selo? they asked one another. Besides the royal family, only Anna Vyrubova had attended. The tsar and Alexei had traveled all the way from Stavka to be there. Before closing the coffin, the grand duchesses had placed an icon on Rasputin's chest, their tears falling on the oak casket. Alexandra, too, had left behind a token—a pitiful little note that read "My dear martyr, give me thy blessing that it may follow me always on the sad and dreary path I have yet to follow here below. And remember us from on high in your holy prayers. Alexandra."

Members of the nobility expressed shock over the harsh punishment given to Rasputin's murderers. Incredibly, Nicholas had ordered his own cousin, Grand Duke Dmitri Pavlovich, to leave Petrograd and join the Russian army. And Yusupov? The man married to the tsar's dearest niece had been exiled to one of his huge estates in the center of the country. Only Purishkevich had been lucky. He went free, not because he wasn't guilty, but because he'd become such a big hero in the Duma that even the tsar was afraid to punish him. No one seemed to know what happened to Dr. Lazovert or Officer Sukhotin.

Instead of returning to Stavka after the funeral, the tsar remained in Tsarskoe Selo. People who had seen him claimed he acted tired and confused. Said one minister, "He listened to me with a strange, almost vacant smile, glancing nervously about him." When asked a question, he was "reduced to a state of helplessness. . . . For a long time he looked at me in silence, as if trying to collect his thoughts, or recall what had escaped his memory."

All these rumors were true. Suddenly unable to make any decisions at all, Nicholas simply stared for hours on end at the battlefield maps he'd spread out on his pool table. So changed was he that many people claimed Alexandra was giving him drugs. But Ambassador Paléologue knew better. "The Emperor's words, his silences . . . his grave, drawn features and vague, distant thoughts confirm in me the notion that Nicholas II feels himself overwhelmed by events . . . and is now resigned to disaster."

Even though the tsar was back in the palace, Alexandra remained in control of the government. Rumor had it that the palace's main telephone was removed from Nicholas's desk and put in her lilac drawing room, and ministers' reports were still handed to her. Some claimed she'd even taken to eavesdropping on her husband's conversations with advisers and generals, hiding behind thick velvet curtains on a balcony located just above the tsar's study. Later she gave Nicholas her opinions.

Remarked Grand Duchess Maria Pavlovna at one of the nobility's many parties that winter, "It seems the empress has the emperor entirely under her thumb. . . . I can't tell you how downhearted I feel. Everything seems black. . . . I badly need sun and rest. The emotions of recent times have worn me out."

THE WORKERS

If Maria Pavlovna had bothered to look out her palace window, she would have seen others far more worn out than herself. Thousands of poor working women shivered in the subzero temperatures outside Petrograd's bakeries. They often stood in line all night for a loaf of bread, just to be told in the morning that there would not be any for sale because there wasn't any flour. But what else was there? A worker could buy little else because of shortages and exorbitant prices. "These exhausted mothers," noted one policeman, "having suffered so much in watching their half-starving and sick children are perhaps closer to revolution than anyone else . . . and more dangerous."

Meanwhile, their husbands wandered the snow-packed streets. Bellies grumbling, their expressions dark and angry, they complained about the lack of food, the war, and a government that did not care about its people. More and more, workers began marching behind banners that read "Down with the War." The city, recalled

Ambassador Paléologue, now struck him as a "lunatic asylum," filled with a "poisonous atmosphere" and "profound despondency and fear."

The danger of revolution was growing. Indeed, a police report from this time stamped TOP SECRET noted that the food shortages combined with an inflation rate of 300 percent had pushed the country to the edge of rebellion. If something dramatic wasn't done to avert it immediately, a "hungry revolt" was bound to happen, followed by "the most savage excesses."

If Nicholas read this report, he did not respond.

And in the Duma, yet another deputy stood. This time it was Alexander Kerensky, an outspoken champion of the worker. "To prevent a catastrophe," he cried, "the tsar himself must be removed, by force if there is no other way."

Only months earlier, Kerensky's words would have landed him in jail. A man of the government was advocating the tsar's over-throw! But in the dark mood now gripping Petrograd, his speech did not seem out of the ordinary. Kerensky was simply saying out loud what so many others were thinking.

LAST-DITCH EFFORT

On February 10, 1917, the tsar's old friend and cousin Sandro made a final effort to ward off disaster. Traveling to Tsarskoe Selo, he insisted on speaking with Alexandra. He was shown into her bed-room.

The empress reclined on one side of the big double bed in a white dressing robe. With her lips pressed tightly together, she looked cold and angry. On the other side of the bed sat the tsar, his slip-pered feet crossed on the satin comforter, smoking silently.

Sandro spoke bluntly, beginning with the people's grim mood.

But Alexandra interrupted him. "That's not true. The nation is still loyal to the tsar." She turned to Nicholas. "Only the treacherous Duma and St. Petersburg society are [our] enemies."

Sandro corrected her. "I am your friend and so I point out to you that *all* classes of the population are opposed to *your* policies. . . . Please, Alix, leave the cares of state to your husband."

Alexandra's eyes narrowed.

Nicholas continued to smoke.

And Sandro went on. The only way to end "the nation's wrath" was to immediately appoint leadership acceptable to the people. That meant removing all of Rasputin's "suspicion-provoking ministers" and replacing them with men of talent and ability. "Don't let the nation's wrath reach the explosion point," he begged.

Alexandra bristled. "All this talk of yours is ridiculous."

"Remember, Alix," snapped Sandro, struggling to keep the anger out of his voice, "I remained silent for thirty months. For thirty months I never said . . . a word to you about the disgraceful goings on in our government, better to say *your* government. I realize you are willing to perish, and your husband feels the same, but what about us?"

Alexandra did not reply.

"Must we all suffer for your blind stubbornness?" Sandro exploded. "No, you have no right to drag your relatives [down] with you. . . . You are incredibly selfish!"

"I refuse to continue this dispute," said Alexandra coldly. "You are exaggerating the dangers. Some day, when you are less excited, you will admit that I knew better."

Remaining silent, Nicholas lit another cigarette.

Sandro realized there was nothing more to say. "It's enough to drive you mad," he later wrote his brother. "Up here at [Tsarskoe Selo] it's like water off a duck's back, all is submission to God. How else can I explain . . . such total blindness and deafness? The tsar has ceased to rule Russia."

REVOLUTION AND THE RESTING TSAR

Three weeks later, on Thursday, March 8, 1917, the women on breadlines snapped. Shouting *"Daite khleb*—Give us bread!" they broke into the bakeries and cleared out the shelves. Masses of angry factory workers quickly joined the women. Marching toward the center of town, chanting *"Daite khleb! Daite khleb!"* the mob broke windows, halted streetcars, and urged others to join them.

While all this was happening, Nicholas's train was carrying him back to Stavka. As he chugged eastward, he blithely wrote to his wife: "I will miss my half-hourly game of cards every evening, but vow to take up dominoes again in my spare time."

In Petrograd the next day, even bigger crowds flowed into the streets. Again they chanted, "Give us bread." This time, though, shouts of "Down with the war!" and "Down with the tsar!" were mixed in. Moving as one, the mob headed for the center of the city. That's when two squadrons of Cossack patrols moved in to disperse them. But because the Cossacks sided with the workers, they came without whips, the weapon they traditionally used when controlling mobs. Seeing this, the crowd applauded. The Cossacks gallantly bowed in return. "Don't worry," they assured the crowd. "We won't shoot."

At Stavka, Nicholas gave little attention to reports streaming in from Petrograd. Instead, he noted that the fresh air was doing him good. "My brain is resting here," he wrote to Alexandra, "no ministers, no troubling questions, or demanding thought."

Back in Petrograd, his ministers faced huge new problems. By Saturday, March 10, most of the city's workers were on strike, bringing the capital to a standstill. Electricity and water were shut off. Immense crowds of strikers, housewives, and college students crammed the streets. Unfurling revolutionary red banners, they screamed, "Down with the war! Down with the German woman!" They hurled rocks and chunks of ice at police.

Frantically, the ministers tried to deal with it all. They wrestled with the food problem, hoping the promise of more bread would disperse the crowd. They telegrammed Nicholas and begged him to return, believing that the sight of the tsar might end the violence. They even offered their resignations, urging Nicholas to replace them with a government more acceptable to the people.

But at Stavka, Nicholas continued to "rest" his brain. After a late breakfast, he listened to an army staff report, then took an afternoon stroll. It wasn't until early evening that he learned of the situation in Petrograd. But he still did not grasp its seriousness. Believing it was just another strike in a long line of strikes, he refused to return to the capital or accept his ministers' resignations. As for more bread, feeding revolutionaries was out of the question. There was only one way to suppress the rebellion. He sent a stern telegram to his military chief in Petrograd: "I command you tomorrow to stop the disorders in the capital, which are unacceptable in the difficult time of war with Germany and Austria."

The tsar's order meant he would be unleashing soldiers with rifles and machine guns on his own people! This at a time when he still expected their support in waging a war against Germany and Austria-Hungary. And he did not have the slightest idea he'd just taken such a drastic step. Instead, he believed Alexandra's description of the events. "It's a hooligan movement," she wrote him, "young boys and girls running about and screaming that they have no bread, only to excite. . . . But this will all pass and quiet down."

As the pale wintry sun washed over Petrograd that Sunday morning, March 11, the first demonstrators moved into the streets.

Posters hung overnight by the police met them. The posters forbade them from assembling, by command of the tsar. Strikers, they warned, would be forcefully disbanded.

Demonstrators ignored the warning. Again, they surged through the streets, chanting and waving banners. In response, columns of soldiers closed in on them. An officer ordered the crowd to halt. When it didn't, he gave the command. "Fire!"

Machine guns crackled. When they stopped, workers' blood reddened the snow. Two hundred lay dead, and forty were wounded.

The sight sickened the soldiers, most of whom were just country boys fresh from their villages. Not only did these young men understand the demonstrators' frustrations, they sympathized with them. And so, as the crowd continued to surge, many troops emptied their rifles into the air. One company even refused to fire. When their enraged commanding officer insisted they "aim for the heart," they shot him instead. Encouraged by the soldiers' actions, the crowd grew larger . . . louder . . . angrier.

Desperate, Duma president Rodzianko sent Nicholas a frantic telegram: "The hungry, unemployed throng is starting down the path of elemental and uncontrollable anarchy. . . . State authority is totally paralyzed. . . . Your Majesty, save Russia; she is threatened with humiliation and disgrace. . . . Urgently summon a person in whom the whole country can have faith and entrust him with the formation of a government that all the people trust. . . . In this terrible hour . . . there is no other way out and to delay is impossible."

But when the telegram arrived, Nicholas didn't even bother to read it. Setting it aside, he said, "That fat Rodzianko has written all sorts of nonsense to me, to which I shall not even reply." And he spent the rest of the evening playing dominoes.

IGNITED

Monday, March 12, dawned in eerie silence. Meriel Buchanan, daughter of the British ambassador, looked out her window. Everywhere were "the same wide streets, the same great palaces, and same gold spires and domes rising out of the pearl-colored mists, and yet ... everywhere emptiness, no lines of toiling cars, no crowded scarlet trams, no little sledges. ... [Only] the waste of deserted streets and ice-bound river ... [and] on the opposite shore the walls of the Fortress and the Imperial flag of Russia that for the last time fluttered against the winter sky."

Suddenly, there came a loud roar, and a mob of demonstrators appeared. Armed and ready to fight with the tsar's soldiers, they rushed for one of the bridges. At that moment, a regiment stormed toward them. "It looked as if there would be a violent collision," recalled one eyewitness. But instead, the two groups became one. The tsar's army had *joined* the revolution!

Now events moved quickly. Together, citizens and soldiers seized the arsenal, arming themselves with the guns and ammunition that had been stored for the capital's protection. Soon, men and women draped in cartridge belts and carrying weapons raced down the street, firing wildly into the air. They flung open jails and set the prisoners free, looted shops and bakeries, torched police stations and other government buildings. When firemen arrived at these scenes, rather than fighting the blazes, they cheered and watched the structures burn.

Distraught, the tsar's younger brother, Grand Duke Michael, telephoned Stavka. Nicholas had to appoint a government acceptable to the people ... *now!* But the grand duke was not allowed to speak with Nicholas directly. Instead, he was forced to leave a message with one of the generals. "I see," said the general after Michael explained the dire situation. "Please wait while I speak with the tsar." Forty long minutes later, the general called back. "The Emperor wishes to express his thanks," he told Michael. "He is leaving for Tsarskoe Selo [where he can confer with his wife] and will decide there."

Nicholas *still* did not understand.

Government ministers finally gave up. Adjourning themselves, they simply walked away.

Duma president Rodzianko tried one last time. "Sire, do not delay," he telegrammed to Stavka. "[This] will mean the end of Russia. Inevitably, the dynasty will fall with it. Tomorrow [will] be too late."

It was already too late. By midafternoon, the first crowd of workers and soldiers waving red flags and singing revolutionary songs arrived at the Tauride Palace, where the Duma was meeting. It was, wrote one historian, "a motley, exuberant mob. There were soldiers tall and hot in their rough, wool uniforms; students shouting exultantly; and a few gray-bearded old men just released from prison, their knees trembling, their eyes shining." They had come looking for a government that would be responsive to the people.

Some deputies wavered. It would be illegal, they claimed, to assume the tsar's powers without his permission. Shouldn't they cable and ask for his approval first? Otherwise, any government they formed would be illegitimate.

But others, including Alexander Kerensky, the Duma member who just days earlier had called for the tsar's removal, realized the ridiculousness of their argument. This was a revolution, and all revolutions are by definition illegal: forcible uprisings against an established government. The people had swept away the tsar's authority, and the only real power now lay with them. And as the hours passed, the capital was sinking deeper into anarchy. The people needed leadership. Kerensky turned to President Rodzianko. "Can I say the Duma is with them?" he asked. "That it stands at the head of the government?"

Still loyal to the tsar, Rodzianko vacillated, unsure of what to do. "I don't want to revolt," he admitted.

"Take the power," advised another member. "If you don't, someone else will."

Rodzianko had no choice. Russia would continue to burn if the Duma did not step up. Reluctantly, he addressed the crowd. "The Duma accepts responsibility for the government."

Then members got to work. Before the day was done, twelve deputies of the former Duma created what they called the Provisional Committee of Duma Members for the Restoration of Order and for the Relations with Individuals and Institutions (Provisional Government for short). It was meant as a temporary government, one that would restore order and end the revolutionary chaos. And it would rule only until a national "constituent assembly" could meet, where representatives from all across the country would decide on the type of government Russians would live under. Led by men from the nobility and the middle class, the Provisional Government hoped to establish a democracy modeled on England's government, with two houses of parliament and a fair court system. Many still wanted a tsar—but one without any dictatorial power.

On the very day the Provisional Government organized in the Tauride Palace, labor leaders—many of them just released from prison by the revolutionary mob—reorganized the Petrograd Soviet, forming a union of workers and soldiers. As night fell, representatives from both groups (one for every thousand workers, and one from every company of Petrograd soldiers) arrived at the soviet's first meeting. Held in another room of the Tauride Palace, the meeting swelled to three thousand delegates, many of them still toting rifles.

The Petrograd Soviet saw the goals of the revolution far differently from the Provisional Government. Power, it believed, had *not* been wrested from the tsar so that the nobility and middle class could simply rule the workers through another form of government. No, the revolution had been fought for "the people"—the poor and the marginalized.

The soviet was an organization to be reckoned with. Among its many members were railroad men, enabling the soviet to stop trains whenever it wanted; bank clerks so it could control the flow of money; and soldiers who could carry out the soviet's will.

Members of the Provisional Government—most especially Alexander Kerensky—knew they needed the soviet's support to govern. Peeling off his formal morning coat and rolling up the sleeves of his starched dress shirt to look more like a man of the people, Kerensky strode down the hall to the soviet meeting. "Comrades!" he cried in a voice both fiery and dramatic, his bright, birdlike eyes looking out over the assembly. "I speak . . . with all my soul, from the bottom of my heart. . . . [The Provisional Government and the soviet] must come to settle side by side."

The soviet agreed. It would let the Provisional Government take the lead while it sat back as a kind of watchdog of the revolution. This fit in with Marxist political theory, which assumed that after a revolution, a backward peasant country like Russia needed a long period of capitalism and democracy before it could move toward a communist state. During this time, people would learn to relinquish what Marx had called "their petty notions of small property." Additionally, a long period of capitalism would allow the illiterate, politically inexperienced masses time to gain knowledge before taking up government's reins. Until this happened, the leadership of the upper classes was essential.

But the soviet did not relinquish leadership without some concessions. The Provisional Government agreed, among other things, to abolish the police and in its place create a "people's militia"; to release all "politicals" still imprisoned or in exile; and to dissolve all the bureaucracy set up by the tsar to run his government.

These concessions had disastrous consequences. Eliminating bureaucratic institutions left the Provisional Government without an
effective way to govern the country at a time when it desperately
needed leadership. The well-intentioned Provisional Government
would find itself unable to stop Russia from falling into even greater
chaos.

Meanwhile, at Stavka, completely unaware that his throne had
toppled, Nicholas made plans to leave the next morning for Tsarskoe Selo. "Leave tomorrow. . . . Always near you. Tender love to
all," he telegrammed to Alexandra. Then he headed for bed.

Beyond the Palace Gates:
Molecule in a Storm

*Juvenale Tarasov, a farmer from a nearby village, was visiting Petrograd
on business when the revolution erupted. Soon afterward, he recalled his experiences for American journalist Ernest Poole, who was covering events in
Russia for the* New Republic. *Said Tarasov:*

> With a jubilant shout of freedom arising from every cor-
> ner of the city . . . the long-expected revolution which . . .
> had gathered for fifty years, was suddenly upon us at
> last! Eagerly I burst out into the street and hurried to
> the palace square. . . . I found it like a beehive, black
> with swarming thousands of people and soldiers. I made
> my way deep into the crowd, listening, watching, all my
> thoughts and feelings gripped by a force gigantic—like
> the world! But a new world! It was like a dream! Then
> suddenly I heard the word go 'round to burn the Palace.
> At once I thought of the Hermitage [a public art mu-

seum] which stood so close to the Palace one could not burn without the other—the Hermitage with its Rembrandts and all its other treasures of art. My father and I had been there often. The place had been like a holy cathedral, my only religion as a child. And now, as I stood in a trance, something strange happened inside of me—and what took place I cannot recall. I remember shouting to two men to hoist me up on their shoulders. Then I began speaking to the crowd. And as I noticed that thousands of eyes were turning in my direction, I seemed to lose all consciousness. Now I was speaking down to them from somewhere in the cloudy sky. . . . When I regained my senses I was lying on the pavement. There was cool dirty snow on my face, and a soldier [was] on his knees beside me. . . . The Winter Palace was not burned. I do not mean in the least to say that the Hermitage was saved by my speech. That doubtless played but one little part in the thoughts and passions deep and . . . surging through such a multitude. I was simply a molecule in a storm.

Chapter Thirteen
❧ "YE TYRANTS QUAKE, YOUR DAY IS OVER" ❧
MARCH 1917

ANXIOUS DAYS AT THE PALACE

While Nicholas slept and Petrograd burned, Alexandra fretted about her children. Olga, Tatiana, and Alexei had all been sick with measles for the last two days. They lay in their darkened bedrooms, their fevers soaring and their bodies covered in red splotches. Things were so serious Dr. Botkin had left his house in town and moved into the palace to be near them. Alexandra had barely rested since that first red flush spread across Olga's face. Donning her nurse's uniform and ignoring her own ailments, she had cared for her children around the clock.

She knew little about the events erupting outside the palace—not until the evening of Monday, March 12. That's when Anna Vyrubova's father limped into the lilac drawing room. "Petrograd is in the hands of the mob!" he panted. "They are stopping the cars. They commandeered mine, and I've had to walk every step of the way!"

Hours later, the palace phone rang. It was Rodzianko. The empress and her children were in danger, he warned, and should leave Tsarskoe Selo immediately. There was no telling what the angry mob might do, and with so many soldiers in revolt, he had no way of protecting her.

Alexandra refused. The children were too ill. Besides, she had just received word from her husband. He was on his way home.

"When a house is burning," argued Rodzianko, "the invalids are the first to be taken out."

But the empress was firm. She would wait. Little did she know that the rebels had already seized the railroads around Tsarskoe Selo. All escape routes were gone.

Tuesday, March 13, dawned with a thick snowfall and an icy wind that rattled the palace windows. Upstairs in their sickbeds, the half-conscious children burned with fever. They were getting worse.

And so were events outside the palace gates.

Hours earlier, a mob of rebellious soldiers from Petrograd had arrived in the town of Tsarskoe Selo. They had come, they shouted, for "that German woman" and her son. But before storming the palace, they sacked the town. "Drunken soldiers . . . were running back and forth carrying off all they could lay hands on in the shops," recalled Dr. Botkin's daughter, Tatiana. "Some carried bales of dry goods, others boots, still others, though already quite drunk, were making off with bottles of wine and vodka."

Even with the howling wind, Alexandra could hear the soldiers whooping and shouting. She could hear the sounds of breaking glass and gunshots. What would happen if the mob reached the palace?

"We shall not, must not be afraid," she said to her friend Lili Dehn, who was visiting the family. "Everything is in the hands of God. Tomorrow the Emperor [will] come. I know that when he does, all will be well."

Besides, they weren't entirely helpless. That morning fifteen hundred men, a battalion of the still-loyal Garde Equipage, the marine guard that had protected them on the *Standart,* had arrived to defend the palace. Most of the Cossack guards and the other soldiers who had protected the Imperial Park had deserted to join the revolution. Looking out at the battalion, fifteen-year-old Anastasia felt reassured. "It's just like being on the yacht again," she declared.

Poised tensely, the troops waited as night fell. At nine p.m. the telephone rang. The voice on the other end warned that the rebels were on their way. Minutes later a sentry fell, shot through the neck by sniper fire. The sounds of shouting and gunfire echoed through the Imperial Park. They grew closer and closer.

During those anxious hours, Anastasia began to feel tired and her muscles ached. It was the first sign of oncoming measles. Hoping her symptoms would go away, she went upstairs and lay down. But nerves and the occasional gunshot made it impossible to sleep. Once, when the shooting sounded especially close, she got up and looked out her window. A huge field gun had been dragged into the courtyard, and soldiers were dancing around it, stamping their feet and trying to stay warm.

"How astonished Papa will be," the girl whispered to Lili Dehn.

Night dragged on, but the attack never materialized. Instead, the mob turned back after hearing rumors that a huge force of troops armed with machine guns protected the imperial family.

It was still dark the next morning when a feverish Anastasia dragged herself out of bed. Nicholas had cabled he'd be home by six a.m. and measles or not, she wanted to be waiting when he arrived.

But he did not come.

"The train is late," Alexandra explained. "Perhaps the blizzard detains him." But her voice shook, and worry lined her face.

"The train is *never* late," Anastasia exclaimed, suddenly panicked. "Oh, if only Papa would come quickly."

It wasn't until midmorning that they learned Nicholas's train had been stopped en route. Alexandra quickly sent a cable from the palace telegraph office to the imperial train. She received no reply. Anxiously, she sent another message. And another. And still another. Each one came back marked "Address of person mentioned unknown."

Sick and frightened, Anastasia broke down. "I'm beginning to be ill," she sobbed to Lili Dehn. "What shall I do if I get ill? I can't be useful to Mama. . . . Oh, Lili, say I'm not going to be ill." And then, "Please don't keep me in bed. Please, don't. Please."

Smoothing the girl's hair and murmuring reassuring words, Lili persuaded her to lie down.

Early the next morning, March 15, the battalion guarding the palace deserted. And Alexandra's self-control finally broke. "My sailors," she sobbed. "My own sailors. I can't believe it."

It was not just the troops who deserted. Many of the palace's hundreds of maids, chauffeurs, cooks, and footmen vanished from the marble hallways. That same day the electricity and water were cut off, as well as its telegraph and telephone. The remaining servants were forced to break ice on the pond for water. And without electricity, the little elevator between the empress's drawing room and the children's rooms above no longer worked. Exhausted and in pain, Alexandra had no choice but to climb the stairs. Gasping for breath, she dragged herself up the dark staircase. "I must not give way," she confided to Lili Dehn. "I keep on saying, '*I must not*'—it helps me."

WHERE IS THE TSAR?

That same morning, Nicholas's train chugged into the town of Pskov. For days, his route home had been slowed or detoured as revolutionaries seized control of the tracks. Now, learning from advisers that the palace guard had deserted, he finally grasped the situation. There was, he concluded, no other choice. He would have to give in and appoint a government acceptable to the people. He immediately telegraphed Rodzianko with his offer. Minutes later, Rodzianko answered: "His Majesty . . . [is] apparently . . . unable to realize what is happening in the capital. A terrible revolution has broken out. . . . The measures you propose are too late. The time for them is gone. There is no return."

Now telegrams began to pour in from Nicholas's generals—those men of the nobility whose opinions he valued most. They all urged a bleak course of action. To save the army, the war campaign, the country, and, perhaps most important, the Romanov dynasty, the tsar needed to resign his throne. They believed his abdication in favor of a different ruler would be enough to appease the people.

Nicholas chain-smoked as he read these messages. Then he stood and looked out the train window. There was a gloomy silence. "I have decided that I will give up the throne in favor of my son, Alexei," he finally said. Then turning to face the three attendant generals with him, he crossed himself and went to his bedroom.

Why did he give it all up so easily? Some historians have speculated that his abdication was an extraordinary act of patriotism, that he cared more about winning the war than keeping his throne. Others have suggested he was simply tired and longed to be left in peace. Whatever his reasons, that night in his diary, he wrote, "For the sake of Russia, and to keep the armies in the field, I decided to take this step. . . . I left . . . with a heavy heart. All around me I see treason, cowardice and deceit."

But just hours later, Nicholas reconsidered his decision. How could he possibly leave his sick twelve-year-old son in charge of the country? He could not. With heavy heart, Nicholas sat down at the desk and wrote his Abdication Manifesto. In it, he gave up the throne in favor of his brother Grand Duke Michael.

His attendant generals rushed to the train's telegraph room to forward the news to Petrograd.

In Petrograd

Outside the Tauride Palace—now headquarters of the newly established Provisional Government—a crush of people jammed the gardens and courtyard, waiting for news of the tsar. An official stepped triumphantly onto the balcony. Explaining what had happened, he ended his speech with "Long live the Emperor Michael!"

The mob erupted in anger. They had not overthrown Nicholas simply to replace him with his brother! The people no longer wanted or needed a tsar. What they wanted was a republic, the type of government where the people held the power and their will was expressed through their elected representatives. Raising their fists in the air, they shouted, "Down with the dynasty!" and "Long live the Republic!"

Surging into the streets, the people attacked any and all tsarist symbols, toppling statues and burning double-headed eagles. In the Winter Palace, Nicholas's official portrait was slashed with bayonets. A huge demonstration of soldiers marched to demand an end to the Romanov dynasty. Their angry expressions and loaded rifles quickly convinced the new government that keeping the monarchy (as Britain had) was impossible. If a new tsar was forced on the people, there would surely be further violence, perhaps even a civil war.

Convinced all the Romanovs had to go, Rodzianko, along with Alexander Kerensky, set out to persuade Grand Duke Michael to also abdicate.

Michael listened closely to their arguments. Then he turned to Kerensky. Could the new government guarantee his safety if he took the throne?

No, answered Rodzianko.

Wanting time to think, Michael stepped out of the room. But only five minutes later, he returned. Tears in his eyes, he said simply, "I have decided to decline the throne."

Rodzianko pulled out a prepared document, and Michael signed it. With that, 304 years of Romanov rule came to an end.

SCENES OF REJOICING

The end of Romanov rule was greeted by joyous demonstrations in Petrograd. Crowds hung red flags from roofs, balconies, windows, and statues. There was singing, parades, and rousing speeches. Cannons boomed. Bells pealed.

The revolution had taken place entirely in Petrograd, unknown to the rest of the country. But as news spread to Moscow and other cities and towns in the last days of March, reaction was much the same. "The entire city became like a wild street carnival that one could not wait to get outside to see," recalled one citizen.

The soldiers at the front were wild with joy, too. When the news arrived, a mighty "Huzzah!" rose from the trenches like a song. Flinging their caps into the air, they pounded each other on the back. Some even fired a few precious rounds of ammunition into the air. Overnight, red ribbons appeared on almost everything— rifle butts, horse saddles, cannons. Most hoped that revolution also meant the end of the war. As a fighting force, the Russian army had completely collapsed. It hadn't launched an offensive since June 1916, and its war aims had been reduced to protecting its borders. With news of the revolution, tens of thousands of peasant soldiers, tired of sitting around with empty bellies, simply walked away from the war. Others, believing the revolution put them on an equal footing with their officers, formed committees to decide whether or not to obey a command. Some refused to salute; others insisted on choosing their own officers. Explained one soldier to his fellow troops, "Haven't you understood? Don't you know what a revolution is? It's when the people take all the power. And what's the people without us, the soldiers, with our guns? Bah! It's obvious—it means that the power belongs to us!"

The news, as it slowly spread across the vast and remote countryside, frightened some of the villagers. "The church was full of crying peasants," one citizen recalled. "What will become of us?" others wailed. "They have taken the tsar away from us." But as the weeks passed, and their lives went on as usual, many peasants celebrated. "Our [village] burst into life," recalled one. "Everyone felt enormous relief, as if a heavy rock had suddenly been lifted from our shoulders." Remembered another, "People kissed each other from joy and said that life from now on would be good." They praised God for "the divine gift of the people's victory." Like that, the reign of the Romanovs vanished.

BEYOND THE PALACE GATES:
"YE TYRANTS QUAKE, YOUR DAY IS OVER"

In his autobiography, Story of a Life, *Konstantin Paustovsky vividly recalls the moment his little town of Yefremov—located 640 miles south of Petrograd—received word of the revolution weeks after it happened:*

It was one o'clock in the night, a time when Yefremov was usually fast asleep. Suddenly, at this odd hour, there sounded a short, booming peal of the cathedral bell. Then another, and a third. The pealing grew faster, its noise spread over the town, and soon the bells of all the outlying churches started to ring.

Lights were lit in all the houses. The streets filled with people. The doors of many houses stood open. Strangers, weeping openly, embraced each other. The solemn, exultant whistling of locomotives could be heard from the direction of the station. Somewhere far down one street there began, first quietly, then steadily louder . . . singing:

> Ye tyrants quake, your day is over,
> Detested now by friend and foe!

The singing brass sounds of a band joined the human voices in the chorus.

BACK AT THE PALACE

On the evening of March 16—one day after Nicholas's abdication—his uncle Grand Duke Paul arrived at the Alexander Palace. He went straight to Alexandra with the news.

"It's all lies!" she cried when he finished. "The newspapers invented it. I believe in God and the army."

"God and the army are on the side of the revolution now," replied the grand duke.

Minutes later, recalled Lili Dehn, "the study door opened and the empress appeared. Her face was distorted with agony, her eyes were full of tears."

Stumbling forward, Alexandra grabbed the edge of a nearby table to steady herself. *"Abdiqué,"* she croaked, using the French word for *abdicated.* And then, in a whispered sob, she added, "The poor dear . . . all alone down there . . . what he has gone through, oh my God, what he has gone through. . . . And I was not there to console him."

PART FOUR

FINAL DAYS

You are filled with anguish
For the suffering of others.
And no one's grief
Has ever passed you by.
You are relentless
Only to yourself,
Forever cold and pitiless.
But if only you could look upon
Your own sadness from a distance,
Just once with a loving soul—
Oh, how you would pity yourself.
How sadly you would weep.
—Grand Duchess Olga Nikolaevna Romanova,
poem dedicated to her mother, April 23, 1917

CHAPTER FOURTEEN

❧ "SURVIVORS OF A SHIPWRECK" ❧

WHAT TO TELL THE CHILDREN?

On March 21, the day before Nicholas returned to Tsarskoe Selo, Alexandra summoned Pierre Gilliard to her drawing room. The children had to be told about the abdication. Would the tutor explain to Alexei?

Gilliard said he would.

"I am going to tell the girls myself," said the empress. Calm, but pale, she climbed the stairs to their sickroom. What she said is not known, but the news caused them all to burst into tears.

Across the hall, Pierre Gilliard sat beside Alexei. He began by telling the twelve-year-old boy that his father would never be returning to Stavka.

"Why?" asked Alexei.

"Your father does not want to be Commander-in-Chief anymore," replied Gilliard. Then he added, "You know, your father does not want to be tsar anymore."

"What? Why?" cried Alexei.

"He is very tired and has had a lot of trouble lately," answered the tutor.

Alexei struggled to understand. "But who's going to be tsar then?"

"I don't know," answered Gilliard. "Perhaps nobody now."

"But if there isn't a tsar," said Alexei, fidgeting beneath his blankets, "who's going to govern Russia?"

Gilliard explained about the Provisional Government.

What he didn't tell Alexei was that they were all prisoners of this new government. Just that morning, the entire family had been placed under house arrest!

ARRESTED

Their arrest was purely for security reasons, a representative of the Provisional Government, General L. G. Kornilov, had explained to Alexandra earlier that day. It was the only way to protect her and the children from the angry mobs. As for Nicholas, he was headed home as they spoke, accompanied (for safety's sake) by an armed guard. Once back at the palace, he, too, would be placed under house arrest. It was the government's plan, Kornilov continued, to send the whole family to England as soon as the children's health improved. In the meantime, they would all remain together under guard at Tsarskoe Selo.

After speaking with Alexandra, General Kornilov dismissed the few troops still remaining at the palace. He replaced them with soldiers faithful to the new regime. Then he spoke with the servants and courtiers. They, too, should leave, he advised. Otherwise, they would be placed under house arrest with the imperial family. His words sent most people scurrying for the door. But nearly one hundred of the more than five hundred who had worked at the palace—ladies-in-waiting, valets, grooms, cooks, tutors, maids, and footmen—remained. This included the empress's friend Anna Vyrubova, Pierre Gilliard, and the devoted Dr. Botkin. They were, noted Anna, "like survivors of a shipwreck."

Not long afterward, soldiers of the Provisional Government closed and locked the high iron fence surrounding the Imperial Park. In the palace, all entrances except the kitchen and front door were sealed shut. Sentries were posted in the hallways, and all letters going in and out of the palace were examined. Use of the telephone and telegraph was prohibited. "No longer was there the coming and going of the outside world," recalled one courtier. "The pulse of life had stopped."

WELCOME HOME, NICHOLAS

March 22 dawned bitter cold and overcast. Nerves on edge, Alexandra sat beside Alexei's bed, whispering prayers and watching the clock. Every so often, the still-recuperating boy called out the minutes until "Papa" arrived.

Finally, there came the crunch of tires on the ice-crusted driveway. Minutes later, the door to the family's private rooms flew open. "His Majesty the Emperor," announced the family's faithful butler, refusing to acknowledge recent events. Then Nicholas pounded up the stairs. Alexandra gave a little squeal as she leaped from her chair to meet him.

Together at last, husband and wife clung to one another. Tears streaming, Alexandra reassured him of her love. "My beloved, Soul of my soul . . . I wholly understand your action, oh my hero."

And Nicholas broke down. Recalled Anna Vyrubova, "He sobbed like a child on the breast of his wife."

CHANGES

Silver strands now streaked forty-eight-year-old Nicholas's beard, and dark shadows circled his blue eyes. And yet, to those around him, he acted "like a schoolboy on vacation." Walking. Sawing wood. Breaking ice. This was how the former tsar filled his days. And he felt invigorated. No more meetings with ministers. No more war reports to read or documents to sign. The only thing he admitted to missing about his old life was visiting with his mother and sisters. Otherwise, he reveled in spending time with his family and having "plenty of [hours] to read for my own pleasure." When told that they might be imprisoned at Tsarskoe Selo for several months, he replied, "A pleasant thought."

Forty-four-year-old Alexandra found life less pleasant. She spent most of her days on her sofa. Whatever glue had been holding her together since the start of the war seemed to vanish overnight. Now the family had the sickly Alexandra back. Her features suddenly aged and gaunt, her hair almost completely gray, she constantly grumbled about the hardships imposed on the family. In truth, changes in their material lifestyle were few. Footmen in elaborate livery still bowed and served meals; expensive wines from the imperial cellar still appeared on the table; maids still came to help her change into lace gowns and lengths of pearls. It was the mental strain Alexandra found intolerable. Suddenly, she was a prisoner in her own home, with parts of the palace and its grounds completely off-limits.

Far worse were the family's walks. For a few hours each day, the Romanovs were allowed outside. But every afternoon, just before they stepped out, angry crowds gathered along the iron fence. They shouted insults and obscenities. Some even hurled sticks and clods of dirt.

The soldiers did little to stop this. Not long ago, just a glimpse of the tsar would have sent them to their knees. But years of hardship had left them with little sympathy for Nicholas. "Too many hard, terrible things had been connected in the past with his name," explained one soldier. One could hardly blame them for their gaping and mocking. Sometimes they went even further, poking him in the back with their bayonets, and turning rudely away when he offered to shake hands. Once a soldier even stuck a rifle into the spokes of his bicycle as he pedaled past. The tsar flew over the handlebars, crashing to the ground. He managed to accept it all without complaint.

The soldiers targeted the others, too. They snatched away Alexei's toy rifle, told crude jokes about Alexandra within her earshot, and made fun of the way the girls spoke. "What an 'appetizing book' you have in your hand," one soldier drawled in imitation of Anastasia, who was overheard complaining about lunch. "One is tempted to eat it."

At first, these incidents humiliated Alexandra and her children. But Nicholas helped them get over it by laughing at his new title. "Don't call me a tsar anymore," he would joke. "I am only an ex." Soon the rest of the family began using the expression. One day when an overcooked ham was placed on the lunch table, Nicholas declared, "Well, this may have once been a ham, but now it's nothing but an ex-ham." Everyone—even Alexandra—giggled.

And so, slowly, the empress began to accept her fate. "It is necessary to look more calmly on everything," she said three months after her husband's abdication. "What is to be done? God has sent us such trials, evidently he thinks we are prepared for it. It is a sort of examination—to prove we are ready for His grace."

LENIN'S RETURN

Just before midnight on April 16, 1917, a train pulled into Petrograd's Finland Station. In the waiting area, hundreds of workers and soldiers buzzed with excitement. After twelve years in exile, Vladimir Lenin was coming home!

He'd been following events in Russia closely. "It's staggering!" he'd exclaimed when he learned of Nicholas's abdication. "It's so incredibly unexpected!" With the tsar gone, Lenin believed now was the time for the soviet to finally seize power.

It took six weeks and lots of political wrangling for Lenin to cross the war zone from Switzerland. But at long last, he arrived, his well-tailored wool coat and formal felt hat contrasting sharply with the workers' gray tunics. Catching sight of him, the crowd cheered as a military band struck up a revolutionary anthem:

> We renounce the old world,
> We shake its dust off our feet,
> And we don't need a Golden Idol,
> And we despise the Tsarist Devil.

Hurrying out into the station square where even more workers waited, Lenin climbed onto the hood of an armored car. He declared the war a "shameless imperialist slaughter," and called the Provisional Government who still supported the war "capitalist pirates" full of "lies and frauds." Bolsheviks should not, he shouted, "support in any way the new government."

The crowd cheered.

But just because Lenin had been greeted as a returning hero did not mean the Petrograd Soviet—the majority of whom were more moderate Mensheviks—agreed with him. Only two months earlier, it had agreed to support the Provisional Government. Thus many were flabbergasted when Lenin appeared before the soviet's members the morning after his arrival and demanded an immediate overthrow of the Provisional Government. "We don't need any parliamentary republic!" Lenin shouted. "We don't need any [rich man's] democracy! We don't need any government but the Soviet of worker and soldiers!"

Boos and whistles met his words. "That is raving!" hollered one listener. "That is the raving of a lunatic!" It seemed Lenin, who had lived comfortably in Europe, did not understand how hard they'd struggled to reach this place. "[He] is," snorted one member, "a hopeless failure."

But Lenin, who loved a fight, now launched what he called his "drive to power." Through the spring and summer of 1917, he appeared before Petrograd crowds, giving passionate speeches. Even though he could not pronounce his *R*s, his use of easy slogans and repetition made his message memorable. "Bread, peace, land, and all power to the Soviets. That is what we . . . want. That is what we . . . deserve. Bread, peace, land, and all power to the Soviets." Thumbs shoved under his armpits, swaying back and forth to the rhythm of his staccato words, Lenin possessed, said a listener, "a curious, hypnotic power."

His message was strengthened by the continued ineffectiveness of the Provisional Government. The cost of living had continued to skyrocket; food supplies remained scarce; and no steps had been taken to help the peasants toward their hearts' desire of more land. The war, citizens believed, was to blame for all these problems. So why weren't their new leaders doing something about the conflict? Could those rich, upper-class ministers in the cabinet be continuing the war for their own purposes? Mistrust growing, the Petrograd Soviet demanded to know the government's war policy.

In early April, leaders responded with their Declaration on War Aims. Russia's role in the conflict, the document claimed, would be purely defensive. She would protect her borders and nothing more.

But the soviet was not entirely assured. It insisted the Provisional Government send a diplomatic note to their allies declaring the same.

Government leaders agreed.

But just weeks later, on May 3, newspapers defiantly published the contents of that note. And it contradicted what leaders had told the soviet. Instead, the government's foreign minister, P. N.

Milyukov, had assured allies that Russia would go on fighting Germany to the bitter end.

The next day, mass demonstrations broke out in Petrograd and Moscow. Angry mobs carrying guns and banners denounced the foreign minister. They declared the government deceitful and hypocritical. They demanded change.

To calm the chaos, Milyukov quickly resigned. But it wasn't enough. The people demanded more representation in the new government. After a long and heated debate, the Petrograd Soviet decided, much to Bolshevik members' disgust, to participate in the Provisional Government. Five moderate members of the soviet now joined the reorganized ministry.

But the people's trust in their government was evaporating. By midsummer 1917, Bolshevik slogans began to resonate with many soviet members. Recalled one soviet member, "[Lenin] was followed unquestioningly as [the Bolsheviks' chosen] leader . . . a man of iron will and indomitable energy, capable of instilling fanatical faith in the movement and the cause."

SPRING DAYS

In May—as Lenin fanned the flames of insurrection against the Provisional Government—Nicholas and his children planted a vegetable garden. Happily, they moved sod, turned soil, and poked seeds into muddy furrows. Their clothing grew dirt-streaked and their fingernails turned black. But they didn't care. Working in the sunshine was bliss. And incredibly, some soldiers even offered to help. After weeks of standing over the Romanovs, they began to see them as ordinary people. Soon, wrote Gilliard in his diary, "several guards even [came] to help us!" Hatred softening, they laid down their rifles and picked up hoes. Before long, the family was chatting with the soldiers as they all weeded and tilled together.

ENTER KERENSKY

While the Romanovs tended their cabbages, the Provisional Government wrestled with the question of what to do with the family. At first, everyone believed they would be sent to England. Not only was King George V related to Nicholas and Alexandra (he was first cousin to both of them), he had even offered them refuge in his country. That spring, however, King George received thousands of letters from incensed British citizens. With the war against Germany and Austria still raging, they saw German-born Alexandra as an enemy. Worried that public opinion might boil over as it had in Russia, King George withdrew his invitation.

The next best thing to do, decided Alexander Kerensky, was to move the Romanovs someplace far from Petrograd. Just an hour's car ride away, the capital seethed with angry citizens. Seeking revenge, many demanded the family be imprisoned in the small, dark cells of the Peter and Paul Fortress. Shouts of "To the palace! To the palace!" were repeatedly heard in the streets. Kerensky feared a vengeful mob might attack the family.

The city's atmosphere grew even more dangerous in July 1917, when the Provisional Government decided to launch a military offensive against the Austrians. It had been two years since the Russian army had gone on the attack. Morale among the soldiers had never been lower; mass desertions continued and many refused to fight. The Provisional Government, however, was encouraged by the United States' entry into the war. This powerful new ally, they hoped, would somehow help Russia defeat Germany. Kerensky—

who had recently become minister of war—toured the front, making eloquent speeches to rally the troops. The offensive began in early July and soon turned into a rout, not for the Austrians and the Germans who helped them, but for the Russians, as hundreds of thousands of peasant soldiers were killed.

Passionate antiwar feelings erupted. In Petrograd, half a million people took to the streets on July 16 and 17. "Down with the war!" they shouted. "Down with the Provisional Government!" Among them marched twenty thousand sailors, many of them Bolsheviks, armed with rifles and revolvers. Eager for instructions from the man whom they considered their leader, they headed to Lenin's house. If he approved, they intended to march on the Winter Palace, where the Provisional Government was now headquartered, round up the ministers, and proclaim soviet power. But when they arrived, Lenin refused to even speak to them. Finally persuaded to say a few words, he stepped onto the balcony and mumbled briefly about the future of soviet power. Why didn't he fire up the crowds to topple the government? No one knows for sure. Minutes later, the discouraged sailors marched away. That's when soldiers of the Provisional Government began firing on them from rooftops and the upper windows of buildings. When it was over, hundreds of people lay dead or wounded. Recalled one witness, "It is clear that the crowds on the street had absolutely no idea of what they were doing—it was all a nightmare. Nobody knew the aims of the uprising or its leaders. Were there any leaders at all? I doubt it."

This uprising convinced Kerensky that the imperial family needed to be moved immediately. "The Bolsheviks are after me," he told Nicholas, "and then will be after you." But where could the family live safely?

Nicholas and Alexandra wanted to be sent to their palace in the Crimea. But Kerensky knew this was impossible. Their train would have to pass through Central Russia, where angry peasants were burning down manor houses and killing landowners. After much thought, Kerensky picked a quiet river town called Tobolsk in western Siberia. "I chose Tobolsk because it was an out-and-out backwater," Kerensky later wrote, "[with a] population which was prosperous and contented. . . . In addition . . . the climate was excellent and the town boasted a very passable Governor's residence where the family could live with some measure of comfort."

On August 11, Kerensky visited Tsarskoe Selo. "Start packing," he told the royal couple. "Be prepared to leave . . . within a few days."

"Where are we going?" asked Alexandra.

"For your safety, it must remain a secret," replied Kerensky.

Kerensky kept his secret from almost everyone else, too. "Only five or six men in all of Petrograd knew about it," he later wrote. "I made all the plans to move the family myself."

First, he handpicked the men who would accompany the family and act as guards once they reached their destination—loyal men who would follow Kerensky's orders to the letter. "Behave like gentlemen, not like cads," he advised them. "Remember, [Nicholas] is a former Emperor and neither he nor his family must suffer any hardships."

Next he made the travel arrangements. Knowing he could not transport the family in their easily recognizable blue imperial train, he had an ordinary one fitted out with Japanese flags and placards that read "Japanese Red Cross Mission." Kerensky hoped this disguise would reduce the chances of the family being recognized and captured.

BEYOND THE PALACE GATES:
THE "TSAR'S SURPRISE PARTY"

In the summer of 1917, American journalist Albert Rhys Williams was traveling across Siberia when his train came to an abrupt stop. In his book Through the Russian Revolution, *he reported what happened next:*

Suddenly from behind a snow-bank a figure shoots up . . . and comes running violently for the train. . . . From other snow-piles and bushes and from the far horizon, more and more figures keep emerging, until the whole plain is dotted with men racing headlong for the train . . . carrying . . . guns and grenades. . . . They are a harsh, determined lot. Many of them are grimy, nearly black. All of them have black looks for the train. . . .

[I] thrust my head out [the train window] and . . . address [their leader.] . . . "Where did all these men suddenly spring from? Why is the train held up?"

[He replied, laughing,] "These men are miners from the great coal mines less than half a mile away, and peasants from the village. Thousands more will be along directly. . . . We [intend] . . . to take off of it the Tsar and the Royal Family."

"Tsar and Royal Family? On this train? Here?" [I] shouted.

"We don't know that for sure. . . . [But] every man dropped his tools, snatched up his gun and rushed for the train. . . . You see how deeply we feel for our Tsar? Only twenty minutes advance notice, and we got this nice, big [surprise] party ready for him. He likes military displays.

Well, here it is. Not in regulation style, but quite impressive, is it not?"

It was! Never have I seen such a beweaponed set of men. . . . In their hands were missiles enough to blow a thousand Tsars into eternity, and in their hearts and eyes vengeance enough to annihilate ten thousand. . . . They combed the train from end to end, opening trunks, ransacking beds, even shifting the logs on the engine tender to see if His Imperial Majesty might be hidden in the woodpile. There were two white-bearded peasants who . . . would run their guns under [each train car], ram their bayonets around, and then withdraw them, shaking their heads sadly. The Tsar of All the Russias they hoped to find riding the bumpers. . . . Each time disappointed, they would hope for better luck at the next car and repeat the proddings. But there was no Tsar, and so their bayonets did not puncture him.

FAREWELL, TSARSKOE SELO

How does one choose among the belongings of a lifetime? In his study, Nicholas sorted through his papers. Some he destroyed. Others he locked in a file cabinet, taking the key into exile with him. And still others—all fifty of his diaries as well as the over six hundred letters Alexandra had written to him since their courtship—went into two crates marked A.F. (for Alexandra Feodorovna) and N.A. (Nicholas Alexandrovich).

In her dressing room, Alexandra emptied the contents of her closets onto the floor. Then she picked through the huge mound of clothing, making two piles. Into the smallest one went the items she was taking along; the other, much larger pile would be donated to war victims. Afterward, she packed her family photographs, prayer books, and icon collection. Unlike Nicholas, she had no diaries or letters to pack. She had burned these during the tense days just before Nicholas's abdication.

Overhead, the children bustled about. Along with their clothes, the girls packed books, art supplies, photograph albums, and their Brownie box cameras. Alexei added his tin soldiers, a chessboard, and his toy gun. Even the army cots with their thin mattresses and satin comforters would be folded up and taken along.

August 13, 1917, was their last day at Tsarskoe Selo. While Alexandra did some last-minute packing, the children drifted through the palace for the final time. Already, the rooms felt empty, the dustcloth-covered furniture looking like forlorn ghosts. They rowed across the pond to visit Children's Island one last time, and walked between the furrows of the now lush vegetable garden. "What shall the future bring for my poor children?" Alexandra wondered that day. "My heart breaks thinking of them."

As ordered, at five o'clock that evening, the family gathered in the semicircular hall to wait for word that the train arranged for by Kerensky had arrived at the station. Around them, fifty soldiers grunted and cursed as they moved the family's mountain of luggage. Besides clothing, toys, and personal papers, there were crates of books, rolled-up Turkish rugs, reams of bed linen marked with the imperial crest, silverware, fine porcelain dinner plates, clocks, fragile vases, silver pencils, and velvet cushions. Anything to preserve the appearance of their former luxurious lives. Other necessary items included the tsar's portable chin-up bar, Alexandra's nursing kit, and the electroshock machine Dr. Botkin used on Alexei's weak leg muscles. There were vials of holy water; boxes of smelling salts; laxatives, morphine, and even a year's supply of bath oil and cologne.

But more than luggage accompanied the family. In addition to several courtiers who had chosen to share their exile, the Romanovs went with two valets, six chambermaids, ten footmen, three cooks, four assistant cooks, a clerk, a nurse, a doctor, a barber, a butler, a wine steward, two pet spaniels, and a bulldog.

Now the Romanovs sat among the detritus of their lives, and waited. But as the hours passed with no word of the train, the family grew more and more nervous. Finally, at eleven p.m., Kerensky arrived to take the situation in hand. He found the grand duchesses huddled together "weeping copiously" while the tsar stood at one of the windows stonily smoking cigarette after cigarette. Even the usually stoic Alexandra was affected by the nerve-racking delay. Sitting in her wheelchair, "she wept and worried like any ordinary woman," recalled Kerensky.

As the hours continued to pass, Kerensky also grew pale and tense. The train ordered for one a.m. did not arrive. It did not come at two a.m. either. When three a.m. came and went, Kerensky picked up the phone. The problem, he learned, was the rail workers. On strike, they refused to couple the cars together. Kerensky desperately tried to work out a deal with them, but two anxious hours passed before the group finally heard cars pull into the driveway. Their train was ready, Kerensky told them. It was time to head to the station.

Alexandra, her face ashy white, took Nicholas's arm and walked out the door. Behind them came the children, all five of them in tears. Overhead, the sky was a rosy pink, the first rays of sunlight bathing the palace and the park in a golden haze. As the cars pulled away, the family turned and watched until their beloved Tsarskoe Selo faded into the distance.

They would never see it again.

CHAPTER FIFTEEN

❧ INTO SIBERIA ❧

TOBOLSK

The journey to Tobolsk took a week, the train clacking over a ribbon of rails that stretched across the empty Siberian grasslands before crossing the Ural Mountains and chugging into the river town of Tyumen. Here the family transferred to a steamer for the last leg of their trip down the Tura River. It took forty hours to cover the last two hundred miles. Nicholas and the children spent most of their waking hours on the steamer's upper deck, playing with the dogs, basking in the sunshine, and gazing out across the barren landscape. It was all so different from the ornate palaces and manicured parks they knew. The countryside seemed to stretch forever, broken only by an occasional village of mud roads and simple log huts. Just before sunset on the first day, the steamer passed the village of Pokrovskoe, where Rasputin had lived. Years earlier, the *starets* had predicted they would see it for themselves. Now, standing at the boat's railing, the entire family watched as his village glided past. Alexandra was especially moved. Crossing herself, she took the sight as a sign of her destiny.

Finally, Tobolsk came into view. As the boat slipped into the wharf, the passengers saw a town of dirt roads and whitewashed churches, log huts and wooden plank sidewalks. It was a far cry from cosmopolitan Petrograd some two thousand miles away.

The Romanovs' new home was a two-story mansion that had once belonged to the governor of the province. The family and their servants quickly decorated it with the furniture, rugs, and other items they had brought with them. It was "arranged all quite cozily," said Olga.

Even though the mansion had fourteen rooms, it could not house everyone who'd accompanied the Romanovs. The imperial family took up the entire first floor, the grand duchesses sharing a corner room next door to their parents while Alexei lived opposite, and Pierre Gilliard settled into the study on the ground floor. Most of the servants had to live across the street in a sprawling pink house that had been commandeered from a wealthy merchant.

Both houses sat on a dusty avenue that the townspeople of Tobolsk had renamed Freedom Street after the revolution. Sometimes they even called the Governor's Mansion the Freedom House. But without a doubt, the place was now a prison. Armed guards stood at all the entrances, and not long after the family moved in, a tall wooden wall was built. Extending all the way around the house, the wall also enclosed the greenhouse and a little-used side street meant as a sort of courtyard for exercise. The Romanovs were used to living behind fences. But always before they'd been erected to keep people *out*. This was the first one built specifically to keep the family *in*.

Still, life was far from uncomfortable. Just as Kerensky had said, the townspeople remained respectful of the tsar. Whenever they walked past the house, they removed their hats and crossed themselves. Just a glimpse of Nicholas sent them to their knees. Spotting Alexandra in her second-story window, they bowed. And whenever the grand duchesses stepped out onto the second-floor balcony, so many people gathered below on the sidewalk that the guards were forced to wave their rifles to shoo them away. Recalled one resident, "We were all amazed at the girls."

So attached to the imperial family were some of the shopkeepers that they regularly sent gifts of bread and meat. Peasant farmers arrived with fresh butter and eggs. And to dessert-loving Anastasia's joy, nuns from the local convent brought sugar and cakes. While much of the country starved, the youngest grand duchess grew "very fat . . . round and fat to the waist," remarked her mother.

Perhaps Anastasia overate because she was bored. The family tried everything it could think of to keep busy. They sawed and chopped wood. They snapped photographs of each other, played card games, knit or did needlework, and listened as Nicholas read aloud from *The Three Musketeers* or *The Scarlet Pimpernel*. He even built a small wooden platform on top of the greenhouse roof, where he and the children could sit, secluded and above it all. There in the sunlight, they could close their eyes and conjure up images of Tsarskoe Selo's shaded footpaths and sweet-smelling lilacs. They could dream about home and freedom.

Still, time dragged. "The whole day was just like yesterday," Alexei complained time and again in his diary. "Everything is the same!" "Boring!!!" "It's still boring."

What a relief it was when the children's English tutor, Sydney Gibbes, arrived.

A FACE FROM THE OUTSIDE WORLD

Gibbes had been away when the Romanovs were placed under house arrest in Tsarskoe Selo. Returning to the Alexander Palace, he discovered he'd been locked out. Dismayed, he repeatedly petitioned the Provisional Government for permission to rejoin the family. Seven months later, in October 1917, he finally received it. Taking the first available train to Siberia, the tutor arrived in Tobolsk just before winter did.

The tsar, who had been lunching with the children when Gibbes turned up at the Governor's Mansion, hurried forward to grip the tutor's hand. "He absolutely pounced on me," recalled Gibbes, so eager was he to hear the most recent war news. (Nicholas received newspapers weeks, sometimes even months, late.) Were the Germans being held back? How many troops had the Americans, who'd entered the conflict in April 1917, sent to Europe? As Gibbes spoke, he couldn't help but notice how "extremely . . . cheerful" the tsar looked. He still depended on Alexandra for even the most trivial decisions. "I will ask my wife; her wishes are mine," he said whenever he was asked for an opinion. But months of working outdoors had left him looking fit and healthy.

Not so Alexandra. In his diary, the tutor expressed shock at how much she had aged. Stooped and thin, she looked achingly tired and there was an expression of pain and anguish in her eyes.

Gibbes found the children changed, too. Olga, who would celebrate her twenty-second birthday in Tobolsk, had "got[ten] much thinner," he recalled, and was "easily irritated."

As for twenty-year-old Tatiana, "you could hardly find anyone so thin. Haughty and reserved . . . it was [now] impossible to guess her thoughts."

Eighteen-year-old Marie, however, was as earnest and open as ever. "She liked Tobolsk," he wrote, "and told me she could have made herself quite happy there."

Anastasia, at sixteen, was "short and stout, the only ungraceful member of the family," claimed Gibbes. Even in captivity she had retained her sense of humor. "She had a comedienne's talent, and she made everyone laugh."

And Alexei? He now let his emotions rule and "rarely did what he was told," noted Gibbes. Additionally, "he had [developed] some odd fancies." One of them was a constant and obsessive search for old nails, pieces of tin, bits of string. "This may be useful," Alexei would say, tucking them into his already full pockets. Whatever unpleasant thoughts were in his head, Gibbes said, the boy "bore them silently."

BACK IN PETROGRAD

Even though the Provisional Government had put down the July uprising, its problems were far from over. The bloody war still ground on. And the economy was in shambles. In Petrograd, jobs were hard to find, and bread even harder. "Week by week food became scarcer," wrote American journalist John Reed. "The daily allowance of bread fell from . . . a pound, then [to] three-quarters, then half, and a quarter pound. Toward the end there were weeks without any bread at all." As for sugar, milk, and meat, they were rarely seen.

Many people blamed the Provisional Government. They believed it had intentionally kept back the promises of the revolution—food, land for the peasants, and an end to the war. For this, they said, the government must be considered an enemy of the people, and overthrown.

The Petrograd Soviet agreed. In the months since Lenin's return to Russia, more and more members had come around to his beliefs. Now Bolsheviks held the majority in the soviet. "History will not forgive us if we do not take power [soon]," urged Lenin.

Two weeks later, on November 6, 1917, a few thousand Bolshevik-leaning soldiers under soviet orders seized control of the electric power station and the main post office as well as the main bridges and railroad stations. The majority of Petrograd's citizens didn't even notice. The streetcars continued to run; restaurants and shops were open for business; people even attended the opera and theater.

Hardly anyone realized the Bolsheviks were overthrowing the Provisional Government.

Inside the Winter Palace, ministers of the Provisional Government huddled around a table, smoking nervously and waiting for word from Kerensky, who had gone east to the front in hopes of raising an army to stop the mobs. They had known the insurrection was coming. Bolsheviks had been openly discussing it for days. In fact, just twenty-four hours earlier, the ministers had issued several orders: shut down Bolshevik newspapers, arrest Lenin and his fellow revolutionaries, and cut phone service to the Smolny Institute (a former girls' school now being used by the soviet). Problem was, there was nobody to carry out these orders. The only soldiers the government had on hand were a single unit of female troops and a few untrained military cadets. That was all that stood between them and the rebels.

At nine p.m., the *Aurora,* a ship operated by Bolshevik sailors, slipped down the Neva River. It fired just one blank shell at the Winter Palace. But it was enough to terrify the ministers' measly troops into instantly surrendering. A few hours later, the Bolsheviks seized the Peter and Paul Fortress and fired twice more at the palace. Again, no damage was done, but it was enough to scare the still-waiting ministers. At two a.m. on November 8, 1917, they surrendered.

The event, which became known as the October Revolution (according to the old-style Julian calendar, it took place on October 25), was dramatically different from the one that had occurred the previous March. The March Revolution had happened spontaneously, without any planning whatsoever. But the October Revolution was a well-organized and quiet coup. In later years, the Soviet Union would mythologize the October Revolution, inventing stories of fierce battles and daring exploits. But in truth, there was little drama. That night, the Provisional Government vanished with barely a whimper. All power had indeed passed to the soviets.

BEYOND THE PALACE GATES:
SWARMING THE PALACE

American journalist John Reed sailed to Russia in September 1917 to report on events there for The Masses, *a socialist magazine. Allowed to join the Bolsheviks as they swarmed into the Winter Palace after ministers of the Provisional Government surrendered, he recalled the scene in his book* Ten Days That Shook the World:

> Like a black river, filling all the street, without song or cheer we poured through the Red Arch, where the man just ahead of me said in a low voice, "Look out, comrades! Don't trust them! They will fire, surely!" In the open, we began to run, stooping low and bunching together, and jammed up suddenly behind the pedestal of the Alexander Column. . . .
>
> After a few minutes huddled there, some hundreds of men, the army seemed reassured and without any orders suddenly began again to flow forward. By this time, in the light that streamed out of all the Winter Palace windows, I could see that the first two or three hundred men were Red Guards [armed workers], with only a few scattered soldiers. Over the barricade of firewood we clambered, and leaping down inside gave a triumphant shout as we stumbled on a heap of rifles thrown down by the *yunkers* [military students opposed to Bolsheviks] who

had stood there. On both sides of the main gateway the doors stood wide open. . . .

Carried along by the eager wave of men we were swept into the right hand entrance . . . from which issued a maze of corridors and staircases. A number of huge packing cases stood about, and upon these the Red Guards and soldiers fell furiously, battering them open with the butts of their rifles, and pulling out carpets, curtains, linens, porcelain plates, glassware.

One man went strutting around with a bronze clock perched on his shoulder; another found a plume of ostrich feathers, which he stuck in his hat. The looting was just beginning when somebody cried, "Comrades! Don't touch anything! This is the property of the People!" Immediately twenty voices were crying, "Stop! Put everything back! Don't take anything! Property of the People!" Many hands dragged the spoilers down. Damask and tapestry were snatched from the arms of those who had them; two men took away the bronze clock. Roughly and hastily the things were crammed back in their cases. . . . Through corridors and up staircases the cry could be heard growing fainter and fainter in the distance, "Revolutionary discipline! Property of the People!"

AND BACK IN TOBOLSK

Word of the October Revolution arrived in a bundle of old newspapers delivered to the Governor's Mansion several weeks later. Nicholas read the accounts with despair. "I had never seen the Emperor so shaken," recalled Sydney Gibbes. "For a moment he was completely incapable of saying or doing anything." When he finally did speak, he expressed for the first time regret over giving up his throne. He had done so, he told Pierre Gilliard, "in the hope that those who wished to get rid of [me] would be capable of making a success of the war and saving Russia." But now he believed he had done Russia "an ill turn" by making way for the Bolsheviks. "This idea," added Gilliard, "haunt[ed] him."

By Lenin's Decree

Lenin had promised workers and peasants that, under Bolshevik rule, he would replace the unjust social order with a system of equality. So almost immediately after assuming power, he declared "a war to the death against the rich, the idlers and the parasites." Between November 1917 and March 1918, he decreed dozens of new policies that transferred much of the country's public and private wealth into the government's hands. There were so many, claimed one Moscow citizen, that the streets "smelled of printer's ink. . . . Day by day, these sharp, ruthless decrees were cutting away whole layers of a way of life, throwing them away, and laying the basis for a new life." Among them was the Decree on Land, making private ownership of land illegal. Within weeks, 75 percent of all estates had been confiscated. The new government did not compensate the noblemen for their losses. Instead, the land passed directly to peasant committees whose job it was to divide it. When divvying up these estates, committees often left the former owner enough acreage to live on. Believing, as they did, that the land belonged to those who plowed it, peasants now provided a way for the nobleman to earn a living. Many took the peasant committees up on their offers. In the mid-1920s, there were still some ten thousand former landowners laboring beside the peasants.

Additionally, Lenin decreed that private homes be seized. Bolshevik officials now arrived at upper-class homes waving warrants that allowed them to seize anything—furniture, books, carpets, silverware. Said one looter as he meticulously plucked every jewel-tipped pin from Countess Sheremetev's pincushion, "This is how we take everything." Across the country, palaces, mansions, and town houses were turned into government offices, or living space for workers. Taking the best rooms, workers typically forced the previous owners into one small room in the servants' quarters (as sanctioned by another of Lenin's laws). To most workers, this seemed fair. "I've spent all my life in the stables while they live in their beautiful flats and lie on soft couches playing with their poodles," said one ex-servant. "No more of that, I say! It's my turn to play with poodles now."

Around the same time, Lenin issued more than thirty other decrees nationalizing private industry and manufacturing. Factories were wrested from their owners. Shipping and foreign trade were declared a state monopoly. And the banks were nationalized. On December 27, 1917, government soldiers occupied twenty-three private banks and arrested their directors. After cleaning out the vaults, they ordered anyone with a safe-deposit box to report with their key. When the boxes were opened, they confiscated everything inside—jewels, money, property deeds. They even took personal items like marriage certificates and lockets of baby hair. Additionally, the government formed a State Treasury for Storage of Valuables, charged with collecting everything from art, antiques, and precious stones to rare books and expensive wines. Lenin was determined that no personal wealth would remain in anyone's hands—not even the Church's.

In January 1918, he issued the Decree on the Separation of Church and State, allowing for the seizure of all property belonging to the Russian Orthodox Church. Gold was stripped from altar walls. Jewels were pried from holy icons. And cathedrals and monasteries were converted into hospitals, schools, and orphanages.

All these policies were directed at those who had once been socially privileged. Now Lenin gave them a new title—"former people." And he ordered the mandatory registration of all "former landowners, capitalists and persons who held positions of authority in either the tsarist or the provisional government." These "former people" were forced to work, and any who refused, starved. By Lenin's decree, every month "former people" had to show proof of having performed community jobs (other Russians did not have to do this). And they were purposely given the most degrading tasks— cleaning public toilets, digging graves, cleaning trash off the streets. As they struggled with their brooms and shovels, groups of bystanders mocked them. "For centuries, our fathers and grandfathers have been cleaning up the dirt and filth of the ruling class," said one Bolshevik official, "but now we will make them clean up our dirt."

This miserable existence forced many "former people" to pack up and abandon their homeland. They moved to Western Europe or America. Some moved to southern cities in Russia, where Bolshevik authority did not yet reach. Many were jailed. Others were killed. So effective was Lenin's attack on the former elite that the communist newspaper *Pravda* would soon write: "Where are the wealthy, the fashionable ladies, the expensive restaurants and private mansions, the beautiful entrances . . . all the corrupt 'golden life'? All swept away."

BEATING THE WINTER DOLDRUMS

At first, the new Bolshevik-controlled government had little effect on the Romanovs, and their days went on as before—meals, books, card games . . . boredom! Then winter roared in, bringing both snow and a break in the monotony.

For ten whole days in January 1918, everyone except Alexandra worked to build a mountain of snow in the little yard. Gibbes and Gilliard joined in the fun, along with a handful of servants and even a couple of the guards. Together, they shoveled snow and piled it high. Then they carried gallons of water to pour and freeze over the mound. With the temperature dipping below zero, they had to sprint from the kitchen tap, trying to reach the mountain before the water froze in their buckets. When they finished, the mountain stood almost as tall as the wooden fence—an icy and fast sled run. Soon everyone (except Alexandra) could be seen wrestling, sliding, tumbling, and racing up and down the hill. "We often take very funny falls," reported Tatiana. "Once Monsieur [Gilliard] ended up sitting on my head. . . . It was terribly silly and funny. . . . Another time I was going down the hill backwards and banged the back of my head really hard across the ice. I thought nothing would be left of the hill, but it turned out that neither it nor my head burst. . . . I've got a hard head, don't I? Eh?"

CHANGES

February brought blizzards as well as changes to Tobolsk. On the twenty-seventh, the new government ordered the family placed on "soldiers' rations." After all, they asked, why should "Bloody Nicholas" live so luxuriously while others starved? Almost immediately, butter, sugar, coffee, and eggs vanished from the family's table. Indeed, any kind of luxury—silver teaspoons, bone china cups, linen napkins—the soldiers considered aristocratic could be snatched away without warning.

At the same time, the family's monthly allowance from the state was slashed. The family would have to cut its living expenses. But how? Nicholas had never needed to draw up a family budget before. He asked Pierre Gilliard and two courtiers who had followed him into exile for help. "We held a 'sitting' this afternoon," Gilliard wrote in his diary, "and came to the conclusion that the personnel must be reduced." Nicholas reluctantly agreed to let ten servants go.

Yet these were minor changes compared to what was happening with the guards. Emboldened by all the Bolshevik talk of class revenge, they "became cruder," noted Nicholas, and "began to act like hooligans." Forming a soldiers' committee and proclaiming authority over the Romanovs, the guards now provoked a series of trivial, yet menacing incidents. When a shipment of wine arrived for the family from Tsarskoe Selo, the soldiers seized it and poured it into the river. They demanded that Nicholas remove his officer's epaulets from his uniforms and jackets. Since they bore his father's monogram, their forced removal was a deep affront to the entire family. Perhaps worst of all, they mean-spiritedly destroyed the family's snow mountain. "To stop us from climbing up onto it and looking over the fence," admitted Nicholas. Said Gilliard, "The children are disconsolate."

Toward the end of March, a detachment of Red Guards arrived to replace those who had traveled with the family from Tsarskoe Selo. Fresh from Petrograd with its rebellious atmosphere, the men were tough, hardened radicals. In his diary, Gilliard described them as "a pack of blackguardly-looking young men" whose behavior was positively "indecent." One day, he recalled, they carved "filthy, stupid, crude words and pictures with [their] bayonets" into the wooden seat of a swing used by the grand duchesses. Alexei found them first. But before he had a chance to study the graffiti, Nicholas quickly took down the seat. This did not stop the soldiers.

They simply carved obscene messages onto the boards of the fence, instead. Did the sheltered girls understand their meaning? Probably not, but they surely grasped the soldiers' anger. "It is obvious that [they were] deeply affected," said Gilliard.

These soldiers imposed even more restrictions. They limited the family's time outdoors, searched their belongings, and—at Moscow's insistence—forced the remaining servants and courtiers to move out of the house across the street and squeeze into the Governor's Mansion with the imperial family. Since the house was already overcrowded, this caused "a great inconvenience," said Dr. Botkin, with some servants sleeping three to a bed.

"I should like to be a painter, and make a picture of [a] beautiful garden," Alexandra wrote to Anna Vyrubova around this time. "Sometimes we see men with the most awful faces. I would not include them in my garden picture. The only place for them would be outside, where the merciful sunshine could reach them and make them clean from all the dirt and evil with which they are covered."

ONE WAR ENDS AND ANOTHER BEGINS

Not all Russians backed Lenin. Many hated both him and his policies, and this hatred soon spurred the formation of a group intent on overthrowing him. Known as the White Movement, it was a collection of former tsarist officers, soldiers, and nobles. In the forests of Siberia, these men formed the White Army and marched on Moscow, the new Russian capital. As they marched, former landowners and factory owners angry over Bolshevik seizure of their property joined them. So did devout members of the Russian Orthodox Church who still believed the tsar was God anointed; supporters of the Provisional Government who wanted democracy rather than communism; and twenty-five thousand Czech prison-ers of war who were fighting their way out of Russia in hopes of being reunited with Czech troops on the front.

In response, the Bolsheviks created their own army, known as the Red Army.

Civil war, Lenin realized, had erupted.

But how could he fight this new conflict when Russia remained at war with Germany? He knew he couldn't.

Back when the Provisional Government was still in power, "Peace" had been Lenin's key slogan. Workers had rallied around him because of his promise to end the war. Peace, they believed, would bring prosperity. Now, Lenin knew, he had to make good on his promise. He *had* to end hostilities. Otherwise, he risked being overthrown himself.

So he sent a delegation to meet with the German High Com-mand at their military headquarters in the town of Brest-Litovsk (located in modern-day Belarus). There, on March 3, 1918, the delegates gave in to *all* of Germany's demands, signing away Po-land, Finland, the Baltic states, Ukraine, and the Crimea. This amounted to 32 percent of Russia's land, 54 percent of its factories, and 89 percent of its coal mines. It also placed more than one-third of its population—sixty million Russian citizens—into Germany's hands. In return, Russia was allowed to put down her guns and walk away.

NICHOLAS HEARS THE NEWS

The news, when it reached Tobolsk, could not have come at a worse time. For days, Alexei had suffered with a bad cough. According to Nicholas, he "developed a pain in the groin" from it. It was, said Alexandra, "an awful internal hemorrhage ... reminding me of

Spala." Day and night, the boy screamed as both the pain and swelling grew worse.

Without Rasputin, Alexandra felt helpless. "He is frightfully thin and yellow," she wrote. "I sit all day beside him, holding his aching legs, and I have grown almost as thin as he."

Nicholas was growing thin, too. "It is such a disgrace for Russia," he gasped when he learned of the treaty, "and amounts to suicide." His mood swung between anger and sadness. "To think they called [Alexandra] a traitor," he cried indignantly one moment, only to moan in the next, "How much longer will our unfortunate motherland be torn and ripped apart? Sometimes it seems as if [I] have no more strength to stand it. I don't even know what to hope for, what to desire." He tried to comfort himself. "Everything is in the hands of God! He is our only recourse," he repeated over and over.

THE BOLSHEVIK AGENT

Busy with other, more pressing issues, officials in Moscow had put off making any decisions about the imperial family. But by March 1918 they turned their attention to the Romanovs. What should be done with them? Some of Lenin's advisers insisted on tossing Nicholas into the fortress dungeons in Petrograd. Others wanted to drag him to Moscow and put him on trial for crimes against the people. But all worried he would be rescued by the White Army now marching across Siberia. If that happened, there was a chance Nicholas would be returned to his throne. There was only one option, those closest to Lenin advised: secretly move the family to a new location. They sent Commissar Vasily Yakovlev to Tobolsk to do just that.

Yakovlev arrived at the Governor's Mansion on April 22, 1918. There he found a weak and bedridden Alexei. The sight of the former heir lying so still in his bed shook the commissar. "The yellow-complexioned, haggard boy seemed to be passing away," he later wrote. It was obvious Alexei could not be moved.

Hurrying to the telegraph office, Yakovlev sent a coded message to Moscow: "Only principal part of baggage can be transferred." *Baggage* meant the imperial family, while *principal part* referred to Nicholas. What, Yakovlev asked, did the government want him to do?

Moscow answered immediately: "Removal [of] only principal part is approved."

The following day, Yakovlev interrupted the imperial couple's breakfast. He came right to the point. "I must tell you that . . . my mission is to take your family from Tobolsk, but as your son is ill, I have received a second order that says [Nicholas Romanov] alone must go."

"I refuse to go," said Nicholas.

"Then I must take you by force," replied Yakovlev. He let his words sink in a moment before adding, "Be calm, I am responsible with my life for your safety. If you do not want to go alone, you can take with you any people you wish . . . [but] be ready. We are leaving tomorrow at four a.m."

Alexandra's face turned scarlet. Her fists clenched. Taking a step toward the commissar, she screamed, "You want to tear him away from his family! How can you? How? His son is sick! He can't go, he must stay with us! This is too cruel!"

"Like an animal," recalled Yakovlev, she began pacing back and forth. Under her breath she muttered, "If [Nicholas] is taken alone, he'll do something stupid, like he did before. Without me, they can force him to do whatever they want."

But how could she leave Alexei?

Rushing to her bedroom, she sent for Pierre Gilliard. When he arrived, she wailed, "I can't let the tsar go alone. . . . I ought to be at his side in this time of trial. . . . But the boy is still so ill. . . . Oh, God, what a ghastly torture. . . . For the first time in my life I don't know what I ought to do; I've always felt inspired whenever I've had to take a decision, but now I can't think."

All morning, she muttered, raged, wept, and paced.

Her behavior frightened her daughters. They'd never seen her act like this before. Even during the worst of times—Alexei's illness in Poland, Rasputin's murder, Nicholas's abdication—Alexandra had kept her regal composure.

Finally, Tatiana spoke up. "Mother," she said soothingly, "something must be decided."

Gilliard agreed. He suggested Alexandra go with the tsar. He and the others, he promised, "would take great care of [Alexei]."

At last, Alexandra gave in. "Yes, that will be best; I'll go with the tsar."

But who would go with the empress and tend to her needs? Not Olga, Alexandra decided. She was too dispirited. And certainly not Tatiana. Her superior nursing skills were needed to care for Alexei. Anastasia? She was just "too young to be taken into account." That left Marie, "an angel and the best of us."

Their decision made, the family spent the rest of the evening together at Alexei's bedside. It was a long, dreadful night. Faces swollen from crying, the girls clung to one another's hands. Yakovlev had promised to fetch the rest of the family in three weeks. But could the Bolshevik be trusted? The family had never been separated this way before, and they were terrified. Again and again, one or another burst into tears.

"God won't allow the tsar's departure," said Alexandra, tears streaming down her face. "It can't be. It mustn't be." Bowing her head, she desperately prayed that the frozen rivers, which they would have to cross on their journey, would suddenly thaw and overflow their banks. "I know, I am convinced [it will happen]," she said. "I am sure a miracle will take place."

But no miracle came. Just before four a.m. the next morning, an assortment of horse-pulled carts, wagons, and carriages rolled into the courtyard, followed by a long line of soldiers. Soon the front door of the Governor's Mansion opened, and the three Romanovs stepped outside. Yakovlev escorted them and the handful of servants accompanying them to their vehicles. Then he gave the signal, and the procession moved forward—out through the wooden fence and down the frozen street, the sound of the rumbling wheels fading into the gray light.

On the steps, left behind and feeling utterly alone, stood Anastasia, Olga, and Tatiana. "[They] gazed for a long time into the distance," recalled one witness, "then turned and slowly, one after the other, entered the house."

As they passed their brother's room, where Gilliard sat with a distraught Alexei, the tutor heard the girls weeping.

CHAPTER SIXTEEN

❧ THE HOUSE OF SPECIAL PURPOSE ❧

LEFT BEHIND

With Nicholas and Alexandra gone, "sadness . . . descended on the house," said valet Alexei Volkov. The children waited nervously for news of their parents. What was happening to them? Even Anastasia turned solemn and fretful. "These days I am boring, and not pretty," she admitted.

Finally, on May 3, a week after the family's separation, Commissar Yakovlev cabled with news. The group was in Ekaterinburg, a city located in the Ural Mountains.

The news stunned those in Tobolsk. "Why Ekaterinburg?" wrote one household member. "We always thought that Moscow was their destination."

Moscow *had* been their destination. But while Yakovlev and his "baggage" were en route, Bolshevik officials suddenly changed their minds. They ordered Nicholas and his family to the Urals. No one knows exactly why. Certainly, leaders in Ekaterinburg—a town with fierce anti-tsarist sentiments—had pressured the government to hand over the Romanovs to them. They claimed their remote location eight hundred miles east of Moscow would keep the family safe. But Moscow also knew that Ekaterinburg's soviet was, according to one official report made in 1918, undisciplined and violent. Many of its town leaders eagerly spoke of "finishing off the butcher [Nicholas II]." So brutal was their reputation that Commissar Yakovlev grew worried about delivering the family there. Aware that Lenin was considering putting Nicholas on trial for crimes against the Russian people, Yakovlev cabled Moscow as soon as he received the new orders. "I consider it my duty to warn [you]," he began. If the family was left in Ekaterinburg, not only would Moscow never be able to get them back, but "[the Romanovs] will be in utter danger at all times." His warning did not change Moscow's mind.

Days later, a letter written by Marie but dictated by Alexandra finally arrived in Tobolsk. "It is not clear how things will be here," read the letter. Unable to give many details about their new surroundings because all ingoing and outgoing mail was read by the Ekaterinburg guards first, the empress did warn that all their belongings had been searched, even their "medicines."

Medicines was the Romanovs' code word for jewels. Before she left, Alexandra had instructed the girls to conceal the family's jewelry if they ever received this message. Now they took up needle and thread and cleverly sewed close to $14 million worth of diamonds, rubies, sapphires, and pearls into the hems of skirts and the belts of dresses; behind jacket buttons and under hat rims, and deep inside pillows and cushions. Most of the "medicines" were concealed between double layers of cotton in the girls' camisoles—almost nineteen pounds of diamonds alone in each of these undergarments. The jewels were all the family had left of their vast fortune, their financial future if they escaped Russia.

While they sewed, another letter arrived, this one from Marie. "We get nasty surprises here every day," she wrote ominously. "Who would think . . . we would be treated like this? We hope you have it better."

The children didn't. In mid-May, the Bolshevik government had sent another commissar to Tobolsk—Nicholas Rodionov. Described by one courtier as a "right snake of a man," Rodionov hated the imperial family and enjoyed inflicting petty humiliations on the grand duchesses. Armed from head to toe with revolvers, rifles, and knives, the new commissar stalked about the house, keeping careful watch over his prisoners. His orders were to bring the rest of the family to Ekaterinburg as soon as Alexei could travel. In the meantime, the Governor's Mansion would become "a strict prison," he announced.

On his first day, he ordered the doors inside the house to remain open at all times, even the one leading to the grand duchesses' bedroom. Prisoners, he declared, must always be watched. When valet Volkov protested—"Your soldiers would pass by there all the time!"—Rodionov pulled out his revolver and pointed it at the servant. "If you do not do as I have ordered . . . I [will] shoot you where you stand," he warned. From then on, the girls had little privacy.

Rodionov also instituted a daily roll call. Every morning, the prisoners were made to line up in the ballroom, facing the commissar. "Are you Olga Nikolaevna? Tatiana Nikolaevna?" he shouted into their faces. Stepping forward, they obediently answered his questions. "Darling," Olga wrote in one of the last letters she sent to Anna Vyrubova, "you must know how dreadful it all is."

These changes—so obviously and frighteningly a taste of what was to come in Ekaterinburg—forced Gibbes and Gilliard to question whether or not the children should be sent to their parents. "We feel we ought to delay [their] departure as long as possible," Gilliard wrote in his diary.

The girls refused to hear of it. In the three weeks since their parents' departure, Alexei, though still unable to walk, had grown strong enough to travel. All four were eager to be reunited with their family. "In our thoughts we are with you all the time," Anastasia wrote Marie. "It is terribly sad and empty [here] and I have whole trainloads of things to tell you all."

And so the prisoners began packing. "The rooms are empty," Alexei scrawled in his diary. "Little by little everything is [put] away. The walls look bare without their pictures."

On their final night in the Governor's Mansion, as a maid wrapped the last of the knickknacks, Rodionov suddenly appeared at her side. "Life down there [in Ekaterinburg]," he whispered, "will be very different."

LAST STOP

On May 23, after a three-day journey, the train carrying the imperial children pulled into the Ekaterinburg station. Despite an icy drizzle, a large crowd had gathered. "I cannot describe the faces I saw," said one courtier. "Fat faces, lean faces, but all with deadly, intense hatred stamped on them."

As the luggage was being taken out, one man grabbed a box and tore it open. Out spilled boots and shoes. "Look! [The tsar] has six pairs and I have none," cried the man. In response, the mob began chanting, "Death to the tyrant!" and surged forward. A second box, full of Alexandra's gowns, was ripped open. The sight further enraged the crowd. "The dresses . . . of wanton women," shrieked a woman, pointing toward the train. "Off with their heads!"

In response, the mob screamed, "Down with them! Hang them! Drown them in the lake!"

From the train window, the children watched as the soldiers worked to hold back the mob. Finally, Rodionov ordered them out of the train. As they gathered up their things and went out into the gray Siberian day, their expressions, recalled one eyewitness, were "a tragic symphony . . . nervous, emotional . . . trying to suppress [their] pride, but also trying to suppress [their] fear in front of hostile strangers."

Pierre Gilliard, who had been placed in a separate car for the entire journey, saw them go. "Nagorny the sailor . . . passed my window, carrying the sick [Alexei] in his arms; behind him came the grand duchesses, loaded with valises and small personal belongings. . . . Tatiana Nikolaevna came last, carrying her little dog and struggling to drag a heavy brown valise. It was raining, and I saw her feet sinking into the mud at every step." The girls climbed into a waiting carriage and drove away. Added Gilliard, "How little I suspected that I was never to see them again."

THE HOUSE OF SPECIAL PURPOSE

Stretching across a cluster of small hills, Ekaterinburg was a city of iron-smelting factories, soap works, and tanneries. Its wide boulevards were lined with fine houses and golden-domed churches, as well as a natural history museum, two theaters, and even an opera house.

Near the center of this town, on an unpaved street lined with linden trees, a wealthy engineer named N. N. Ipatiev had built himself an ornate, two-story stone house. But in April, just as Nicholas and Alexandra were being taken from Tobolsk, Ipatiev had received orders from the Bolshevik government to leave. He'd had time to pack just a few belongings before workmen arrived to transform his home into a prison. Hastily, they built a tall wooden fence that not only reached the windows on the upper floors, but entirely hid the house and its garden from the street. Later, this fence would be extended even higher—all the way up to the house's eaves. They sealed off five rooms on the upper floor as a prison and whitewashed all the windows so the captives could not see out. "It [always] looks as if there is a thick fog outside," complained Nicholas. Only one of these windows could be opened. Without much ventilation, the rooms, said Nicholas, were very "hot and stuffy." When all was ready, the house had received its new and ominous name, the House of Special Purpose.

Now the carriages carrying the children rolled into the House of Special Purpose's courtyard. For the last time, they saw the outside world. Then the fence's heavy wooden doors slammed behind them, and they raced through the rain into the house, where their parents eagerly waited.

IN FIVE ROOMS

The children found themselves crammed into five interconnecting rooms with their parents and their servants—Dr. Botkin, the maid Anna Demidova, cook Ivan Kharitonov and his fourteen-year-old kitchen assistant Leonid Sednev, and footman Alexei Trupp. The empress had hoped to squeeze in Gibbes and Gilliard, too. But officials denied the men permission to enter the house. Instead, they were returned to Tobolsk, along with many of the others who had accompanied the grand duchesses.

Nicholas and Alexandra occupied the corner bedroom. With its couch and armoire, it was small but "cosy," said Marie. This room's only exit was through the girls' cramped bedroom (actually a former dressing room) with its floral wallpaper and oriental rug. Until their army cots arrived from the train station, the girls snuggled together on a mound of coats and blankets on the floor, whispering late into the night.

There was little other furniture in their room—a table, a few upright chairs, and a large mirror in one corner. As the weeks passed, the girls had less and less use for this last item. Even though they'd left Tsarskoe Selo with boxes of clothing, they hadn't been allowed to bring most of them into the House of Special Purpose. Instead, their luggage had been tossed unopened and haphazardly into a storage shed located behind the house. Soon, the few clothes they had grew threadbare and faded. Did they find themselves standing before the mirror, longing for the white lace dresses they used to wear?

The girls' room was connected to the dining room with its wooden floors and solid oak furniture. At Nicholas's insistence, all of the prisoners—royals and servants alike—sat together for meals at the big table. But there was not enough silverware to go around. This was because their fine tableware also sat unopened in the shed. Other things sat untouched in the shed, too—boxes of Alexei's baby clothes, riding crops, binoculars, and most disappointing to the children, their beloved Brownie box cameras. Even in Tobolsk, the family had been allowed to use them. But guards had confiscated the cameras here in Ekaterinburg. There was something else in the shed, too—Nicholas's diaries and letters, neatly stacked in crate number nine marked A.F. and crate number thirteen marked N.A.

The final space was the drawing room. Here, Alexandra made an altar by covering a table with her lace bedspread and the family's icons. Here, too, the girls played the mahogany piano left behind by Comrade Ipatiev, while Nicholas sat reading beneath an ornate chandelier of Italian glass. At night, this room became Dr. Botkin's bedroom, while Trupp, Kharitonov, and young Leonid slept in the stairway hall. Anna Demidova was given a closet-size room toward the back of the house.

Also located on the house's top floor, but separate from the prisoners' rooms, was Commandant Alexander Avdeev's office. A former factory worker, Avdeev was tall and thin-faced, and behind Nicholas's back called him "Nicholas the Blood-Drinker." He had gotten the job of overseeing the Romanovs' imprisonment because of his dedication to the Bolshevik party. In the elegant office that had once belonged to Comrade Ipatiev, the commander smoked and drank and scrawled an occasional order on stationery he'd had engraved with the words "House of Special Purpose." Between shifts, guards squeezed into the office, flinging their rifles onto the rich carpets before reclining on the sofa's plush cushions. These guards, noted Nicholas sarcastically, "are original in both composition and dress."

Indeed, the forty men guarding the imperial family were not professional soldiers or hardened Bolshevik revolutionaries. Most were young factory workers between the ages of seventeen and twenty-three (some the same age as the grand duchesses). They did not have any fighting experience, or know how to handle guns. They had not taken the job out of hatred for the tsar but rather for the "money," explained a twenty-one-year-old guard named Alexander Strekotin.

Young and immature, these guards made "all kinds of mistakes," admitted Strekotin, "like sleeping at their posts, leaving their posts, [and] letting people in for a peek [at the imperial family]." One guard accidentally fired his rifle into a storeroom ceiling directly beneath the grand duchesses' bedroom, causing the girls to scream with fear. Another dropped a hand grenade into the garden, where it exploded, rattling both windows and nerves. And one day while Anastasia stood at the prison's one open window, hoping to catch a scrap of breeze, a bullet whizzed past her head and lodged in the wall behind her. Had one of the guards shot at her on purpose? Nicholas refused to believe it. No one would dare fire at the tsar's daughter, not even in revolutionary Russia . . . would they? "In my opinion," he said with mock bravado, "[the sentry] was just fooling around with his rifle the way guards always do."

But was he really? Days later, according to an often-repeated but unsubstantiated story, Anastasia asked the commandant's assistant for permission to visit the storage shed. She wanted to fetch a pair of shoes from her luggage. The assistant laughed nastily. "The shoes [you have] on," he said, would easily "last the rest of [your] life."

A MONOTONY OF DAYS

Days passed, each one the same. Rising between eight and nine every morning, the family dressed and joined the rest of the prisoners before the makeshift altar. After prayers (led by Alexandra), they headed into the dining room for a breakfast of black bread and tea. This was also the time when Commandant Avdeev took roll call, making sure that each prisoner was accounted for. Once in a while, the family received a cup of hot chocolate or a slice of cold meat for breakfast. But for the most part, they received the same rations as any other Russian citizen.

At first, a workplace cafeteria called a canteen delivered the family's meals every day, usually an unvaried menu of soup and pork cutlets. In mid-June, worried about the imperial family's diet, nuns from a nearby convent began bringing eggs, milk, cream, and bread to the house's gates each morning, which the family's cook, Ivan Kharitonov, turned into simple meals. The nuns also brought sausages, vegetables, and the occasional meat pie. These last items never reached the imperial table. Instead, Avdeev and his guards gobbled them up.

During the day, the family filled their hours by reading or sewing. They played cards. Anastasia taught the dogs tricks. And all the girls helped Anna Demidova with the household chores. They swept floors, washed dishes, and gathered up the family's dirty laundry so it could be sent out for cleaning. But this last task quickly became a problem. The grand duchesses "insisted on changing their bed linen every day," recalled Avdeev. In just a few weeks, they racked up a whopping 87-ruble laundry bill (around $428)!

When soviet officials saw the bill, they flew into a rage. It was outrageous, absurd, "astronomical!" From now on, they ordered, the imperial family would have to wash its own bed linens. After all, "a little work never hurt anyone."

The grand duchesses were willing. But they didn't know the first thing about doing laundry. They asked Avdeev for directions. But the commandant knew as little as they did. So he headed to the library in search of a manual. But "[I] could find no written instructions on how to do laundry." Anxious to carry out the soviet's order, Avdeev finally hired the girls a laundry instructor, bestowing upon him the title "Comrade Laundry Teacher to the House of Special Purpose." Recalled the commandant, "[He] proved rather clever with this work, and got on well with the grand duchesses."

A few weeks later, the bored grand duchesses begged Ivan Kharitonov for bread-baking lessons. With the commandant's permission, they spent an entire morning in the upstairs kitchen, happily mixing and kneading. The results, noted Alexandra in her diary, were "excellent."

The family's evenings were filled with more reading, more card games, more prayers.

The only break in this routine came in the late morning and again in the afternoon. That's when the family was allowed to walk for thirty minutes outside in the small, weed-choked garden.

Why so little time outdoors? Nicholas had asked his captors. Summer had finally come to Siberia, hot and sunny. How could they be so cruel as to leave the family trapped indoors all day with the sealed-in smells of cigarette smoke and sweat? "It [is] unbearable to [be] . . . locked up, and not be in a position to go out into the garden . . . and spend a fine evening outside," Nicholas said. Couldn't he and the children clean up the garden or chop wood?

Avdeev's assistant denied his request.

"Why?" persisted Nicholas.

"So that this resembles a prison regime," replied the assistant.

Still, the two youngest grand duchesses must have relished this brief chance to feel the sun on their skin. At these times, the guards heard them laugh as they chased the dogs through the scraggly flower beds or around the few trees.

Alexei, too, must have enjoyed the fresh air. Although the boy could no longer walk, Nicholas "hugged him to his broad chest" and carried him outside to a waiting wheelchair. Then Leonid Sednev, the fourteen-year-old kitchen assistant, would push Alexei into the garden. Sometimes the boys played with toy soldiers. Other times, Nicholas would bring his son pebbles or flowers to examine. "Being a child," recalled one of the guards, "[Alexei] would look at them and then toss them into the bushes."

When the family first arrived, all the guards (even those not on duty) had pressed into the garden to get a look at them. Soon, recalled guard Alexander Strekotin, "everyone had a chance to see [the grand duchesses]." They quickly became the topic of conversation between the young men, who "passed some sleepless nights speaking of them when they were off duty."

"There is nothing special about them," declared one guard.

They are "stuck up and stupid," said another.

But Strekotin disagreed. "There was something very special about them," he argued. "You could look at them in their old and tattered clothes . . . like any poor girls, but yet there was something especially sweet about them. They always looked good to me, and I thought they would not have looked better even if they had been covered in gold and diamonds."

Strict rules prohibited prisoners and guards from talking to one another. But Anastasia and Marie didn't care. They were used to speaking with soldiers, and felt a natural ease in their company. And so they drew the young men into lighthearted conversations.

Flirtatious and giggling, the "Little Pair" would stroll across the garden, their spaniel, Jemmy, scampering along at their feet. Approaching a guard on duty, Anastasia would pretend to yawn. "We're so bored!" she would say. "In Tobolsk there was always something to do. I know! Try to guess the name of this dog."

How could the guards resist?

Some joined eagerly in the banter, answering the girls' questions about their lives and hobbies. Others, with smiles and winks, said, "Don't try to distract me with your smooth talk—just keep walking."

The girls, "pretending fright," said Strekotin, "would hurry along the path, then burst into giggles."

Soon, "everyone relaxed more and began to talk and laugh with each other," remembered Strekotin.

HAPPY BIRTHDAY, MARIE

On the afternoon of June 27, the "Little Pair," along with Tatiana and Nicholas, carrying Alexei, went for their scheduled walk in the courtyard. Noted the tsar in his diary, "Our dear Marie is 19 years old."

One of the guards had also noted the grand duchess's birthday, and he had smuggled in a cake for her. Somehow, after his shift ended, he managed to pull Marie aside. The two slipped away.

Where did they go? The kitchen? The hallway? One of the storerooms on the lower floor? The historical record doesn't indicate, but obviously the other guards—sympathetic to their comrade's feelings—looked the other way as he grabbed his chance to give Marie his gift.

They were soon discovered. Little did the guards know that local Bolshevik authorities had chosen this day to inspect the house. Walking in on the couple, the officials were outraged. Obviously, security had completely collapsed. It was time for a clampdown. Authorities called in Yakov Yurovsky.

CHAPTER SEVENTEEN

❧ DEADLY INTENT ❧

"THE DARK GENTLEMAN"

"Today there was a change of commandant," wrote Nicholas in his diary on July 4. That afternoon, just as the family sat down to lunch, a government official unexpectedly appeared.

"Because of an unpleasant episode that had occurred in [the] house," the official announced, Commandant Avdeev had been dismissed. He gestured to a tall, dark-haired man standing beside him. Here was the Romanovs' new captor—Yakov Yurovsky.

Yurovsky greeted the family politely. In fact, he was so respectful and mannerly that at first Nicholas called him "the dark gentleman."

But behind those impeccable manners, Yurovsky burned with hatred for the imperial family. Raised in Siberia by a father who had been exiled for theft, he grew up in a cramped, stinking apartment above a butcher shop. These years of poverty and deprivation sowed the seeds for a deep-seated hatred of the tsar. When the revolution came, he backed the Bolsheviks with zealous enthusiasm, rising up quickly through the party ranks. He believed his new job—commandant in control of the imperial family's lives—was his destiny. "It was left to *me,* son of a worker, to settle the Revolution's score with the Imperial [Family] for centuries of suffering," he later said proudly.

Making security his top priority, he replaced the young factory-worker guards with a squad of war-hardened guards. These men, like Yurovsky himself, were "all obedience and command and [they] burned with the Red Fire," recalled one eyewitness. Talking with the prisoners was now strictly forbidden, and any unauthorized conversations were immediately reported to Yurovsky. In the courtyard, the new guards watched the family closely, constantly on the alert for any word or gesture that might mean the family was trying to signal someone on the street. In addition, Yurovsky installed a new system of alarm bells throughout the house, and reorganized the guard posts. Now a machine gun pointed straight down the street, while a second one set up in the spire of a nearby cathedral was aimed directly at the prisoners' rooms. Last but not least, Yurovsky had the family's one open window covered by a thick iron grate. "Always fright[ened] of our climbing out, no doubt," Alexandra remarked sarcastically.

In fact, he was. Forty-five thousand White Army troops were advancing on Ekaterinburg. Already they had seized control of Tyumen, cutting railroad lines and creating chaos. "Constantly hear artillery passing," Alexandra wrote in her diary on July 12. "Infantry and twice cavalry during the week. . . . Also troops marching with music." The untrained Red Army could do little to stop the advance. Bolshevik officials knew the city would fall. And when it did, the White Army would free the Romanovs. Unless the Bolsheviks murdered them first.

JULY 12

Outside the iron grille of the prisoners' only open window, thunder rumbled and rain poured down. Alexandra lay in bed with an excruciating backache. But the pain medication Dr. Botkin had brought from Tsarskoe Selo had long been used up. In hopes of soothing her mother, Marie offered to read aloud from the family's favorite collection of sermons. But time and again, she was interrupted by the sound of marching soldiers and military bands from the street below. Both mother and daughter knew what these sounds meant—the Bolsheviks were losing their hold on Ekaterinburg.

Meanwhile, down the road at Bolshevik headquarters, an urgent meeting was taking place. Nicholas had to be "liquidated" before the city fell. But Lenin and other high-ranking Bolsheviks in Moscow refused to authorize an execution. They still thought of putting Nicholas on trial, where his crimes against the people would be broadcast to the entire country. Of course, Moscow expected the trial to end in a sentence of execution for the tsar. It was, they believed, the only proper punishment for "Bloody Nicholas."

Even though most officials believed Alexandra was to blame for much of the country's disintegration, they had no intention of charging her—or the children—with any crimes. Lenin was adamant on this last point. He vehemently opposed murdering the entire imperial family, not because he cared what happened to them but because he believed it would have a bad effect on public opinion across Russia and abroad. Bolsheviks, he insisted, must not be perceived as barbaric or bloodthirsty.

Ekaterinburg officials disagreed. They resented the fact that the tsar and his family were still living in relative comfort at the Ipatiev house while they continued to scrape out a meager living. After all, at the heart of the Bolshevik Revolution lay the notion that all privilege must be destroyed. Moscow or no Moscow, they resolved to murder the entire family, as well as their servants. They knew Lenin's regime, mired as it was in civil war, was not strong enough to punish them for the act.

The only decisions that remained were how and when.

The how they left up to Yurovsky. As for when, they would let him know. But with the White Army marching ever closer, it would be soon.

JULY 13

"It has to be said," Yurovsky later noted, "that it's no easy thing to arrange an execution, contrary to what some people may think."

In the early-morning hours, long before the Romanovs woke, Yurovsky rode out on horseback to Koptyaki Forest, nine miles west of the city. Few people went there. Not only was the place remote, but with its dense woods, peaty swampland, and abandoned, water-filled mine shafts, it was dangerous. The perfect place, Yurovsky decided, to hide the bodies. But could one drive a truck over the muddy, potholed roads? The commandant believed so. Satisfied, he returned to the House of Special Purpose. In the guard book that day, he coolly wrote, "Everything is the same."

Upstairs, Alexandra was experiencing a rare moment of joy. For the first time since leaving Tobolsk nine weeks earlier, Alexei felt strong enough to take a bath. "Baby . . . managed to get in and out alone," she wrote in her diary. "Climb[ed] also alone in and out of bed." Alexei still could not straighten his leg "but can only stand on one foot," she noted.

Nicholas, too, wrote in his diary. "Today," he noted, "we have absolutely no news from the outside." It was his last recorded statement. After almost forty years of daily journal keeping, Nicholas Romanov simply stopped.

JULY 14

On this bright Sunday morning, just after the family finished breakfast, Father Ivan Storozhev arrived at the House of Special Purpose. Hours earlier he'd been summoned by Yurovsky to conduct a church service for the Romanovs. This had surprised Father Storozhev. Their captors had repeatedly denied the family's request for a priest to say Mass with them. So why now? The priest feared to ask. Donning his vestments, he made his way to the prisoners' drawing room.

They were waiting before the makeshift altar. Propped up in his mother's wheelchair, Alexei looked ghostlike in his paleness. Alexandra sat beside him in an overstuffed armchair, her face creased with pain. Behind them stood Nicholas and the girls. Recalled Storozhev, they "gave the impression . . . of being exhausted." Even Anastasia, her hand resting on her father's arm, appeared "in depressed spirits." Yurovsky planted himself in a corner of the room. Crossing his arms over his chest, he never took his eyes off the group as the priest moved through the liturgy.

At last, Father Storozhev came to the part in the service where the traditional prayer for the dead is recited: "With the saints give rest, O Christ, to the souls of your servant, where there is neither pain, nor sorrow, nor suffering but life everlasting."

Spontaneously, unexpectedly, all but Alexei sank to their knees. Looking across their bowed heads, the priest realized how deeply comforted the prisoners were by the prayer. Then one by one, each came forward to kiss the cross. Tears stood in the grand duchesses' eyes.

Minutes later, Yurovsky walked the priest to the front gate. Both men knew that the family had just been given their Last Rites. And Yurovsky seemed pleased. It was one more item off his to-do list.

JULY 15

Upstairs, the Romanovs went about their usual morning routine—prayers, breakfast, reading. They had just gathered around the dining room table to play cards when the double doors of their prison opened. There stood four women from the Union of Professional Housemaids. They had come to wash the floors. Why? Yurovsky was trying to create a sense of normality so the doomed family would not suspect their time was short.

Smiling, happy to see faces from the outside world, the grand duchesses dropped their cards on the table. They hurried to help the women move the beds and other furniture.

Following the group to the doorway of the bedroom, Yurovsky glared at them for several minutes. When he finally moved away, Anastasia thumbed her nose at his back. Both grand duchesses and cleaning women laughed. Then the girls got down on their hands and knees to help the women scrub. No matter, Tatiana whispered. They welcomed this brief chance for some exercise. The girls, recalled one cleaning woman, "were spirited and breathed [a] love of life." Their hair was "tumbled and in disorder, their cheeks were rosy like apples."

Not so the others. The cleaning women had grown up with the idea that the tsar was a god, "a giant among men," while the empress was a beauty with a voice "like a flute from paradise." Instead, they found a "drab man with a large balding spot [and] legs too short for his body." His wife looked "tired and sick . . . and lacking color." And their son was "the color of wax," his eyes "with great dark circles under them." When the women left ninety minutes later, they took with them a new view of the imperial family. "They were not gods," said one, "but . . . ordinary people like us, simple mortals."

JULY 16

The day—Nicholas and Alexandra's seventy-sixth in the House of Special Purpose—dawned gray and rainy. As usual, the family said their morning prayers before sitting down to yet another dismal breakfast of tea and black bread.

Around the same time, Yurovsky was summoned to Bolshevik headquarters. When he returned an hour later, he pulled his assistant, Gregory Nikulin, into his office. "It's been decided," Yurovsky told him. "Tonight. . . . We have to carry out the execution tonight, execute everyone [including the servants]."

He appeared, recalled Nikulin, "to be in a state of near-panic." There was still much to do, and little time to do it. Picking up the telephone receiver, Yurovsky called the military garage. He needed a driver and a large truck, he told the person on the other end. Come to the house at midnight.

Next, he ordered a handful of guards to clear all the furniture from one of the house's cellar rooms. This, Yurovsky decided, was where the execution would take place. The small space would keep his victims confined and unable to escape, while the room's wallpaper-covered stone walls would muffle the sounds of gunshots.

As guards cleaned out the basement room, the Romanovs took their morning walk. The sun had come out, chasing away the rain clouds, and now Nicholas carried Alexei into the overgrown garden, while Anastasia and Marie ran ahead, the dogs chasing happily at their heels. As usual, Alexandra stayed inside. Olga kept her company. The two spent their time "arranging [their] medicines," making sure the jewels they'd sewn into their clothing in Tobolsk remained safely hidden.

Around one o'clock, as the family sat down to lunch, the Ekaterinburg Bolsheviks sent a telegram to Moscow. They had decided to let Lenin know their plans.

Did Lenin cable back? And if so, did he finally authorize the execution? Most historians believe he did, although he never admitted it. After all, he did not want to be linked with the children's murder. Still, as one official close to Lenin explained, "the execution of the tsar's family was needed not only to frighten, horrify and dishearten the [White Army], but also to shake up our own ranks to show them that there was no turning back, that ahead lay complete victory or complete ruin. . . . This Lenin sensed well."

Midafternoon, the Romanovs headed outside for their second walk. This time, Tatiana stayed inside with Alexandra, reading Bible verses while her mother made lace. There wasn't, reported one guard, "anything out of the ordinary with them."

That evening, just as the prisoners were sitting down to dinner, Yurovsky appeared. He ordered the kitchen boy, Leonid Sednev, to pack his things.

Where was he going? Alexandra demanded to know. Was he not returning?

Yurovsky explained that the boy's uncle wanted to take him home. This was a lie. In truth, the commandant did not want the fourteen-year-old to be among the murder victims. Leonid was taken to a house across the street.

Afterward, Yurovsky returned to his office. He still had one important decision to make: who would do the shooting? After some thought, he picked several (the precise number is unknown) of his most ruthless guards to join him and Nikulin on the execution squad. But when Yurovsky explained what was expected of them, at least two of the men balked. "[They] said they did not feel able to shoot at the girls and refused to do it," Yurovsky later recalled. These men quickly joined the kitchen boy in the house across the street. They spent the rest of the night, remembered one of their comrades, "complaining about the murders."

Around nine o'clock, the prisoners gathered for evening prayers. Afterward, Alexei was carried to his bed in his parents' room while the girls went to their own. Putting on their nightgowns, they slid beneath the sheets of their army cots.

From the drawing room came the snap and shuffle of cards as their parents played one last game of cards before bed.

In the distance, artillery echoed.

At ten-thirty, Nicholas and Alexandra went to their own room. Sitting at her corner table, the empress took a few minutes to make one last entry in her diary, noting the temperature: "15 degrees" (58 degrees Fahrenheit). Then she switched off the light and lay down beside her husband.

Darkness shrouded the rooms.

The family slept.

JULY 17

At one thirty in the morning, Yakov Yurovsky tucked a Colt pistol into his pocket. Then he went out to the landing and knocked on the prisoners' door.

A sleepy Dr. Botkin answered. What was happening? he asked.

"Everyone [must] be woken up right away," Yurovsky told him. With the White Army's approach, "the town [is] uneasy." It would be dangerous for the family to remain in the upstairs rooms. What if an artillery attack was launched? For precautionary reasons, everyone was being moved to the safety of the cellar. As for their personal belongings, added the commandant, "they [should not] bring anything with them." The guards would bring them down later.

While Dr. Botkin went to wake the others, Yurovsky returned to his office. For the next forty minutes, he waited impatiently for the prisoners to dress. Every so often, a member of the execution squad, Peter Ermakov, crept down the hall to check on their progress. Pressing his ear to the closed double doors, he could hear the family moving and talking. But what was taking so long?

On the other side of the door, the family prepared for what they believed would be an evacuation from the house. In their bedroom, the girls carefully slipped into their jewel-lined camisoles, making sure every tiny eye hook was securely fastened before donning their plain white blouses and black skirts. Alexei, too, put on an under-shirt concealing gems, while Alexandra tied a cloth belt containing several rows of large pearls around her waist. High up on her arm, she wound a length of solid gold wire.

At last the double doors opened, and the prisoners stepped out onto the landing. First came Nicholas wearing his usual soldier's tunic and military cap, his still-strong arms carrying thirteen-year-old Alexei. The boy, also dressed in a soldier's tunic, winced with every step his father took.

Alexandra came next, walking with difficulty. Rail thin, her gray hair untidy from her being awakened at such an hour, she leaned heavily on Olga's arm.

Olga, too, was "all skin and bones," remembered one of the guards. She appeared faded and sad. But not the other girls. Following behind their mother, "they smiled naturally at us in their usual cheerful manner."

Rounding out the group was Alexei Trupp, the family's footman, Ivan Kharitonov, the cook, and Anna Demidova, the parlor maid. Demidova clutched two pillows she claimed were for the empress's back. Only the captives knew the truth—buried deep within the cushion's feathers lay two boxes containing even more jewels.

Yurovsky inspected the prisoners. "They still did not imagine anything of what was in store for them," he later recalled. Added one of the guards, "None of the members of the imperial family asked . . . any questions. . . . There were no tears, no sobbing either."

Yurovsky, along with the other men, steered the group toward the narrow stairs leading to the ground floor. At that moment, the family's dogs—Joy, Jemmy, and Ortipo—scampered after them. Wiggling and whining, they begged to come along.

No dogs, Yurovsky instructed.

But Anastasia refused to leave Jemmy behind. Although the dog had been a gift to Tatiana from a family friend, he'd become Anastasia's constant companion during their captivity. She couldn't abandon him now. Scooping up the little King Charles spaniel, she hugged him to her chest.

Not wanting to create a scene and alarm the Romanovs, the commandant ignored Anastasia's disobedience and let her take the dog. He led them down the stairs.

At the bottom, Nicholas turned to the others. "Well, we're going to get out of this place," he said.

Yurovsky pushed open the door, and the prisoners filed out into the early-morning darkness. For the first time in months, they felt the cool night breeze tickling their cheeks. Overhead, stars twinkled like a thousand watching eyes in the dark Siberian sky.

Across the sloping courtyard at the corner of the house lay an open door, and behind it, more steps leading into a labyrinth-like cellar. Down they went, twenty-three steps—one for every year of Nicholas's ill-fated reign. At the bottom, Yurovsky took them through a series of hallways toward a storeroom at the opposite end of the house. Opening another set of double doors, he waved them inside.

The space—just eleven by thirteen feet—was lit by a single naked lightbulb hanging from the low ceiling. A heavy iron grille barred the room's only window, and a piece of wood had been nailed over it from the inside. Faded wallpaper covered the walls, and the yellow painted floor was without rugs. There was no furniture.

"What, there isn't even a chair?" said Alexandra. "One isn't even allowed to sit down?"

Ignoring her haughty tone, Yurovsky turned to one of the guards. He asked for chairs to be brought down.

Grumbling under his breath, the guard obeyed, returning minutes later with two straight-back chairs. Alexandra lowered herself onto one while Nicholas gently settled his son on the other.

The maid, Anna Demidova, hurried over. She tucked the pillows she'd been carrying behind the empress's bony back.

Now Yurovsky began giving instructions. "Please, you stand here," he said, spreading the group against the wall. "And you here . . . that's it, in a row."

When he finished, there were two rows: Nicholas stood next to his son's chair in the front, while Alexandra sat in her own chair on the other side of the boy. The girls—Anastasia still clutching the dog—stood behind their mother, while Dr. Botkin and the servants stood behind Alexei and the tsar.

Yurovsky looked them over. "They [still] had no idea what was taking place," he later recalled. Then, lying yet again, he asked the prisoners to wait there until the truck taking them to safety arrived. No one was to speak. He stepped from the room, closing the door behind him.

From outside came the rumble of a truck—the one Yurovsky had ordered earlier—pulling into the courtyard. Did the family believe it had come to take them from the house? Disobeying the commandant's order, Alexandra whispered something in English to her daughters.

The cellar door reopened. There stood Yurovsky. Behind him, crowding into the room, came the others.

Nicholas, obviously thinking this motley group was a special detachment sent to escort them to safety, took a step forward.

And Yurovsky moved farther into the room. In his left hand, he clutched a piece of paper. He asked the prisoners to stand.

Unable to obey, Alexei remained seated. Alexandra, "with a flash of anger in her eyes," according to one squad member, pulled herself to her feet.

Yurovsky began reading from the paper: "In light of the fact that your relatives in Europe [are] continuing their aggression against Soviet Russia [it] has been decreed that [you are] to be shot."

"Lord, oh, my God!" stammered Nicholas. He turned to his family. "Oh, my God! What is this?"

"So we're not going to be taken anywhere?" cried Dr. Botkin.

"I can't understand you," said Nicholas. "Read it again, please." Yurovsky did.

"What?" Nicholas cried again. "What?"

Yurovsky let go of the paper. As it fluttered to the floor, he jerked the Colt pistol from his pocket. "This!" he said. He shot the tsar.

Nicholas crumpled to the floor just as the other men raised their guns and fired. Alexandra died as she tried to cross herself. Dr. Botkin, Trupp, and Kharitonov also died instantly.

But the others were still alive. Incredibly, bullets aimed directly at both the girls' and Alexei's chests merely bounced off and "jumped about the room like hail," remembered Yurovsky. It was the jewels sewn into camisoles and T-shirt. They had unwittingly turned the garments into bulletproof vests.

As the men shot, Alexei—unable to get up and run—gripped his chair in terror. In the chaos, it toppled over, flinging the boy to the floor. He moaned and clutched his father's arm. Minutes later, Yurovsky shot him in the head.

Meanwhile, the others dropped to the floor, instinctively trying to protect themselves. Crawling through the thick cloud of gun smoke that now filled the room, they searched frantically for a way out. Only their outlines could be seen, and the men began firing randomly at anything that moved. The bullets ripped into the wallpaper, "sending dust flying in the air and bullets flying about the room," remembered one squad member.

Olga and Tatiana, arms around each other, huddled in a corner. Bullets soon took their lives.

In another corner, Anastasia and Marie pressed themselves together. Both girls screamed for their mother. The murderers moved forward. They slashed at the "Little Pair" with bayonets before silencing them both with gunshots.

Anna Demidova was the last to die.

Then an eerie quiet settled over the room. The imperial family lay still. Calmly, Yurovsky checked for pulses. Then the men wrapped the bodies in sheets taken from the girls' army cots, and carried them up the stairs to the waiting truck. That's when someone found the body of Anastasia's little dog. They tossed it into the truck, too.

Under cover of darkness, they headed for Koptyaki Forest.

Chapter Eighteen
"The World Will Never Know What Has Become of Them"

"But the Children—the Children!"

Eight days later, on July 25, 1918, the White Army captured Ekaterinburg, and a group of officers raced to the House of Special Purpose to free the tsar and his family. What they found was an empty house, save a few remnants that lay scattered about the prisoners' rooms—thimbles, icons, a jewelry box covered in lilac silk, an ivory hairbrush with the initials A.F. carved on its handle. On a small side table sat a box of dominoes, along with a heavily underlined prayer book titled *Patience in Suffering*. Next to the fireplace sat a wheelchair.

But it was a room in the cellar that shook the officers. Although scrubbed clean, the wooden floor still showed the nicks and gouges made by bullets and bayonets; the walls were pocked with holes; and smears of dried blood could be seen on the baseboards. It was obvious something awful had happened here.

Three day after the murders, Bolshevik officials in Ekaterinburg had bluntly and publicly announced: "The . . . Soviet passed a resolution to execute Nicholas Romanov and carried it out on July 16." But they did not confess to killing the rest of the family. Instead, they claimed Alexandra and the children had been "sent to a safe place." That's because the Bolsheviks, afraid of losing the public's support, did not want to admit to murdering innocent children and servants. Without any bodies to contradict their lie, "the world will never know what has become of them," remarked one official.

In truth, it didn't appear as if most Russians cared. They "received the news [of Nicholas's death] with amazing indifference," reported British journalist Bruce Lockhart. And rumors that the rest of the family had been killed didn't elicit much emotion either. Only some former noblemen mourned. Admitted a tearful General Brusilov, he prayed each night for the "missing Romanovs."

Announcement made, Bolshevik officials in Ekaterinburg fled before the White Army could capture them. Yurovsky skipped town, too. He took with him a black leather suitcase full of diamonds, rubies, sapphires, and pearls—jewels he'd discovered hidden in both the children's and empress's clothing while disposing of their bodies. He also loaded up seven trunks of the family's belongings, including Nicholas's diaries and letters, as well as their photograph albums. Then he headed to Moscow, where, days later, he made a full report to high-ranking Bolsheviks. The rest of the Romanovs' belongings were hastily crated by the remaining guards and sent to the capital by train just hours before Ekaterinburg fell.

Without witnesses or evidence, White officers did not know what to believe. Desperate to learn the truth, they launched an investigation. And they put a hard-nosed detective named Nicholas Sokolov in charge. Sokolov did not doubt that an assassination had taken place in the cellar. But had everyone been killed? Or was it possible, as Bolsheviks claimed, that some members of the family had survived? The only way to know for sure was to find their bodies.

The following spring, after the snows had melted, the detective turned his attention to Koptyaki Forest. Not only had local peasants reported seeing men in the woods around the time of the murders, but deep ruts made by a truck still showed in the dirt path that ran through the woods. Following these tracks, Sokolov came to the mine shafts Yurovsky had scoped out the previous summer.

Around the surface hole of the deepest one were hundreds of boot prints. Close by, he found evidence of two bonfires. Convinced he'd found the place where the bodies had been dumped, he ordered the water siphoned from the pit. He began to excavate.

Helping with this grim job were Sydney Gibbes and Pierre Gilliard. Having rushed back to Ekaterinburg when the city fell, the men now offered to help identify anything Sokolov might find at the site.

Among the dozens of objects discovered were a child's military belt buckle identified by the tutors as belonging to Alexei; an emerald cross worn by Alexandra; the metal case Nicholas always carried his wife's picture in; Dr. Botkin's glasses and the upper plate of his dentures; shoe buckles like the kind worn by the grand duchesses; and remnants of six sets of corsets. There were also some bone fragments.

But there were no bodies.

This tragic evidence, however, convinced Sokolov that the entire family had been killed. Their bodies, he hypothesized, had been burned and dissolved with sulfuric acid, and the ashes tossed into the mine shaft.

"But the children—the children!" cried Pierre Gilliard when he heard the detective's verdict. They couldn't *all* be dead, could they? "I could not believe it," he said. "My whole being revolted at the idea."

I AM ANASTASIA . . . AND ALEXEI . . . AND MARIE

Without bodies, rumors of escape swirled.

Suddenly, the imperial family was spotted everywhere—in the Crimea, Japan, even America. But the most frequently sighted family members were Alexei, Anastasia, and Marie. Fascinated by tales of miraculous survival, the public claimed to have seen the youngest Romanovs in hospitals, prisons, peasant huts, and remote monasteries. One day, Anastasia was spied strolling down Nevsky Prospect in Petrograd; the next, she was glimpsed on a streetcar in Moscow.

It wasn't long before people began claiming to *be* the imperial children. The first Anastasia pretender appeared in Siberia in 1920, but was quickly exposed. Others stepped forward to take her place. Over the years, more than two hundred people, most saying they were Marie or Alexei, claimed they'd escaped the massacre in the cellar.

But had they?

Only time would tell.

AFTER THE STORM

After overthrowing their tsar, smashing two systems of government, and launching the country into what would be three years of civil war, had Russians improved their lives? Hardly. By 1920, the Bolsheviks—who had recently changed their official name to the Communist Party—were beginning to establish policies that would eventually oversee every aspect of a citizen's daily life. Citizens became subject to "labor conscription"; that is, they had to work where, when, and at what the government told them. Factories came under the control of government managers, while in the countryside Red troops seized peasant crops and livestock at gunpoint. Shortages continued, and practically everything was rationed—food, clothing, even books and tobacco. In the cities, the government doled out food in canteens. Only those registered by the state to eat in

Выходъ Его Императорскаго Величества Государя Императора на балконъ Зимняго дворца къ народу послѣ молебствія 20-г Іюля 1914 г.

Standing on a balcony of the Winter Palace the day he declared war in 1914, Nicholas bows his head emotionally as the crowd below bursts into the national anthem.

ROMANOV COLLECTION, BEINECKE RARE BOOK AND MANUSCRIPT LIBRARY, YALE UNIVERSITY

Russian troops stand in a trench on the Eastern Front, 1915. Since tsarist generals scorned trench warfare, they never learned the technological art of properly constructing them. Nothing more than holes in the ground, Russian trenches constantly filled with water while unsupported dirt walls crumbled under artillery bombardment. The primitive nature of these trenches was a major cause of Russia's huge loss of life.

LIBRARY OF CONGRESS

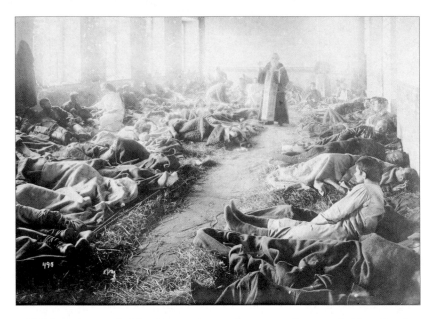

Raising his cross in blessing, a priest walks among the wounded in a Russian field hospital, 1915. While officers recuperated in mansions that had been converted into hospitals, ordinary soldiers were not so lucky. Recalled one war observer, "I went around several wards, rooms in vacated houses where the sick and wounded lay on the floor, on straw, dressed, unwashed and covered in blood." Because of this, diseases such as cholera, typhoid, and dysentery decimated Russian troops even further.

Russian dead. The number of the country's casualties was staggering—more than three million by 1917.

A peasant woman mourns the death of her soldier son, 1916.

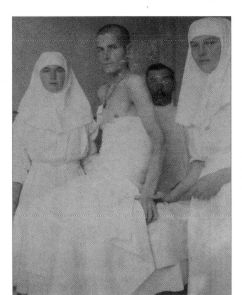

Olga (left) and Tatiana in their nurses' uniforms, ministering to wounded officers.

Marie (left) and Anastasia pose with a group of recovering officers in their hospital, c. 1915.

Alexei (in uniform) presides over a military luncheon at Stavka in 1916. Third from the left sits Nicholas. Between him and Alexei is the deposed, but still consulted Nicholasha.

Rasputin at his full powers, looking both commanding and controlling, c. 1915.

This snapshot of an imperious Alexandra was taken in 1916 when the reins of government were firmly in her hands.

ROMANOV COLLECTION, BEINECKE RARE BOOK AND MANUSCRIPT LIBRARY, YALE UNIVERSITY

This 1916 cartoon depicts Rasputin as an evil puppet master, pulling both Nicholas's and Alexandra's strings.

THE STATE ARCHIVES OF THE RUSSIAN FEDERATION, MOSCOW

Prince Felix Yusupov, the mastermind behind Rasputin's murder, c. 1915.

A photograph of Rasputin's battered corpse after being pulled from the Neva River three days after the murder.

Somber, hungry Petrograd citizens line up outside a bakery for bread, c. 1915.

Carrying a red banner reading "Long Live the Council of Workmen's and Soldiers' Deputies," a group of mostly women and children, along with former tsarist soldiers, marches through the streets of St. Petersburg in February 1917.

LIBRARY OF CONGRESS

Alexander Kerensky in 1917. Just thirty-six years old, he took on the hard task of maintaining a link between the Provisional Government and the Petrograd Soviet.

LIBRARY OF CONGRESS

The Petrograd Soviet of Workers' and Soliders' Deputies meets in the Tauride Palace, February 1917.

COURTESY OF THE AUTHOR

After Nicholas's abdication, citizens jubilantly dismantled tsarist symbols in and around cities. Here children gaze at the giant bronze head of Alexander III—Nicholas's father—after crowds pulled it off the statue.

Nicholas poses for a photograph aboard the imperial train, site of his eventual abdication.

PART IV: FINAL DAYS

Enthusiastic crowds welcome Lenin back to Petrograd, April 1917.

Nicholas under guard at Tsarskoe Selo, 1917.

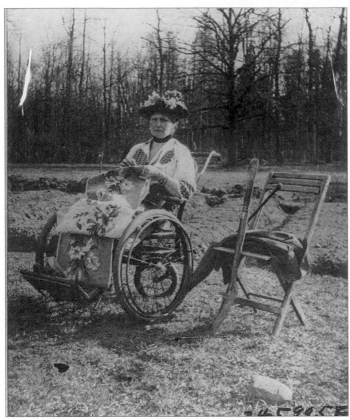

Alexandra sits in her wheelchair while watching her family (not pictured) working in the garden at Tsarskoe Selo, 1917.

From left to right: Olga, Alexei, Anastasia (holding Jemmy in her lap), and Tatiana resting after gardening in May 1917.

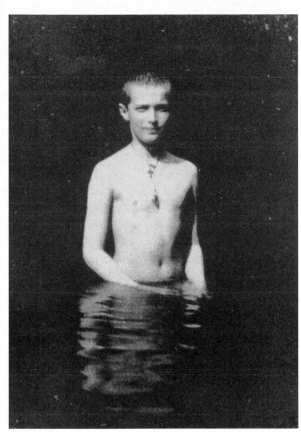

Alexei, just hours before the family's removal from Tsarskoe Selo, takes one last swim in the estate's lake, August 1917.

Forces of the Provisional Government fire on Bolshevik rioters, necessitating their lying down in the street to avoid being shot, July 1917.

The Governor's Mansion in Tobolsk, where the Romanovs were imprisoned. This picture was taken before the tall wooden fence was built, although guards can be seen patrolling the street. From the balcony, the family could sit and wave to the passersby below.

Perched on the platform that Nicholas built on the roof of the greenhouse in Tobolsk are (from left to right): Olga, Anastasia, Nicholas, Alexei, and Tatiana. Marie is standing.

Штурм зимнего дворца 25 октября 1917 г.

This retouched photograph shows a column of Bolshevik soldiers seizing the Winter Palace after the Provisional Government's surrender.

The House of Special Purpose surrounded by its fence, which would later be extended to the house's eaves.

White Army troops move through the forests of Siberia in January 1918.

The man who planned and carried out the murder of the Romanovs, Yakov Yurovsky, c. 1920.

A soldier of the Red Army captured by the Whites. He confesses he is a Communist and is bound to a stake to be shot.

Captured by White Troops, a soldier of the Red Army is tied to a stake after confessing that he is a Communist. He would later be shot.

A photograph of the cellar room, taken after the family was killed, shows bullet holes and bayonet scars in the walls and floor.

Investigators in Koptyaki Forest search at the mine site. Sheets were laid out to receive bodies that were never found.

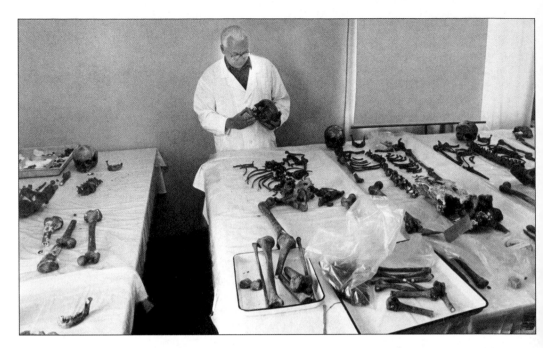

Skeletons of the Romanovs (Nicholas, Alexandra, and three of the girls) being examined by a forensic scientist in Ekaterinburg, 1992.

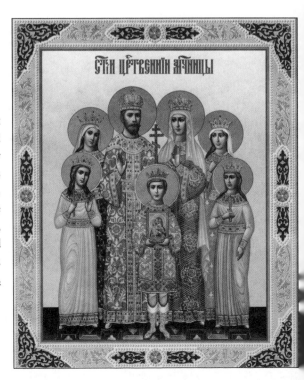

In 2000, the Orthodox Church in Russia declared Nicholas II and his family saints. This holy icon shows them together and haloed. Alexei himself holds the icon of Our Lady of Kazan, one of the most revered icons in Russian history.

these canteens were allowed to line up for a meal, if one could call it that. A ladleful of gruel was the usual fare. But even this meager meal was hard to come by. People spent hours each day searching for a meal, as well as the goods their ration coupons promised. Many came up empty-handed, their bellies still grumbling.

Like food, fuel was also in short supply. To survive the freezing winters, city dwellers ripped up wooden houses and fences for firewood. They chopped down the trees in city parks and burned their own furniture and books. Electricity was rationed. In Petrograd, the city was divided into sectors. Because of the power shortage, each sector took its turn having its lights turned on in the evening. The rest of the time, citizens sat in the shadowy darkness of candles or homemade lamps. Streetlights didn't work. Trams didn't run. At times, the cities felt like ghost towns.

"The houses looked like broken old tombs upon neglected and forgotten cemeteries," wrote one Petrograd citizen. "The people walked about [the city] like living corpses; the shortage[s] . . . slowly sapping [it]; grim death was clutching at its heart."

So bad did things become that in March 1921, thousands of sailors—once the most enthusiastic supporters of the Bolsheviks—openly rebelled against Communist authorities. Disillusioned by the treatment workers and peasants had received under Lenin's dictatorship, they took to the streets, demanding freedoms the soviet government had taken away: free elections, free speech, freedom of the press, free trade unions, and freedom for the peasants to harvest their own land for their own benefit.

Lenin refused to let anyone challenge soviet power. Moving the Red Army against the sailors, he launched a bloody attack lasting several days. When it was over, thousands of sailors lay dead; hundreds more were executed later.

Always a realist, Lenin saw the rebellion as a sign of a sick society. And he began to wonder if the soviet victory had not in fact betrayed Marx's vision of a classless utopia. Had he simply replaced the tsar's autocracy with a government that was just as suppressive of the common people? Far from "withering away" as Marx had hoped, the soviet government had grown, extending a totalitarian control over every aspect of an individual's life.

Additionally, Lenin worried about who would succeed him when he died. Although he was just fifty-one years old, his health was waning; he suffered the first of three strokes in May 1922. Looking around at the soviet leadership, he was especially concerned about Joseph Stalin, a man who held the important post of general secretary of the Communist Party. In Stalin, Lenin saw a man whose thirst for power endangered everything for which Lenin had fought. "Comrade Stalin . . . has concentrated in his hands unbounded power," Lenin warned, "and I am not sure whether he will always know how to use this power cautiously enough."

But Lenin died on January 21, 1924, and Stalin seized power. He immediately embarked on what he called a purge, eliminating all his old Bolshevik friends and rivals by exile, execution, or assassination. Now Soviet Russia would rest entirely in the hands of a man ruthlessly bent on making his country a global power—no matter what the cost in lives and freedom. For the next sixty-seven years, until communism fell in 1991, the Russian people would find themselves trapped, once again, by a totalitarian government—politically voiceless, and ruled by repression, fear, and iron-fisted control.

Beyond the Palace Gates:
Life Under Lenin

What was a typical day under Lenin's rule like? In his diary, a Petrograd professor named Vasily Vodovozov describes one:

3 December 1920

I shall describe my day—not because the minor details are of interest in themselves but because they are typical of the lives of nearly everyone—with the exception of a few bosses.

Today I got up at 9 a.m. There is no point getting up before since it is dark and the house lights are not working. There is a shortage of fuel. . . . I drank some coffee (made from oats) without milk or sugar, of course, and ate a piece of bread from a loaf bought two weeks ago. . . . By eleven I was ready to go out. But after such a breakfast I was still hungry and decided to eat in the vegetarian canteen. It is frightfully expensive but the only place in Petrograd I know where I can eat . . . without registration or the permission of some commissar. It turned out the canteen was closed . . . so I went on to the Third Petrograd University, in fact now closed as a university but where there is still a cafeteria in which I am registered to eat. . . . But here too I had no luck: there was a long [line] of hopeful eaters, tedium and vexation written on their faces; the [line] was not moving at all. . . . Anyone reading this . . . may suppose that these people were expecting a banquet. But the whole meal was a single dish—usually a thin soup with a potato or cabbage in it. There is no question of any meat. Only the privileged few ever get that—

i.e., the people who work in the kitchen. . . . There was no choice but to go to work hungry. . . . By 2 p.m. I had reached [my workplace] by foot [the trams were typically not running for lack of fuel]. I stayed for half an hour and then went to the University, where there was supposed to be a ration of cabbage handed out at 3 p.m. . . . But again I was out of luck: it turned out that the cabbage had not been delivered and would be given out tomorrow. And not to professors but only to students. I also found out there would be no bread ration for a week: some people said that all the bread had already been given out to the Communists who run all the committees. . . . I went back to the vegetarian canteen with the hope of eating. Again out of luck: all the food was gone. . . . From there I went back home at 5 p.m. And there I had my first piece of luck of the day: the lights in our sector were switched on. That gave me one precious hour to read—the first hour of the day free from running around for meals, bread, or cabbage. At six I went to my [neighbors'] to eat (at last!), and came back to write these lines. At nine it went dark. . . . I lit a candle . . . drank tea . . . and at eleven went to bed.

THE EARTH REVEALS ITS SECRETS

In 1976, Ekaterinburg historian Alexander Avdonin and Moscow filmmaker Geli Ryabov went in search of the Romanov bodies. "We wanted to do this in order to restore one of the pages of our [Russian] history," explained Avdonin. "We had to look for them." Not only did the men scour archives and historical documents for clues to the bodies' whereabouts, they scoured Koptyaki Forest, too. Three years later, in May 1979, they found what they were looking for—a shallow grave located just four and a half miles from the abandoned mine shaft that had been excavated so many years earlier. "It was frightening! It was frightening!" confessed Avdonin. "All my life I had searched for this. . . . And then, when we first started [digging], I thought to myself, 'Let me find nothing.'"

They unearthed nine skeletons.

But the men were unable to tell anyone what they'd found. The family's murder had long been a forbidden topic, the government clamping down on anyone who discussed the Romanovs. "We swore an oath," recalled Avdonin, "that we would never talk about this until circumstances in our country changed." So the men re-buried their find. And waited.

A decade passed, and the Communist hold in Russia crumbled. Finally, Avdonin and Ryabov's secret could be revealed. In 1991, the Russian government officially opened the grave. Experts from America and Britain were called in to help with identification, and DNA tests were run on the skeletons. The results were conclusive. The remains were those of the Romanovs and their servants.

In a poignant twist, this same series of tests also identified one of the grand duchesses as being a carrier of hemophilia. Unfortunately, while DNA testing could establish that a biologically related family consisting of a father, a mother, and three daughters had been found, it could not identify them more specifically. That is, it could not determine which bones belonged to which daughter. The name of the carrier remains a mystery.

Another mystery also remained. Only five sets of Romanov skeletons had been found. Two remained missing. Scientists identified the missing family members as Alexei, and either Anastasia or Marie. This last discovery fueled speculation. Were the stories true? Had some of the children survived?

FINAL RESTING PLACE

Meanwhile, the Russian government wrestled with what to do with the remains. Most agreed they should be buried in the Cathedral of Saints Peter and Paul in St. Petersburg, where all tsars since Peter the Great had been buried. But there were some touchy issues to sort out first. Should the whole family be interred together? Traditionally, only the tsar and his wife were given tombs in the central part of the cathedral, while children were relegated to spots farther back. And what about the Romanovs' loyal servants? Nonroyals had never been permitted burial in the cathedral before. Then there was the problem of the missing girl. Was she Anastasia or Marie?

During DNA testing, a controversy had emerged. The Russian scientific team insisted the skeleton in their possession belonged to Anastasia, while the American team concluded it was Marie's. "All the skeletons appear to be too tall to be Anastasia," reported Dr. William Maples, a forensic anthropologist from the University of Florida. Besides, all the other female bones showed "completed growth." But Anastasia was just seventeen at the time of the murders. Her bones would have still been growing. It was compelling evidence, but Russian scientists ignored it. The skeleton in their possession, they declared, belonged to Anastasia.

On July 17, 1998—the eightieth anniversary of the murders— nine miniature coffins were carried into the chapel. Across the Neva River at the Winter Palace, flags flew at half-mast, and boughs of cypress adorned the bridge's iron railings. Inside the cathedral, a choir chanted solemnly while incense from the priest's censers curled toward the ceiling. The servants' coffins were lowered into the vault first—Trupp, Kharitonov, Demidova, and Dr. Botkin. Next came the grand duchesses Olga and Tatiana, and one coffin said by the Russians to contain Anastasia's remains. With music swelling, Alexandra's casket joined her daughters'. Then, as Russia's last tsar was laid to rest, the fortress fired a nineteen-round salute (reduced from the traditional twenty-one because Nicholas had died an abdicated tsar). Some of the Romanovs had finally come home. But where were the two missing children?

FAMILY OF SAINTS

At the same time, the Orthodox Church in Russia was wrestling with a question of its own: should the Romanovs be made saints? Church officials felt pressured to make a decision. Since communism's fall, increasing numbers of Russians were making their way to Ekaterinburg to worship at the site of the Ipatiev house. Even though the structure had been torn down decades earlier, people still knelt on the barren ground, praying to the imperial family for help and guidance. This worship was aided by dozens of Romanov icons that were created when the Orthodox Church Outside of Russia canonized the family as saints a decade earlier.

A separate branch of the Orthodox Church established by Russian emigrés sympathetic to the monarchy, the Orthodox Church Outside of Russia viewed Nicholas through a rosy lens. Largely ignoring his anti-Semitism, poor leadership, and brutal suppression of his subjects, church leaders focused on his piety and devotion to family. And they saw the family's brutal murders as a sort of holy cleansing—the moment when the Romanovs transcended all their earthly flaws and became divine. For these reasons, the Orthodox Church Outside of Russia declared the family "martyred saints." The highest designation of sainthood, martyred saints are those who have been killed specifically because of their faith, and refuse— even after torture and threat of death—to renounce that faith.

But the Orthodox Church *in* Russia was not willing to simply accept this decision. Instead, in 1991, they formed their own commission to study the issue. Focusing their investigation on Nicholas's reign, commission members looked closely at the events leading up to the revolutions. A year later, they concluded that neither Nicholas nor his family deserved sainthood. "His life, his actions . . . all of this is regarded by the Church and Society in a very ambivalent way," explained one church leader.

But the commission did not stop looking. Next they focused on the family's days in captivity. Did they suffer piously without struggle? The Church believed they had. "[Nicholas] could have chosen a safe and . . . peaceful life abroad, but he did not do this, desiring to suffer along with Russia," the commission wrote. "He did nothing to improve his situation, submissively resigning himself to fate."

While this statement stretched the truth—Nicholas had been eager to escape to England—it did allow the church a basis for sainthood. But it still wasn't enough. So the commission began to look for evidence of miracles. Could the family be credited with any? Investigations turned up dozens of Russians claiming to have been cured of illnesses after praying at the Ipatiev house site. One person even asserted that Grand Duchess Marie had materialized with a cup of health-restoring tea! But most convincing of all were stories of an icon of Nicholas that many claimed seeped sweet-smelling myrrh whenever the faithful knelt before it.

Given all this, the commission finally declared the family saints in 2000. But it did not designate them as martyred saints as had the Orthodox Church Outside of Russia. Instead, it gave them the lowest designation of sainthood—"passion bearers"—persons who simply accept their fate piously and submissively. While the Orthodox Church in Russia did consider sainthood for Dr. Botkin and the other servants who died beside the Romanovs, they ultimately decided against it because, as the commission wrote, the four were simply "doing their moral duty by remaining with the Imperial Family." It should be noted that the Orthodox Church Outside of Russia *did* canonize all four servants.

At the Ipatiev house site a wooden cross was quickly erected until money could be raised to build a cathedral there. The Church on the Blood, as it is called, opened its doors just two years later. Meanwhile, close to the site where the bodies were found, the Monastery of the Holy Imperial Passion Bearers sprang up. In memory of the tsar and his family, the monks planted thousands of white lilies—a church symbol of resurrection. These days they sway in the summer breeze, perfuming the air with their thick scent. In front of these lilies stand seven wooden churches. Built in the Russian style, each with its own gold cupola and green roof, they are individual shrines, one for each of the now haloed Romanovs.

FINAL SECRETS

On a warm afternoon in July 2007, Sergei Plotnikov was searching Koptyaki Forest not far from the Romanovs' grave site when he stumbled on a small hollow covered with nettles. Using a large, corkscrew-like instrument, Plotnikov—an amateur historian who often spent his weekends searching for the missing imperial children—poked deep beneath the soil's surface. There was a crunching sound. Plotnikov started to dig. Soon he uncovered a pile of bone fragments. DNA tests run on them proved they were the remains of Alexei and one of his sisters. "My heart leaped with joy," Plotnikov said of his discovery. "I knew the Romanov children would finally be reunited with their family."

But as of this writing, the remains of the last two Romanovs have yet to be buried. Instead, they lie in a cardboard box in Moscow's State Archive of the Russian Federation, waiting for the day when all seven Romanovs will once again be together; as Nicholas called them, "a small family circle."

ACKNOWLEDGMENTS

In Russian it's *spasibo*. In English, it's thank you. In either language, I am immensely grateful to the peerless Anne Schwartz for her inspiration and encouragement (not to mention her patience and persistence), as well as to the talented Rachael Cole for her extraordinary book design. Thanks also to everyone at Random House who helped this project come together: Lee Wade, Stephanie Pitts, Adrienne Waintraub, and Colleen Fellingham.

I am also indebted to fellow writer Eugene Yelchin for taking precious time away from his own manuscript to read and comment on mine. He grew up in the former Soviet Union, and his suggestions were not only insightful, but also invaluable.

Special thanks to Sarah Miller (author, librarian, and fellow Romanov geek) for "saving my bacon" in so many ways, and to Laura Mabee for coming to my rescue with that elusive 1903 menu.

Hooray to Holly Pribble for once again aiding me with her artistic skills; cheers to my writing friends Penny Blubaugh, Stephanie Hemphill, and Karen Blumenthal for listening, advising, and occasionally consoling; and hugs to Eric Rohmann, my first, most trusted reader.

Thanks to the following individuals and institutions for their help in obtaining images, documents, and other important resources: Agata Rukowska, picture library assistant at the Royal Collection Trust; Beth Remak-Honnef, head of Special Collections and Archives, University of California, Santa Cruz; Anne Marie Menta, library service assistant for Romanov materials at the Beinecke Rare Book and Manuscript Library of Yale University; Stephanie Stewart, assistant archivist at the Hoover Institution Library and Archives at Stanford University; Susan Halpert, reference librarian at the Houghton Library of Harvard University; and the reference librarians at the State Archive of the Russian Federation and the Prints and Photographs Division at the Library of Congress.

Finally, I owe a huge debt of gratitude to Dr. Mark D. Steinberg, professor of Russian, East European, and Eurasian studies at the University of Illinois at Urbana-Champaign, who not only meticulously vetted the manuscript, but also answered my endless questions with patience and enthusiasm, provided invaluable insight into revolutionary Russia, and challenged my conventional images of Nicholas and Alexandra by pointing me in the direction of additional historical documents. *Spasibo!*

BIBLIOGRAPHY

QUESTIONS AND ANSWERS

Three years ago, I set out to discover the true story of what happened to Russia's last imperial family. I was aware of the facts surrounding their murder. I knew about their bodies' discovery and the results of DNA testing. But the facts did not tell the whole tale. I suspected there was more. After some reading and research, I came to realize, more than anything, that I needed to find the answers to the question that kept nagging me: *How did this happen?* How did this rich, splendidly privileged, and, yes, beautiful family related by blood or marriage to almost every royal house in Europe end up in that Siberian cellar? Something had gone terribly wrong. But what? What forces were at work? What personalities? And was there really nothing Nicholas or Alexandra could have done to change their fate?

These were the questions I set out to answer. But doing so, I realized, would require a wider lens. I would need to look beyond the Romanovs and their fairy-tale existence and examine the lives of lower-class Russians—peasants and workers, revolutionaries and soldiers. The result? A book that is essentially three stories in one. The first is an intimate look at the Romanovs themselves. The second follows the sweep of revolution from the workers' strikes of 1905 to Lenin's rise to power in November 1917. And the third— conveyed in their own words—is the personal stories of the men and women whose struggle for a better life directly affected the course of the Romanovs' lives.

The following bibliography and quote sources reflect just a small portion of the material used to inform my understanding of those three stories. I have bombarded Russian scholars with endless questions; looked at thousands of photographs; scoured dozens of newspapers on microfilm, in bound volumes, and online; and read more Karl Marx than I ever thought possible. With the help of the archivists at both the State Archive of the Russian Federation (GARF) and Harvard's Houghton Library, I've had access to original sources. And in August 2012, I traveled to Russia, where I followed in the Romanovs' footsteps, wandering the shady paths of Tsarskoe Selo and traipsing through the hallways of the Alexander Palace; visiting Rasputin's last apartment; exploring workers' neighborhoods, Lenin's headquarters, and the dark, dank jail cells of the Peter and Paul Fortress. All this and more has significantly contributed to the work you've just read.

PRIMARY SOURCES

The heart of all research is the firsthand accounts and eyewitness testimonies of those who lived through an historical event. For almost seventy-five years, the only primary material we had about the imperial family came from the memoirs of the Russian nobility who had fled the country after Lenin's rise to power. Many of these reminiscences were sympathetic, painting an overly rosy picture of the imperial family. But in 1991, with the collapse of the Soviet Union, all that changed. Diaries, letters, and other documents believed to have been destroyed began emerging from archives and museums. Now we can read Alexei's last diary entries for ourselves, delve into Nicholas's and Alexandra's letters, discover Olga's poetry. More surprising, we can hear directly from ordinary Russians who encountered the family in their final months—Yurovsky's chilling account of the murders; statements from guards; depositions from priests and cleaning women. Certainly, some accounts, especially those of the family's jailers, contradict one another. And because most were originally written in Russian or French, they vary by translator. For this reason, more than one version of the same source is occasionally listed. I have chosen to use the more accessible quote, or the pithier, more poignant translation. It should also be noted that the Romanovs themselves used English when writing to each other. Thus their colorful, sometimes awkward prose is not a creative translation, but exactly how they wrote. Additionally, in citations of letters or diary entries, you will notice two dates. The first is the "old-style" Julian calendar date cited by its creator. The second is the "new-style" Georgian calendar date coinciding with this book's text.

Alexander, Grand Duke of Russia. *Once a Grand Duke*. Garden City, NY: Garden City, 1932.

Alexandra, Empress of Russia. *The Letters of the Tsaritsa to the Tsar, 1914–16*. London: Duckworth, 1923.

Botkin, Gleb. *The Real Romanovs*. New York: Revell, 1931.

Buchanan, Meriel. *The Dissolution of an Empire*. London: John Murray, 1932.

Buchanan, Sir George. *My Mission to Russia and Other Diplomatic Memories*. 2 volumes. Boston: Little, Brown, 1923.

Bulygin, Paul, and Alexander Kerensky. *The Murder of the Romanovs*. London: Hutchinson, 1935.

Buxhoeveden, Baroness Sophie. *Left Behind: Fourteen Months in Siberia During the Revolution*. London: Longmans, Green, 1929.

———. *The Life and Tragedy of Alexandra Feodorovna, Empress of Russia*. London: Longmans, Green, 1928.

Bykov, P. M. *The Last Days of Tsardom*. London: Martin Lawrence, 1934.

"Czar Has Another Daughter." *The New York Times*, 18 June 1901.

Dehn, Lili. *The Real Tsaritsa*. London: Thornton Butterworth, 1922.

de Stoeckl, Agnes. *Not All Vanity*. London: John Murray, 1951.

Elchaninov, Major-General Andrei. *The Tsar and His People*. London: Hodder & Stoughton, 1914.

Gautier, Théophile. "A Ball at the Winter Palace" in *Romantic Castles and Palaces as Seen and Described by Famous Writers*. Edited and translated by Esther Singleton. New York: Dodd, Mead, 1901.

Gilliard, Pierre. *Thirteen Years at the Russian Court*. Translated by F. Appleby Holt. New York: Doran, 1921.

Goldman, Emma. *My Disillusionment in Russia*. Garden City, NY: Doubleday, Page, 1923.

Gorky, Maxim. *Autobiography of Maxim Gorky*. Translated by Isidor Schneider. Amsterdam: Fredonia Books, 2001.

Gudvan, A. M. "Essays on the History of the Movement of Sales-Clerical Workers in Russia" (1925) in *The Russian Worker: Life and Labor Under the Tsarist Regime*. Edited by Victoria E. Bonnell. Berkeley: University of California Press, 1983.

Halliburton, Richard. *Seven League Boots*. Garden City, NY: Garden City, 1942.

(Ilidor) Trufanoff, Sergei. *The Mad Monk of Russia*. New York: Century, 1918.

Kanatchikov, Semën Ivanovich. *A Radical Worker in Tsarist Russia: The Autobiography of Semën Ivanovich Kanatchikov*. Edited and translated by Reginald E. Zelnik. Palo Alto, CA: Stanford University Press, 1986.

Kerensky, Alexander. *The Crucifixion of Liberty*. New York: Day, 1934.

Khrustalev, Vladimir M., and Vladimir A. Kozlov. *The Last Diary of Tsarista Alexandra*. New Haven, CT: Yale University Press, 1997.

Knox, Alfred. *With the Russian Army, 1914–1917*. 2 volumes. London: Hutchinson & Company, 1921.

Kokovtsov, Count Vladimir N. *Out of My Past: The Memoirs of Count Kokovtsov*. Edited by H. H. Fisher. Palo Alto, CA: Stanford University Press, 1935.

Korolenko, Vladimir. "Kishineff: The Medieval Outbreak Against the Jew." www.fighthatred.com/historical-events/pogroms-razzias/1034-the-kishinev-pogrom-of-1093-chaim-nachman-bialik.

Lockhard, R. H. Bruce. *Memoirs of a British Agent*. New York: G. P. Putnam's Sons, 1933.

Marie, Queen of Romania. *Ordeal: The Story of My Life*. 2 volumes. New York: Scribner's Sons, 1934.

Maylunas, Andrei, and Sergei Mironenko. *A Lifelong Passion: Nicholas & Alexandra: Their Own Story*. New York: Doubleday, 1997.

Mosolov, A. A. *At the Court of the Last Tsar*. London: Methuen, 1935.

Nicholas II, Emperor of Russia. *Journal Intime*. Translated by A. Pierre. Paris: Payot, 1925.

———. *The Letters of the Tsar to the Tsaritsa, 1914–1916*. New York: Dodd, Mead, 1929.

——— and Dowager Empress of Russia Marie Feodorovna. *The Secret Letters of the Last Tsar: The Confidential Correspondence Between Nicholas II and His Mother, Dowager Empress Marie Feodorovna*. Edited by Edward J. Bing. New York: Longmans, Green, 1938.

Paléologue, Maurice. *An Ambassador's Memoirs*. 3 volumes. Translated by F. Appleby Holt. New York: Doran, 1925.

Palmer, Svetlana, and Sarah Wallis, editors. *Intimate Voices from the First World War*. New York: William Morrow, 2003.

Paustovsky, Konstantin. *The Story of a Life*. Translated by Joseph Barnes. New York: Pantheon, 1964.

Poole, Ernest. *The Village: Russian Impressions*. New York: Macmillan, 1918.

Purishkevich, Vladimir. *The Murder of Rasputin*. Translated by Bella Costello. Ann Arbor, MI: Ardis, 1985.

Rasputin, Maria. *My Father*. London: Cassell, 1934.

Rasputin, Maria, and Patte Barham. *Rasputin: The Man Behind the Myth*. Englewood Cliffs, NJ: Prentice-Hall, 1977.

Reed, John. *Ten Days That Shook the World*. New York: Boni and Liveright, 1922.

Rodzianko, M. V. *The Reign of Rasputin*. London: Philpot, 1927.

Shulgin, V. V. *Days of the Russian Revolution: Memoirs from the Right, 1905–1917.* Translation of *Dni* by Bruce F. Adams. Gulf Breeze, FL: Academic International Press, 1990.

Skipworth, Sofka [Princess Sophy Dolgorouky]. *Sofka: The Autobiography of a Princess.* London: Hart-Davis, 1968.

Spiridovitch, Alexander. "Murder of Prime Minister Stolypin in Kiev, 1911" in *Les Dernières Années de la Cour de Tzarskoe-Selo.* Paris: Payot, 1928. alexanderpalace.org/palace/stolypin-murder-1911-kiev.html (Translated by Robert Moshein), accessed 6/15/11.

Strekotin, Alexander. "Alexander Strekotin: Statement, 1934." www.kingandwilson.com/FOTRResources/strekotin.htm.

Tian-Shanskaia, Olga Semyonova. *Village Life in Late Tsarist Russia.* Edited and translated by David L. Ransel with Michael Levine. Bloomington: Indiana University Press, 1993.

Trotsky, Leon. *Diary in Exile, 1935.* Translated by Elena Zarudnaya. Cambridge, MA: Harvard University Press, 1958.

———. *The History of the Russian Revolution.* 3 volumes. Translated by Max Eastman. New York: Simon & Schuster, 1932.

Volkov, Alexei. *Souvenirs d'Alexis Volkov, Valet de Chambre de la Tsarine Alexandra Feodorovna 1910–1918.* Paris: Payot, 1928. www.alexanderpalace.org/volkov/ (Translated by Robert Moshein, 2004), accessed 8/1/11.

Vorres, Ian. *Last Grand Duchess: The Memoirs of Grand Duchess Olga Alexandrovna.* London: Hutchinson, 1964.

Vyrubova, Anna. *Memories of the Russian Court.* London: Macmillan, 1923.

Williams, Albert Rhys. *Through the Russian Revolution.* New York: Boni and Liveright, 1921.

Wilton, Robert. *The Last Days of the Romanovs (including Depositions of Colonel Kobylinsky, Pierre Gilliard, Sydney Gibbes, Anatoly Yakimov, Pavel Medvedev, Philip Proskuriakov).* London: Thornton Butterworth, 1920.

Witte, Count Sergei. *The Memoirs of Count Witte.* Translated by Abraham Yarmolinsky. New York: Doubleday, Page, 1921.

(Yusupov) Youssoupoff, Prince Felix. *Lost Splendor: The Amazing Memoirs of the Man Who Killed Rasputin.* Translated by Anne Green and Nicholas Katkoff. London: Cape, 1953.

GENERAL SOURCES

This work stands on the shoulders of dozens of historians who have made the rigorous examination of the Russian past their life's work. Without their books, mine would not have been possible.

Alexandrov, Victor. *The End of the Romanovs.* Translated by William Sutcliffe. Boston: Little, Brown, 1966.

Andrews, Stuart. *Lenin's Revolution.* Humanities E-books, 2007.

Bainton, Roy. *A Brief History of 1917: Russia's Year of Revolution.* New York: Carroll & Graf, 2005.

Bill, Valentine T. *The Forgotten Class: The Russian Bourgeoisie from the Earliest Beginnings to 1900.* New York: Praeger, 1959.

Botkin, Gleb. *The Woman Who Rose Again.* New York: Revell, 1937.

Brewster, Hugh. *Anastasia's Album.* New York: Houghton Mifflin, 1996.

Burleigh, Michael. *Sacred Causes: The Clash of Religion and Politics, from the Great War to the War on Terror.* New York: Harper Perennial, 2007.

Clarkson, Jesse D. *A History of Russia.* New York: Random House, 1961.

Crankshaw, Edward. *The Shadow of the Winter Palace: Russia's Drift to Revolution, 1825–1917.* New York: Viking Adult, 1976.

Essad-Bey, M. *Nicholas II: Prisoner of the Purple.* London: Hutchinson, 1936.

Etty, John. *Primary Sources in Russian History.* Corby Northants, UK: First and Best in Education, 2009.

Ferro, Marc. *Nicholas II: The Last of the Tsars.* Translated by Brian Pearce. Oxford: Oxford University Press, 1995.

———. *The Russian Revolution of February 1917.* London: Routledge and Kegan Paul, 1972.

Fige, Orlando. *A People's Tragedy: The Russian Revolution 1891–1924*. New York: Penguin, 1996.

Fischer, Louis. *The Life of Lenin*. New York: Harper Colophon, 1965.

Fuhrmann, Joseph T. *Rasputin: The Untold Story*. New York: John Wiley, 2012.

Gelardi, Julia. *Born to Rule: Five Reigning Consorts, Granddaughters of Queen Victoria*. New York: St. Martin's, 2005.

Harding, Luke. "Bones Found by Russian Builder Finally Solve Riddle of Missing Romanovs." *The Guardian,* 24 August 2007. The Guardian Archives. Accessed April 12, 2012. www.theguardian.com /world/2007/Aug/25/Russia.lukeharding.

Hosking, Geoffrey A. *Rulers and Victims: The Russians in the Soviet Union*. Cambridge, MA: The Belknap Press/Harvard University Press, 2006.

Keating, John, and Thomas Joseph White. *Divine Impassability and the Mystery of Human Suffering*. Grand Rapids, MI: Eerdmans, 2009.

King, Greg. *The Court of the Last Tsar: Pomp, Power and Pageantry in the Reign of Nicholas II*. New York: John Wiley, 2006.

———. *Empress Alexandra*. New York: Atlantic International Publications, 1990.

———. "Inheritance of Blood: Official Anti-Semitism and the Last Romanovs." Kingandwilson.com/AtlantisArticles/Inheritance.htm.

———. *The Resurrection of the Romanovs: Anastasia, Anna Anderson, and the World's Greatest Royal Mystery*. New York: John Wiley, 2011.

———, and Penny Wilson. *The Fate of the Romanovs*. New York: John Wiley, 2003.

Koslow, Jules. *The Despised and the Damned: The Russian Peasant Through the Ages*. New York: Macmillan, 1972.

Kurth, Peter. *Tsar: The Lost World of Nicholas and Alexandra*. New York: Madison Press, 1995.

Le Blanc, Paul. *Marx, Lenin, and the Revolutionary Experience*. New York: Routledge, Taylor & Francis Group, 2006.

Lincoln, W. Bruce. *In War's Dark Shadow*. Dekalb: Northern Illinois University Press, 1983.

———. *Red Victory: A History of the Russian Civil War, 1918–1921*. New York: Simon & Schuster, 1991.

———. *The Romanovs: Autocrats of All the Russias*. New York: Anchor Books, 1981.

Massie, Robert K. *Nicholas and Alexandra*. New York: Random House Trade Paperbacks, 2011.

———. *The Romanovs: The Final Chapter*. New York: Random House Trade Paperbacks, 1995.

Pares, Bernard. *A History of Russia*. New York: Vintage Books, 1961.

Radziwill, Princess Catherine. *The Intimate Life of the Last Tzarina*. New York: Longmans, Green, 1928.

———. *Nicholas II: The Last of the Tsars*. London: Cassell, 1931.

———. *The Taint of the Romanovs*. London: Cassell, 1931.

Rendell, Matthew. *Defenders of the Motherland: The Tsarist Elite in Revolutionary Russia*. Oxford: Oxford University Press, 2009.

"Revolution: Russia: Area of Study 2, 'Creating a New Society.'" Atar Notes and Study Guides. Vce.atarnotes.com/home/?step=downloader &download=945.

Sablinsky, Walter. *The Road to Bloody Sunday: Father Gapon and the St. Petersburg Massacre of 1905*. Princeton, NJ: Princeton University Press, 1976.

Seward, Deborah. "Researchers: Anastasia and Alexei Mystery Continues." 28 July 1992. AP News Archive. www.apnewsarchive .com/1992/Researchers-Anastasia-and-Alexei-Mystery-Continues /id-ca1c01d799f90b0bd45340dbf1edb38e.

Shelayev, Yuri, Elizabeth Shelayeva, and Nicholas Semenov, editors. *Nicholas Romanov: Life and Death*. St. Petersburg, Russia: Liki Rossi, 1998.

Shipside, Steve. *Karl Marx's* Das Kapital: *A Modern-Day Interpretation of an Economic Classic*. Oxford, UK: Infinite Ideas Limited, 2009.

Smith, Douglas. *Former People: The Final Days of the Russian Aristocracy.* New York: Farrar, Straus, 2012.

Steinberg, Mark D., and Vladimir M. Khurstalev. *The Fall of the Romanovs.* New Haven, CT: Yale University Press, 1995.

Timms, Robert, editor. *Nicholas and Alexandra: The Last Imperial Family of Tsarist Russia.* New York: Abrams, 1998.

Trewin, J. C. *The House of Special Purpose: An Intimate Portrait of the Last Days of the Russian Imperial Family, Compiled from the Papers of the English Tutor Charles Sidney Gibbes.* New York: Stein & Day, 1975.

Ulam, Adam. *The Russian Revolution: Essays, Photographs and Excerpts from Classic Works About the Men and the Ideas That Shaped the Most Significant Revolution of the 20th Century.* New York: Macmillan, 1967.

Victor, Alexander. *The End of the Romanovs.* Boston: Little, Brown, 1962.

Volkogonov, Dmitri. *Lenin: The First Account Using All the Secret Soviet Archives.* New York: Free Press, 1994.

Welch, Frances. *The Romanovs & Mr. Gibbes: The Story of the Englishman Who Taught the Children of the Last Tsar.* Croyden, Surrey, UK: Short Books, 2002.

Wolff, Theodore. *The Eve of 1914.* New York: Knopf, 1936.

Wortman, Richard. *Scenarios of Power: From Alexander II to the Abdication of Nicholas II.* 2 volumes. Princeton, NJ: Princeton University Press, 2000.

Znamenov, Vadim, with Sergei Mironenko and Olga Barkovets. *Nicholas II: The Imperial Family.* St. Petersburg, Russia: Abris Publishers, 2007.

THE ROMANOVS ONLINE

The last imperial family has a large online presence. To explore their world further, try these sites:

Alexander Palace Time Machine

> *The* Romanov website, where you'll find online books, letters, articles, photographs, and much, much more.
> alexanderpalace.org/palace/mainpage.html

Nicholas and Alexandra

> An online exhibit of the State Hermitage Museum, this website features maps, timelines, and a virtual tour by gallery, allowing viewers to see such artifacts as the grand duchesses' white summer dresses, Nicholas's abdication document, and even the imperial couple's costumes from their 1903 ball.
> nicholasandalexandra.com

Romanov Memorial

> A virtual tour of the House of Special Purpose (Ipatiev house), complete with photographs and film footage of the house's exterior.
> romanov-memorial.com

Royal Russia

> A vast repository of over 50 full-length articles, five hundred news articles, three hundred videos, and one thousand photographs, all devoted to the last imperial family. Especially fascinating is the film and video archive, featuring reels of the family on the imperial train, the interior of the Alexander Palace, Prince Yusupov's funeral, and more.
> angelfire.com/pa/ImperialRussian/

Yale Beinecke Albums

> These six photo albums belonging to Anna Vyrubova are chock-full of candid family pictures.
> beinecke.library.yale.edu/collections/highlights/romanov-family.albums

YouTube

Don't miss these three films on YouTube:

> The Romanovs' 1998 funeral: youtube.com/watch?v=8oYHKLHGwvA
> Romanov Home Movies: youtube.com/watch?v=OMHANjJP-M8c
> Parts of the forty-minute Russian film made in commemoration of the tercentary, with a rousing rendition of "God Save the Tsar": youtube.com/watch?v=agILrxmXRjA.

NOTES

Russia

"a natural part . . .": Skipworth, 12.

"a certain quality . . .": Smith, 25.

"C'est la vie.": ibid.

"not sufficiently tall . . .": Alexander, Grand Duke of Russia, 211.

"[She] was just . . .": Vorres, 102.

"She was dressed . . .": Radziwill, *Intimate Life,* 75–76.

"appropriate pomp . . .": Alexander, Grand Duke of Russia, 212.

"The whirling waltz . . .": Gautier, 210.

"She danced badly . . .": Radziwill, *Intimate Life,* 76.

"It was like a living dream!": Timms, 214.

"cheeks glowing with . . .": Lincoln, *War's Dark,* 37.

"vain city women . . .": ibid.

"decked out": ibid.

"Stooping down, I . . .": Koslow, 8.

"It has been . . .": Lincoln, *War's Dark,* 52.

"A cockroach is . . .": ibid., 46.

"Strips [of land] six feet . . .": ibid., 50.

"There are many . . .": ibid., 51.

"Every single peasant . . .": Fige, 106.

"God grew the forests . . .": ibid., 101.

"All the healthy . . .": ibid., 109.

"Everyone is trying . . .": ibid.

"I did not live . . .": Lincoln, *War's Dark,* 109.

"earned the equivalent . . .": ibid., 115.

"In the event . . .": ibid., 113.

"The factory owner . . .": ibid., 114.

"We slept in . . .": Bill, 130.

"I had eleven . . .": Lincoln, *War's Dark,* 121.

"When I am rich . . .": Bill, 133.

"Reflections of a better . . .": Lincoln, *War's Dark,* 121.

Chapter One

"To the palace . . .": Pares, 403.

"My father took me . . .": Shelayev, 7.

"The emperor is dead.": Alexander, Grand Duke of Russia, 60.

"feel the whip": Steinberg, 36.

"presentiment—a secret . . .": Alexander, Grand Duke of Russia, 60.

"The tsar is swift . . .": Mosolov, 4.

"Shut up!": Wortman, 310.

"Nicholas is a *devchonka* . . .": ibid.

"Tell me, have you . . .": Essad-Bey, 26.

"It was my father's . . .": Olga Alexandrovna Memoirs in Maylunas, 42.

"I never show . . .": Steinberg, 10.

"When she did . . .": Marie, Queen of Romania, 331.

"Her attitude to . . .": ibid.

"Life here [on earth] . . .": King, *Court*, 285.

"I'm Nicky . . .": Kurth, 28.

"I sat next to . . .": Nicholas II Diary, 27 May/9 June 1885, in Maylunas, 10.

"My dream—one day . . .": Nicholas II Diary, 21 December/3 January 1891, ibid., 20.

"As always, I don't . . .": Nicholas II, *Journal Intime*, 13.

"[The army] appealed . . .": Alexander, Grand Duke of Russia, 73.

"We got stewed . . .": Massie, *Nicholas and Alexandra,* 19–20.

"The officers carried . . .": ibid.

"Wallowed in . . .": ibid.

"Palaces and generals . . .": Alexander, Grand Duke of Russia, 167.

"Oh, God, what . . .": Nicholas II to the Empress Marie, 10 April/23 April 1894, *Secret Letters*, 76.

"I dreamed that . . .": Nicholas II, *Journal Intime,* 76–77.

"Be firm and make . . .": Nicholas II, ibid., 103.

"your poor little Nicky . . .": ibid., 104.

"Darling boysy . . .": ibid., 103.

"What am I going . . .": Alexander, Grand Duke of Russia, 168–169.

"My poor Nicky's . . .": Buxhoeveden, *Life and Tragedy,* 108.

"invisible trousers.": Alexandra to Nicholas II, 22 August/3 September 1915, *Letters of the Tsaritsa,* 114.

"be all, know all . . .": ibid.

"Beloved, *listen to me* . . .": ibid.

"Alix repeated . . .": Nicholas II Diary, 21 October/3 November 1894, in Maylunas, 99.

"Our marraige seemed . . .": Massie, *Nicholas and Alexandra,* 46.

"the funeral bride.": Gilliard, 48.

"She has come to us . . .": ibid.

"lost her customary . . .": Shelayev, 31.

"She kept herself aloof . . .": ibid.

"perpetually unamused": ibid.

"unwholesomely precocious outlook . . .": Vyrubova, 79.

"corroded by a lack . . .": Shelayev, 44.

"Oh, these young men . . .": Alexandra to Nicholas II, 8 March/21 March
1916, GARF.

"I trust you to . . .": Nicholas II to Alexandra, 10 March/23 March 1916,
GARF.

"spider's net": Wolff, 231.

"own Huzy": Nicholas II to Alexandra, 23–24 February/8–9 March 1917,
GARF.

"sweet Wifey": ibid.

"a world apart . . .": Botkin, *Real Romanovs*, 18.

"charming, dear, precious place": Kurth, 55.

"It is incredible . . .": King, *Court*, 52.

"opal-hued": Vyrubova, 54.

"through and through . . .": Alexandra to Nicholas II, 3 March/16 March
1917, GARF.

"It is inexpressibly . . .": Nicholas II Diary, 20 November/3 December
1894, in Maylunas, 115.

"a sort of everlasting . . .": Crankshaw, 308.

Chapter Two

"utter delight . . .": Nicholas II to Empress Marie, *Secret Letters*, 93.

"[The baby] has become . . .": ibid., 96.

"All the anxiety was over": Nicholas II Diary, 3 November/16 November
1895, in Maylunas, 130.

"God, what happiness!": Nicholas II Diary, 4 November/17 November
1895, ibid.

"precious little one": Buxhoeveden, *Life and Tragedy*, 56.

"humble snub": King, *Empress*, 188.

"sweet baby": Nicholas II to Queen Victoria, 12 November/25 November
1895, in Maylunas, 131.

"She does not look . . .": Nicholas II Diary, 6 November/19 November
1895, ibid., 130.

"You can imagine . . .": Buxhoeveden, *Life and Tragedy*, 56.

"A pity . . .": Nicholas II Diary, 17 December/30 December 1895, in
Maylunas, 133.

"so carefully, so tenderly . . .": Kurth, 58.

"on top of the corpses": Shelayev, 52.

"Mama's emotion was . . .": Grand Duchess Xenia Diary, 29 May/11 June
    1897, in Maylunas, 163.

"The news soon spread . . .": Konstantin Konstantinovich Diary, 29
    May/11 June 1897, ibid.

"The second bright . . .": Nicholas II Diary, 29 May/11 June 1897, ibid.

"And so, there's no . . .": Konstantin Konstantinovich Diary, 14 June/27
    June 1897, ibid., 185.

"Holy Russia abounds . . .": Ilidor, 88.

"moral examination.": Yusupov, 62.

"astral medicine": ibid.

"astrologically auspicious nights": ibid.

"My God, what . . .": Grand Duchess Xenia Diary, 5 June/18 June 1901, in
    Maylunas, 206.

"Czar Has Another . . .": *The New York Times*, 18 June 1901.

"God knows what . . .": Nicholas II to Alexandra, 29 August/11
    September 1902, GARF.

Chapter Three

"fresh white frocks . . .": Vyrubova, 58.

"sweety darling Mama . . .": Olga Nikolaevna to Alexandra, 12 January/25
    January 1909, in Maylunas, 319.

"Remember, elbows off . . .": Alexandra to Olga Nikolaevna, 4 August/17
    August 1905, ibid., 278.

"It is very pleasant . . .": Nicholas II to Empress Marie, 2 October/15
    October 1896, *Letters of the Tsar,* 120.

"Alix cried a lot": Konstantin Konstantinovich Diary, 20 August/2
    September 1902, in Maylunas, 218.

"*Everything* is within . . .": Witte, 204.

"Someday you will . . .": Pares, 131.

"a great never-to-be-forgotten . . .": Nicholas II Diary, 30 July/12 August
    1904, *Journal Intime,* 174.

"The baby was being . . .": Mosolov, 29–30.

"A hemorrhage began . . .": Radziwill, *Taint,* 179–180.

"reach out and . . .": Massie, *Nicholas and Alexandra,* 153.

"Life lost all meaning . . .": Alexander, Grand Duke of Russia, 102.

"My own fate . . .": Etty, 59.

Chapter Four

"When I came in . . .": Lincoln, *War's Dark*, 131.

"was little short . . .": ibid.

"I read Jules Verne . . .": ibid.

"caught sight of . . .": ibid.

"We, the workers . . .": Sablinsky, 251–252.

"The tsar will not . . .": Massie, *Nicholas and Alexandra*, 104.

"And so we have . . .": ibid.

"blood-stained creature" and "common murderer": ibid.

"Remember, son . . .": Sablinsky, 273.

"Lord, how painful . . .": Nicholas II Diary, 9 January/22 January 1905, in Maylunas, 256.

"Yes, the troops, alas . . .": Buxhoeveden, *Life and Tragedy*, 108–110.

"I do not want to die . . .": Lincoln, *Romanovs*, 634.

"There are no labor . . .": Witte, 406–407.

"It makes me sick . . .": Nicholas II to Empress Marie, *Secret Letters,* 183.

"the year of nightmares": ibid., 206.

"Baby Tsar has . . .": Alexandra to Olga Nikolaevich, 4 August/17 August 1905, in Maylunas, 278–279.

"The tragic aspect . . .": Fige, 191.

"sweep away . . .": Nicholas II, *Secret Letters,* 188.

"The heart of the tsar . . .": Steinberg, 16.

"I am not holding . . .": ibid., 10.

"We have sinned . . .": ibid., 11.

"If the Emperor . . .": Pares, 85–86.

"freedom of conscience . . .": Manifesto of 17 October/30 October 1905, at www.dur.ac.uk/a.k.harrington/octmanif.html.

"People have laid down . . .": Lincoln, *Romanovs,* 659.

"buzzed like a huge garden . . .": Fige, 192.

Chapter Five

"uprooted peasants . . .": Fige, 196.

"total success" and "loyal Russians": ibid.

"the Yids must be . . .": King and Wilson, "Inheritance," np.

"Brothers, in the name . . .": www.fighthatred.com>HistoricalEvents>Pogroms&Razzias.

"Good. The Jews . . .": Lincoln, *Red Victory*, 318.

"They have been putting . . .": King and Wilson, "Inheritance," np.

"In the first days . . .": Nicholas II, *Secret Letters,* 190–191.

"It's the Jews . . .": Shulgin, 6–7.

"Excellent in everything!": Fischer, 6.

"It makes me want . . .": Le Blanc, 83.

"Victory? The point . . .": Fige, 199.

"The whole of Moscow . . .": ibid., 200.

"Go ahead and shoot!": Fischer, 54.

"feel the whip": Steinberg, 36.

"teach them a lesson": Fige, 201.

"Don't skimp on the bullets": Lincoln, *Romanovs,* 662.

"This really tickles me . . .": ibid.

"courtesy, friendliness . . .": Smith, 58.

"I am not convinced . . .": Lincoln, *Romanovs,* 664.

"The two . . . sides stood . . .": Fige, 213–214.

"They neither crossed . . .": Grand Duchess Xenia Diary, 27 April/10
    May 1906, in Maylunas, 292.

"The care for . . .": Elchaninov, 106.

"tragic, and her face . . .": Buxhoeveden, *Life and Tragedy,* 276.

"Poor Nicky was . . .": Grand Duchess Xenia Diary, 27 April/10 May
    1906, in Maylunas, 292.

"terrible ceremony . . .": Kokovtsov, 129.

"The peasants looked . . .": Vorres, 121.

"The Duma is such filth . . .": Grand Duchess Xenia Diary, 30 April/13
    May 1906, in Maylunas, 293.

"Slap! And they are gone": Nicholas II, *Secret Letters,* 228.

"The Duma of the Lords and Lackeys": Ferro, *Nicholas II,* 112.

"We made the acquaintance . . .": Nicholas II Diary, 1 November/14
    November 1905, in Maylunas, 284.

"Rasputin was exceptionally . . .": Fuhrmann, 242.

"[It] was at once . . .": Paléologue, *Memoirs,* I: 292.

"There was something . . .": Vorres, 138.

"The poor child . . .": ibid., 142.

"There's a good boy . . .": ibid.

"[He] was not just alive . . .": ibid.

Chapter Six

"etiquette was that . . .": Welch, 38.

"generally behaved like . . .": ibid., 39–40.

"I took my first . . .": ibid., 39.

"a tiny little chap . . .": ibid., 40.

"mediocre": Botkin, *Real Romanovs,* 79.

"Not one of [them] . . .": Mosolov, 59.

"I was amazed that such . . .": Recollection of Vasily Pankratov, "With the Tsar in Tobolsk," in Steinberg, 269–270.

"the grand duchesses had no . . .": Mosolov, 59.

"Four languages is . . .": Buxhoeveden, *Life and Tragedy,* 129.

"[The grand duchesses] had an accent . . .": Botkin, *Woman,* 28–31.

"They never learned . . .": Gilliard, 77.

"possessed a remarkably . . .": ibid., 73.

"You must wait, Mama . . .": King, *Empress,* 93.

"she showed no . . .": Trewin, 73.

"She was not . . .": Gilliard, 75.

"wild and rough . . .": Welch, 40.

"a true genius in naughtiness": Botkin, *Woman,* 23.

"Peter Vasilievich . . .": Trewin, 18.

"What we [children] did . . .": Anastasia to Nicholas II, 13 September/26 September 1915, GARF.

"Anastasia was trying . . .": Alexei to Nicholas II, 22 September/5 October 1914, in Maylunas, 402.

"Now I have to do . . .": Brewster, 26.

"dear one," "wee one," "Sunbeam": Kurth, 73.

"He was the focus . . .": Gilliard, 72.

"He wouldn't sit up . . .": Konstantin Konstantinovich Diary, 18 March/31 March 1912, in Maylunas, 352.

"Can't I have . . .": Vyrubova, 81–82.

"All grownups have . . .": Massie, *Nicholas and Alexandra,* 140.

"When the Heir . . .": Radziwill, *Taint,* 197.

"Now, girls, run away . . .": Buxhoeveden, *Life and Tragedy,* 151.

"trembled for Russia . . .": Kurth, 75.

"governor-general": Marie to Nicholas II, 19 April/2 May 1915, GARF.

"I took [one] picture . . .": Brewster, 5.

"more like a home . . .": Vyrubova, 64.

"was frequently absent . . .": Gilliard, 77.

"My sweety darling . . .": Olga Nikolaevich to Alexandra, 12 January/25 January 1909, in Maylunas, 319.

"My darling Mama!": Tatiana to Alexandra, 17 January/30 January 1909, ibid., 320.

"Mama, at what age . . .": Marie to Alexandra 17 May/30 May 1910, ibid., 334.

"Madam dearest . . .": Anastasia to Alexandra, undated, 1913, ibid., 372.

"I know it's dull . . .": Alexandra to Marie 6 December/19 December 1910, ibid., 335.

Chapter Seven

"coarse barnyard expressions." Massie, *Nicholas and Alexandra,* 206.

"See the gold cross?": Fige, 31.

"Her Majesty sewed . . .": ibid.

"Humble yourself . . .": ibid.

"What's this, little . . .": ibid.

"They accuse Rasputin . . .": Ulam, 78.

"are ours": Fuhrmann, 219.

"There is no need . . .": ibid., 95.

"Everything you say . . .": ibid., 60.

"You have mentioned . . .": Rasputin and Barham, *Man Behind the Myth,* 162.

"I will . . . give . . .": ibid.

"You see, we . . .": Pares, 124.

"Death is after . . .": Massie, *Nicholas and Alexandra,* 226.

"I was obsessed . . .": Spiridovitch, unpaged.

"Each instant I . . .": ibid.

"Papa, don't . . .": ibid.

"He slowly turned . . .": Massie, *Nicholas and Alexandra,* 226.

"slept badly . . .": Nicholas II to Empress Marie, 10 September/23 September 1911, in Maylunas, 344.

"Those who offend . . .": Yusupov, 154.

"She floated like . . .": de Stoeckl, 119.

"She looked like . . .": ibid.

"deep southern sky . . .": ibid., 120.

"God grant that . . .": Olga Nikolaevich to Rasputin, 12 December/25 December 1909, GARF.

"forgive all the sins . . .": Tatiana to Rasputin, 25 March/7 April 1909, GARF.

"let me see you . . .": Marie to Rasputin, undated, 1909, GARF.

"I wish only . . .": Massie, *Nicholas and Alexandra,* 210–211.

"These are not . . .": Kokovtsov, 176–177.

"Now I can rest . . .": Fuhrmann, 135.

"walked barefoot . . .": Brewster, 43.

"The weather is . . .": Massie, *Nicholas and Alexandra,* 181.

"All in all . . .": ibid.

"an experience . . .": ibid.

"was absolutely . . .": ibid., 93.

"Mama, help me . . .": Buxhoevden, *Life and Tragedy*, 132.

"When I am dead it . . .": ibid.

"Seeing his boy . . .": Vyrubova, 93.

"an extraordinary situation . . .": Fuhrmann, 139.

"When I am dead, build . . .": Vyrubova, 93.

"The Little One will not . . .": ibid., 94.

"The doctors notice . . .": Paléologue, I: 148.

"It is wholly . . .": Vorres, 143.

"[The boy] will love . . .": Znamenov, 33.

Chapter Eight

"An officer . . . told me . . .": Botkin, *Woman,* 179.

"lumpy and lacking . . .": ibid.

"Even when grown . . .": Vyrubova, 77.

"When the two . . .": Dehn, 78–79.

"break down the barrier . . .": Buchanan, *My Memoir,* II: 46.

"Thousands of invisible . . .": Fige, 12.

"No hope seems . . .": ibid., 13.

"little real enthusiasms . . .": Vyrubova, 98.

"in a fantastic shower . . .": Kurth, 15.

"Clear out at once . . .": Rodzianko, 76–77.

"Her face was cold . . .": Buchanan, *Dissolution,* 35.

"anxiously and furtively . . .": Kurth, 15.

"A symbol that . . .": Vyrubova, 98–99.

"God Save the Tsar . . .": Kurth, 17.

"You can see it . . .": Fige, 12.

"My people love me": ibid.

"Nobody . . . could have . . .": Massie, *Nicholas and Alexandra,* 239.

"habits of discipline": Gilliard, 38.

"I had a definite . . .": ibid.

"I had a rather . . .": Trewin, 30–31.

"sensitive to the . . .": Gilliard, 40.

"I like to think . . .": Radziwill, *Nicholas II,* 199.

Chapter Nine

"My God! My God . . .": Paléologue, I: 71.

"It is a serious moment . . .": Fuhrmann, 163.

"Her mouth and face . . .": ibid.

"I have killed . . .": Rasputin, *My Father,* 21.

"That hunk of . . .": Fuhrmann, 164.

"We are deeply . . .": ibid.

"should be able . . .": ibid., 173.

"We don't have . . .": ibid.

"give [our enemies] . . .": ibid., 176.

"[Do] not plan . . .": Pares, 188.

"a good thing . . .": Nicholas II to Alexandra, 19 November/2 December 1914, *Letters of the Tsar,* 14.

"an air of weary . . .": Gilliard, 105.

"I say a terrible . . .": Kurth, 118.

"Batiushka, Batiushka . . .": Massie, *Nicholas and Alexandra,* 277.

"For Faith, Tsar . . .": ibid.

"I solemnly swear . . .": Paléologue, I: 51.

"God save the Tsar . . .": Gilliard, 112.

Chapter Ten

"was somber and resigned": Fige, 252.

"[They] don't know . . .": Botkin, *Real Romanovs,* 68.

"Go to the devil . . .": Knox, I: 220.

"Our position is . . .": ibid.

"They haven't given out . . .": Fige, 263.

"morale and equipment": Paléologue, I: 83.

"[the commanders] prepared . . .": Fige, 263.

"became overnight a changed . . .": Vyrubova, 107.

"To some it may seem . . .": Buxhoeveden, *Life and Tragedy,* 192.

"I have seen the empress . . .": Vyrubova, 109.

"dignified and courageous": ibid., 108.

"There was a concert . . .": King and Wilson, *Resurrection,* 43.

"Stand near me . . .": Vyrubova, 110.

"Two more poor . . .": Anastasia to Nicholas II, 28 October/10 November 1914, in Maylunas, 406.

"jumped up and ran . . .": Knox, I: 317–318.

"They've screwed it all . . .": Fige, 268.

"A fish begins . . .": ibid.

"the vital psychological . . .": ibid.

"Yes, do come . . .": Knox, I: 391.

"The Grand Duke is . . .": Paléologue, I: 286.

"If the Grand Duke is . . .": ibid., I: 341.

"Our Friend's enemy . . .": Etty, 79.

"Think, my wifey . . .": Nicholas II to Alexandra, undated, 1915, *Letters of the Tsar,* 71–72.

"Yes, truly you ought . . .": ibid.

"prayers arising . . .": Alexandra to Nicholas II, 22 August/4 September 1915, *Letters of the Tsaritsa,* 114.

"Remember to comb . . .": ibid.

"My field bedstead . . .": Nicholas II to Alexandra, 7 September/20 September 1915, *Letters of the Tsar,* 182.

"See that tiny . . .": Massie, *Nicholas and Alexandra,* 298.

"He . . . walks backward . . .": ibid.

"more of the same": Paléologue, I: 340.

"It is His plan . . .": Nicholas II to Alexandra, 31 March/13 April 1916, GARF.

Chapter Eleven

"My dear and valued . . .": Massie, *Nicholas and Alexandra,* 335.

"All were drawn up . . .": Mosolov, 153.

"Rasputin took part . . .": Massie, *Nicholas and Alexandra,* 337–338.

"Rasputin came home . . .": ibid.

"Rasputin came home at 7 a.m . . .": ibid.

"I fully trust . . .": ibid., 334.

"Forgive me, but I . . .": ibid., 351.

"Long-nozed Saznov . . .": Pares, 341.

"Why do we . . .": ibid.

"Really, My Treasure . . .": Alexandra to Nicholas II, 15 September/28 September 1916, in Maylunas, 439.

"Our Friend begs . . .": Alexandra to Nicholas II, 23 May/5 June 1916, in Maylunas, 468.

"because they liked him . . .": Massie, *Nicholas and Alexandra,* 342.

"Brother, go and . . .": ibid.

"ministerial leapfrog": Rodzianko, 239.

"It is a terrible . . .": Shulgin, 101.

"thief" and "half-educated peasant": Fuhrmann, 251–252.

"the Reign of Rasputin": ibid., 216.

"Dark forces are . . .": Pares, 396–397.

"We will be heroes . . .": Bokhanov, 353–354.

"Play something cheerful . . .": Yusupov, 226.

"Then you wouldn't have . . .": Lincoln, *Romanovs,* 706.

"like a broken marionette": ibid.

"an expression of loathing": Purishkevich, 105.

"That's when I saw . . .": Yusupov, 229.

"Felix! Felix!": Purishkevich, 106.

"He's alive!": ibid.

"I will tell . . .": ibid.

"I fired. The night . . .": ibid.

"In my frenzy . . .": Yusupov, 231.

"People kissed each other . . .": Paléologue Memoirs, 20 December 1916, in Maylunas, 508.

"A patrolman standing . . .": Vyrubova, 179.

"I cannot, and *won't* . . .": Alexandra to Nicholas II, 17 December/30 December 1916, in Maylunas, 493.

"[They] sat on . . .": Mordvinov Memoirs, ibid., 507.

Chapter Twelve

"My dear martyr . . .": Paléologue, III: 136.

"He listened to me . . .": Kokovtsov, 478–479.

"The Emperor's words . . .": Paléologue, III: 151–152.

"It seems the empress . . .": ibid., III: 140–141.

"These exhausted mothers . . .": Reports of the Petrograd Okhrana to the Special Section of the Police, 2 January/26 February 1917, GARF.

"lunatic asylum," "poisonous atmosphere," and "profound despondency and fear": Paléologue, III: 164.

"hungry revolt" and "the most savage excesses": Addendum to Reports of the Petrograd Okhrana to the Special Section of the Police, 26 January/8 February 1917, GARF.

"To prevent a catastrophe . . .": Kerensky, *Crucifixion,* 261.

"That's not true . . .": Alexander, Grand Duke of Russia, 283–284.

"It's enough to drive . . .": Alexander Mikhailovich to Nikolai Mikhailovich, 14 February/27 February 1917, in Maylunas, 530.

"*Daite khleb*—Give us bread!": Steinberg, 47.

"I will miss . . .": Nicholas II to Alexandra, 23 February 1917, *Letters of the Tsar,* 313.

"Down with the war" and "Down with the tsar.": Fige, 310.

"Don't worry. We . . .": Massie, *Nicholas and Alexandra,* 400.

"My brain is . . .": Nicholas II to Alexandra, 24 Februrary/9 March 1917, *Letters of the Tsar,* 315.

"Down with the . . .": Ferro, *Russian Revolution,* 28.

"I command you . . .": Steinberg, 50.

"It's a hooligan . . .": Alexandra to Nicholas II, 25 February/10 March 1917, ibid., 73.

"Fire!" and "aim for the heart": Ferro, *Russian Revolution,* 29.

"The hungry, unemployed . . .": Michael Rodzianko to Nicholas II, 26 February/11 March 1917, in Steinberg, 76.

"That fat . . .": Steinberg, 50.

"the same wide streets . . .": Meriel Buchanan, 164.

"It looked as if . . .": Paléologue, III: 217.

"I see . . .": Bulygin, 78.

"Sire, do not . . .": Gelardi, 254.

"a motley, exuberant . . .": Massie, *Nicholas and Alexandra,* 404–405.

"Can I say . . .": Pares, 449–451.

"Comrades! I speak . . .": Trotsky, Diary, 201.

"their petty notions . . .": Shipside, 63.

"Leave tomorrow . . .": Nicholas II to Alexandra, 27 February/9 March 1917, in Steinberg, 83.

Chapter Thirteen

"Petrograd is in . . .": Dehn, 149.

"When a house . . .": Gilliard, 211.

"Drunken soldiers . . .": Kurth, 144.

"We shall not . . .": Dehn, 151.

"It's just like . . .": ibid., 153.

"How astonished . . .": ibid., 158.

"The train is . . .": ibid.

"Address of person . . .": Vyrubova, 209.

"I'm beginning . . .": Dehn, 158.

"My sailors . . .": ibid., 162.

"I must not . . .": ibid.

"His Majesty . . .": Bulygin, 90–92.

"I have decided . . .": ibid., 93.

"For the sake . . .": ibid., 94.

"Down with the dynasty!" and "Long live the Republic!": Paléologue, III: 238.

"I have decided . . .": Bulygin, 94.

"The entire city . . .": Poole, 53.

"Haven't you understood . . .": Fige, 379.

"The church was full . . .": ibid., 346.

"What will become of us?": ibid.

"Our [village] burst . . .": ibid., 347.

"It's all lies!": Alexandrov, 141.

"God and the army . . .": ibid.

"the study door . . .": Dehn, 165.

"Abdiqué . . .": ibid.

Chapter Fourteen

"I am going . . .": Gilliard, 214.

"Your father does not . . .": ibid., 214–215.

"like survivors . . .": Vyrubova, 218.

"No longer was . . .": Welch, 55.

"My beloved, Soul . . .": Kurth, 149.

"He sobbed like . . .": Vyrubova, 212.

"like a schoolboy . . .": Kurth, 157.

"plenty of [hours] . . .": ibid., 156.

"A pleasant thought": ibid.

"Too many hard . . .": Bulygin, 123.

"What an appetizing . . .": Kurth, 161.

"Don't call me . . .": Dehn, 199.

"Well, this may . . .": ibid.

"It is necessary . . .": Kurth, 161.

"It's staggering!": Volkogonov, 106.

"We renounce the . . .": Fige, 357.

"shameless imperialist slaughter . . .": Trotsky, *History,* I: 309.

"We don't need . . .": Fischer, 128.

"That is raving.": Trotsky, *History,* I: 310.

"a hopeless failure.": Paléologue, III: 302.

"drive to power.": Volkogonov, 222.

"Bread, peace, land . . .": ibid., 231.

"a curious, hypnotic power": Fige, 392.

"[Lenin] was followed . . .": ibid.

"several guards even . . .": Gilliard, 229.

"Down with the . . .": Massie, *Nicholas and Alexandra,* 466.

"It is clear . . .": Fige, 429.

"The Bolsheviks are . . .": Bulygin, Pares in introduction, np.

"I chose Tobolsk . . .": ibid., 120.

"Start packing . . .": ibid., 121.

"Where are we . . .": ibid.

"For your safety . . .": ibid.

"Only five or six . . .": ibid., 128.

"Behave like gentlemen . . .": Massie, *Nicholas and Alexandra,* 469.

"What shall the future . . .": Buxhoeveden, *Life and Tragedy,* 302.

"weeping copiously": Bulygin, 130.

"she wept and worried . . .": ibid.

Chapter Fifteen

"arranged all quite cozily.": Olga Nikolaevna to Anna Vyrubova, 10 December/23 December 1917, in Vyrubova, 309.

"We were all amazed . . .": Kurth, 171.

"very fat . . .": Alexandra to Anna Vyrubova, 15 December/28 December 1917, in Vyrubova, 316.

"The whole day . . .": Alexis Diary, 7 January/20 January 1918, in Maylunas, 601.

"Everything is the same!": Alexis Diary, 18 January/31 January 1918, ibid.

"Boring!!!!": ibid.

"It's still boring.": Alexis Diary, 22 January/4 February 1918, ibid.

"He absolutely pounced . . .": Welch, 66.

"extremely . . . cheerful . . .": Trewin, 72.

"got[ten] much thinner . . .": ibid.

"you could hardly find . . .": ibid., 73.

"She liked Tobolsk . . .": ibid., 74.

"short and stout . . .": ibid.

"rarely did what . . .": ibid.

"Week by week . . .": Reed, 11.

"History will not . . .": Andrews, 59.

"I had never seen . . .": Kurth, 174.

"in the hope . . .": Gilliard, 243–244.

"a war to the . . .": Burleigh, 84.

"smelled of printer's ink . . .": Paustovsky, 506.

"This is how . . .": Smith, 16.

"I've spent all my life . . .": Hosking, 31.

"former people": Rendle, 203.

"former landowners, capitalists . . .": ibid.

"For centuries, our fathers . . .": Leon Trotsky as quoted in "Revolution: Russia: Area of Study 2: Creating a New Society," np.

"Where are the . . .": Bainton, 197.

"We often take . . .": Tatiana to Peter Petrov, 26 January/11 March 1918, in Steinberg, 202.

"Soldiers' rations.": Steinberg, 178.

"We held a 'sitting' . . .": Gilliard, 255.

"became cruder . . .": Nicholas II to Grand Duchess Xenia, 7 January/20 January 1918, in Steinberg, 218.

"To stop us . . .": Nicholas II Diary, 20 February/5 March 1918, in Maylunas, 604.

"The children are disconsolate": Gilliard, 255.

"pack of blackguardly-looking . . .": ibid.

"filthy, stupid, crude . . .": Gilliard testimony of 5–6 March 1919, Houghton Library, Harvard University, Sokolov Archive, vol. 2: document 55.

"It is obvious . . .": ibid.

"a great inconvenience": Kurth, 177.

"I should like . . .": Alexandra to Anna Vyrubova, 30 March/12 April 1918, in Maylunas, 611.

"developed a pain . . .": Nicholas II Diary, 30 March/12 April 1918, in Maylunas, 610.

"an awful internal . . .": Alexandra to Anna Vyrubova, 30 March/12 April 1918, ibid.

"He is frightfully . . .": ibid., 611.

"It is such . . .": Gilliard, 257.

"To think . . .": Bulygin, 202.

"Everything is in . . .": Nicholas II Diary, 9 March/22 March 1918, in Maylunas, 608.

"The yellow-complexioned . . .": Inspection of Freedom House, 23 April/6 May 1918, in Steinberg, 238.

"Only principal part . . .": Negotiations by telegraph between Yakovlev and Moscow, 24 April/7 May 1918, GARF.

"Removal [of] principal . . .": Negotiations by telegraph between Moscow and Yakovlev, 24 April/7 May 1918, GARF.

"I must tell you . . .": Kobylinksy Deposition in Wilton, 205.

"I refuse to go": Bulygin, 208.

"Then I must . . .": ibid.

"You want to tear . . .": King and Wilson, *Fate,* 85.

"Like an animal . . .": ibid.

"I can't let the tsar . . .": Gilliard, 260–261.

"Mother, something . . .": Gilliard, 261.

"would take great care of . . .": ibid.

"too young to be . . .": Kurth, 180.

"an angel . . .": ibid.

"God won't allow . . .": Bykov, 68.

"[They] gazed . . .": Kurth, 181.

Chapter Sixteen

"sadness . . . descended . . .": Volkov, np.

"These days . . .": Anastasia to Marie, 24 April/7 May 1918, in Steinberg, 302.

"Why Ekaterinburg?": Kobylinksy Deposition in Wilton, 207.

"finishing off . . .": Steinberg, 186.

"I consider it . . .": Negotiations by telegraph between Yakovlev and officials on transfer of Nicholas II to Ekaterinburg, 29 April/12 May 1918, in Steinberg, 252.

"It is not clear . . .": Marie to Olga Nikolaevich, 18 April/1 May 1918, in Steinberg, 298.

"right snake . . .": Kurth, 188.

"a strict prison": ibid.

"We get nasty surprises . . .": Marie to Olga Nikolaevich, 27 April/10 May 1918, in Steinberg, 304.

"Your soldiers would . . .": ibid.

"If you do not . . .": ibid.

"Are you Olga . . .": Buxhoeveden, *Life and Tragedy,* 336.

"Darling, you must . . .": Olga Nikolaevna to Anna Vyrubova, nd, May 1918, GARF.

"We feel . . .": Gilliard, 264–265.

"In our thoughts . . .": Anastasia to Marie, 24 April/7 May 1918, in Steinberg, 302.

"The rooms are empty": King and Wilson, *Fate,* 137.

"Life down there . . .": Tegleva testimony of 5–6 March 1913, Houghton Library, Harvard University, Sokolov Archive, vol. 5: document 36.

"I cannot describe . . .": Buxhoeveden, *Left Behind,* 75.

"Look! [The tsar] . . .": ibid.

"Death to the tyrant!": ibid.

"The dresses . . . of wanton . . .": ibid.

"Down with them . . .": ibid.

"a tragic symphony . . .": King and Wilson, *Fate,* 145.

"Nagorny the sailor . . .": Gilliard, 269–270.

"It [always] looks . . .": Nicholas II Diary, 15 May/28 May 1918, in Maylunas, 622.

"hot and stuffy": Nicholas II Diary, 22 May/4 June 1918, ibid., 627.

"cosy": Marie to Olga Nikolaevna, 22 April/5 May 1918, in Maylunas, 618.

"Nicholas the Blood-Drinker": Massie, *Nicholas and Alexandra,* 509.

"are original . . .": Nicholas II Diary, 25 April/8 May 1918, in Maylunas, 620.

"money": King and Wilson, *Fate,* 122.

"all kinds of mistakes . . .": Strekotin, Statement, 1934, np.

"In my opinion . . .": Kurth, 190.

"The shoes [you have] on . . .": Buxhoeveden, *Life and Tragedy,* 342.

"insisted on changing . . .": King and Wilson, *Fate,* 161.

"astronomical!" and "a little work . . .": ibid.

"[I] could find no . . .": ibid.

"Comrade Laundry Teacher . . .": ibid.

"[he] proved rather clever . . .": ibid.

"excellent": Alexandra Diary, 18 June/1 July 1918, GARF.

"Hugged him to" and "Being a child . . .": Strekotin, Statement, 1934.

"It [is] unbearable . . .": Krustalev, XLI.

"Why?": Nicholas II Diary, 14 May/27 May 1918 in Steinberg, 324.

"everyone had a chance . . .": Strekotin, Statement, 1934, np.

"passed some sleepless . . .": ibid.

"There is nothing . . .": ibid.

"stuck up and stupid": King and Wilson, *Fate,* 238.

"There was something . . .": Strekotin, Statement, 1934, np.

"We're so bored!": King and Wilson, *Fate,* 240.

"Don't try to . . .": ibid.

"pretending fright . . .": ibid.

"everyone relaxed more . . .": ibid.

"Our dear Marie is . . .": Nicholas II Diary, 14 June/27 June 1918, in Maylunas, 632.

Chapter Seventeen

"Today there was . . .": Nicholas II Diary, 21 June/4 July 1918, in
Maylunas, 633.

"Because of . . .": ibid.

"dark gentleman": Kurth, 193.

"It was left to me . . .": King and Wilson, *Fate,* 258.

"all obedience . . .": ibid., 257.

"Always fright[ened] . . .": Alexandra Diary, 28 June/11 July 1918, in
Steinberg, 333.

"Constantly hear . . .": Alexandra Diary, 29 June/12 July 1918, ibid., 334.

"liquidated": Yurovsky's Account of the Execution of the Tsar, 1
February 1934, in Steinberg, 357.

"It has to be said . . .": Yurovsky's Note on the Execution, 1920, in
Maylunas, 633.

"Everything is the same": The Guard's Duty Log Book, 30 June/13 July
1918, GARF.

"Baby . . . managed . . .": Alexandra Diary, 30 June/13 July 1918, in
Steinberg, 334.

"Today we have absolutely . . .": Nicholas II Diary, 30 June/12 July 1918,
in Maylunas, 633.

"gave the impression . . .": Testimony of Father Storozhev in King and
Wilson, *Fate,* 275–276.

"With the saints . . .": Keating, 146.

"were spirited . . .": Testimony of Eudokia Semyonova in King and
Wilson, *Fate,* 277–278.

"a giant among men": ibid.

"They were not gods . . .": ibid.

"It's been decided . . .": ibid., 290.

"to be in a state . . .": ibid., 291.

"arranging [their] medicines": Alexandra Diary, 3 July/16 July 1918, in
Maylunas, 634.

"the execution . . .": Trotsky, *Diary,* 213.

"anything out of . . .": King and Wilson, *Fate,* 280.

"[They] said they . . .": ibid., 300.

"complaining about the murders": ibid.

"15 degrees": Alexandra Diary, 3 July/16 July 1918, in Maylunas, 634.

"Everyone [must] . . .": Yurovsky's Account of the Execution, 17 February
1934, in Steinberg, 356.

"all skin and bones": King and Wilson, *Fate,* 304.

"they smiled naturally . . .": ibid.

"They still did not imagine . . .": Yurovsky's Account of the Execution, 17 February 1934, in Steinberg, 348.

"None of the members . . .": Interrogation of Pavel Medvedev, 21–22 February 1919, in Steinberg, 348.

"Well, we're going . . .": Testimony of Peter Ermakov in Halliburton, 135.

"What, there isn't . . .": Yurovsky's Note on the Execution, 1920, in Steinberg, 352.

"Please, you stand here . . .": Massie, *Romanovs,* 5.

"They [still] had no idea . . .": Yurovsky's Note on the Execution, 1920, in Steinberg, 352.

"with a flash . . .": King and Wilson, *Fate,* 306.

"In light of the fact . . .": Yurovsky's Note on the Execution, 1920, in Steinberg, 352.

"Lord, oh, my God . . .": King and Wilson, *Fate,* 306.

"So we're not . . .": ibid.

"I can't understand . . .": ibid.

"What? What?": Yurovsky's Note on the Execution, 1920, in Steinberg, 352.

"This!": King and Wilson, *Fate,* 306.

"jumped about . . .": Yurovsky's Note on the Execution, 1920, in Steinberg, 353.

Chapter Eighteen

"The . . . Soviet passed . . .": King and Wilson, *Fate,* 338.

"the world will never . . .": Bulygin, 239.

"received the news . . .": Lockhart, 304.

"missing Romanovs": Fige, 641.

"But the children . . .": Gilliard, 277.

"I could not believe . . .": ibid., 275.

"The houses looked . . .": Goldman, 8–9.

"Comrade Stalin . . . has concentrated . . .": Clarkson, 566.

"We wanted . . .": Massie, *Romanovs,* 27.

"It was frightening!": ibid., 33.

"We swore an oath . . .": ibid., 35.

"All the skeletons . . .": Seward, np.

"His life, his actions . . .": King and Wilson, *Fate,* 497.

"[Nicholas] could have chosen . . .": ibid., 498.

"doing their moral duty . . .": ibid.

"My heart leaped . . .": Harding, np.

Beyond the Palace Gates

"What a stunning impression . . .": Kanatchikov, 7–19.

"My early childhood was not . . .": ibid., 1–6.

"Hush, hush, hushaby . . .": Tian-Shanskaia, 101.

"Grandpa rented . . .": Gorky, 150–151.

"I, too, made . . .": ibid., 161–171.

"About ten in the morning . . .": Korolenko.

"The first thing the shop owner . . .": Gudvan, 195–196.

"I tried to take my son . . .": ibid., 191–192.

"The third [train] whistle . . .": Palmer, 37–44.

"With a jubiliant . . .": Poole, 47–51.

"It was one o'clock . . .": Paustovsky, 474–475.

"Suddenly from behind . . .": Williams, 143–144.

"Like a black river . . .": Reed, 99.

"I shall describe my day . . .": Fige, 727–729.

INDEX